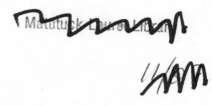

DISCARDED

# Standard Bridge Bidding
# for the Twenty-First Century

All rights reserved. No part of this book may be used or reproduced in any manner whatsoever without written permission except in the case of brief quotations embodied in critical articles or reviews. For information address Vivisphere Publishing, a division of NetPub Corporation, 675 Dutchess Turnpike, Poughkeepsie, NY 12603.

© 2000 by Max Hardy - All rights reserved

ISBN -10: 1-58776-049-5
ISBN -13: 978-1-58776-049-5

Library of Congress Catalogue Number 00-104457

SQueeZe Books

SQZ

SQUEEZE
BOOKS

# PUBLISHER'S NOTE

SQueeZe Books was formed to take advantage of the new print-on-demand technology. This technology has special relevance to the printing of books on contract bridge, our favorite game. Small press runs are not a problem and don't necessarily mean higher prices.

It is the goal of SQueeZe Books to allow the U.S. bridge playing community to see books from England, heretofore difficult to obtain and/or very high priced, and out of print books from everywhere. Old books, new books, established authors, emerging authors—if it's a book that can entertain, amuse, and/or educate, we want to bring it to you.

In 1964, Max Hardy and I were each producing monthly publications for bridge units in the greater Los Angeles area. When a monthly paper for the entire region began, I was a regular contributor and Max was the first editor.

We have come full circle and I am proud and happy that we will be starting the SQueeZe Books catalogue with Max's newest and best effort.

Max has contributed to the game of contract bridge in many ways. His longest lasting effect has been to codify the most popular bidding system (5 card majors) for the tournament playing public.

In this book, Max shows average social bridge players that there is no reason that they can't bid with the same efficiency as tournament types.

You will be using this book as a reference and to settle arguments for years to come.

—Ron Garber
for SQueeZe Books.

*Other Books by Max Hardy*


Five Card Majors – Western Style—1974 (out of print—Replaced by Two Over One Game Force)

Play My Card (with Bill Roney)—1980 (out of print)

Two Over One Game Force—1982 (Original out of print—replaced by Two Over One Game Force Revised and Expanded)

New Minor Forcing – Fourth Suit Forcing – Forcing Notrump Responses—1984

Splinters and Other Shortness Bids—1987

Two Over One Game Force Revised and Expanded—1989
Winner of the award "Bridge Book of the Year for Advanced Players" presented by the American Bridge Teachers' Association

Two Over One Game Force: An Introduction (with Steve Bruno)—1993

Two Over One Game Force Quiz Book—1993

Competitive Bidding With Two Suited Hands—1997

The Problems With Major Suit Raises and How to Fix Them—1998

# ACKNOWLEDGEMENTS

*My sincere thanks to several people who helped me with this book:*

*E.B. Dyer, who convinced me that it should be the first book of a set.*

*Charlotte Behre, who caused me to "demasculinize" the writing.*

*Graham Thomas, who helped organize the Index.*

*Jan Nathan, who worked diligently to be sure that I found the right publisher.*

*Andrew Binstock, who proofed and offered great suggestions.*

*Ron Garber, the finest reviewer of bridge books in the world who was my ultimate editor and publisher.*

*Mike Lawrence, who offered an insightful Introduction.*

*Last—and most important—my wonderful wife, Mary, who spent countless hours helping me improve the manuscript in every possible way.*

*Without the help of these and other people who helped to a lesser extent this effort would have been far more difficult to produce, and most probably would not have been up to the standard that I believe has been presented.*

*I sincerely hope that you, the reader, will find this to be the ultimate textbook on bidding as it presents the true standards for the current age.*

*Sincerely,*

*Max Hardy*
*Las Vegas, Nevada*
*January 2000*
*maxhardy@worldnet.att.net*
*Web page—www.hardybridge.com*

# INTRODUCTION

Thirty years ago, I met Max at a tournament. We discussed a hand or two and from that moment on, I knew Max. First as a player, then as a tournament director, an author, a musician, and finally a publisher. They tell me that he is a teacher and lecturer too. I believe it.

We have each written a number of books and while he published many of mine, we never wrote one together. Still, we have had conversations about what we thought about the game.

Recently, Max wrote me with the news that he is nearly finished with a book on two-over-one bidding for newer players. He sent me a copy to read. This is a necessary book since the current material for new players on Two-over-one bidding is pretty well hidden. Inasmuch as this system is rapidly taking over the game, Max's book is going to fill a large void.

For someone who does not know what Two-over-one bidding is, it is a system devised by one of the greatest players of all time, Alvin Roth. He recognized that standard bidding had so many gaps that it required lots of special little tricks to make it work at all. Key in Alvin's method are two things.

**ONE**—When you respond at the two level in a new suit after your partner's opening bid, you promise enough points to reach game. Your partnership can not stop in a partscore after this start. The strength of this is that your bidding need not include strange bids just in order to keep the bidding going. This lets you bid games and slams extremely well.

**TWO**—Recognizing that these methods created some problems when responder has ten or eleven points only, Alvin invented a brand new tool called the forcing notrump response. This device, truly revolutionary in bidding, defines a one notrump response to a major suit opening as forcing. The idea is that it allows responder to describe all kinds of invitational or otherwise difficult hands he may have.

Well done, Alvin Roth!

Once the system came into being, it remained for someone to describe it in usable fashion. Both Max and I have done that. Now, Max has gone one step further and has created a book on these methods that is not aimed at the experts, but at those that need to start at square one and move on to different levels. His book *Standard Bridge Bidding for the Twenty First Century* starts where it needs to start, at the beginning. It introduces Two-over-one methods, and subsequently ties them all together. In addition, a system is not a system unless it has supporting conventions. These are here, too. Really, a broad and comprehensive book that will turn a lot of not so accurate bidders into players who know how to get the maximum out of their cards.

Well done, Max Hardy!

Mike Lawrence
Berkeley, California
January 2000
77bridge@best.com
Web page—www.michaelslawrence.com

# PREVIEW

This book, *Standard Bridge Bidding for the Twenty First Century*, is the first of a two volume set. Its function is the presentation of a simplified and updated approach to standard bidding as it has evolved throughout the last half of the twentieth century. The companion volume, *Advanced Bridge Bidding for the Twenty First Century*, will follow shortly, and will detail upgrades for the methods shown in simplified form in this first volume.

It is unfortunate that in recent years most bridge columnists and authors have perpetuated assumed bidding standards that have been outgrown in the real arena of serious bridge competition. The masses of social bridge players are still being taught the bidding methods which were standard in 1930. Bridge columns perpetuate those outdated methods, and only serious competitive players have been in a position to grow as bidding ideas have changed.

Most importantly, the outdated methods have been proven both crude and philosophically wrong. The old methods required jumps to show strong hands. Bidding space fell victim to this need, and by the time a reasonable amount of information had been exchanged between hands that might consider slam, the game level had already been reached or surpassed. No space was left for subtle exploration. There was no room in which to find or verify secondary fits. All that was known was that the bidders held a great deal of strength, and the room that remained had to be devoted to determining the adequacy of controls. Many slams were reached because the necessary controls were present, but failed because the fits needed to produce tricks were not present.

Evolution solved this problem. The Roth-Stone and Kaplan-Sheinwold systems emerged in the early 1950's and brought with them a drastic change of philosophy. Instead of using space-consuming jumps to show good hands, the new approach used methods that created forcing auctions at low levels, allowing exploration for secondary fits below the level of game. Instead of using jumps to show strength, these methods use jumps as preemptive actions. Their function is to deprive the opposition of bidding space when it is known that our side holds good fits—offensive potential, but lacks defensive strength. This complete reversal of roles—making slow auctions strong and auctions with jumps preemptive—totally changed the face of what bidding should accomplish.

Why should bridge columns continue to focus on what has become obsolete? Why should bridge teachers of beginners and intermediate players continue to promulgate the crude methods that have been proven inferior? Why should not those beginners and intermediate players have access to the real standard tools of good bidding? It is time for all who teach and purvey information about bidding through writing books and columns to take the step from obscurity to reality.

With this book we believe that we have opened the door to the understanding of the bidding methods WHICH HAVE BECOME STANDARD TODAY IN SERIOUS COMPETITIVE BRIDGE. Let us preview what is presented here.

**INTRODUCTION**—Multiple World and National Champion Mike Lawrence informs the reader that this book has accomplished what we believed we had set out to do. It is a simplified presentation of the updated bidding standards.

**FOREWORD**—In the Foreword we make our case regarding intention. We clearly state that many of the bidding methods that are still promulgated by bridge teachers and columnists ARE NO LONGER STANDARD. We list these items:

1. Four card major suit opening bids in first and second seat.
2. Strong forcing jump raises (e.g.1♠ - 3♠).
3. Strong natural two bids in all four suits.
4. Strong jump overcalls.
5. Two-over-one responses to show at least game invitational values (10 or more high card points (HCP).
6. A non-forcing response of one notrump to a major suit opening bid to show a value range of 5+ to 9 HCP.
7. Cue bids of the opponent's suit to show powerful hands (e.g.Opponent 1♣ - you 2♣).
8. Opening bids in notrump with the ranges of 16 to 18 HCP, 22 to 24 HCP, and 25 to 27 HCP.
9. Natural two level responses to opening notrump bids (except in clubs).

Anyone who believes that any item listed here is standard is living in the dark ages. Yes, the columnists and the teachers keep teaching many (most) of them, and doing the student who wants to bid effectively no favor. If you are such a student of the game, we welcome you to the real bidding standards of today.

**CHAPTER ONE**—The subject of hand evaluation is given a new look. We present the table of defensive tricks and the 4-3-2-1 point count which are staples in current use. However, we emphasize that the numbers game is completely misleading. We ask the student to consider many additional matters when evaluating a hand. We emphasize finding fits in the early auction, and then seeking controls when the fits that exist show the promise of taking tricks. We ask the student to complete the evaluation picture in several ways:

1. Do not count points for short suits. Short suits do not take tricks - they provide controls. Add points for long suits. Long suit cards often do take tricks.
2. Modify your use of the point count to upgrade or downgrade the cards that you hold:
   A. Honor cards are worth more when combined than when isolated.
   B. Honor cards are worth more in long suits than in short suits.
   C. Give credence to good spot cards to which you have not assigned HCP status.
   D. Balanced distribution should downgrade the worth of a hand. Good shape should upgrade the worth of a hand.
   E. Listen to the auction. Your high cards can grow or diminish when their suit is bid in front of you or behind you.

We introduce immediately the most powerful tool for hand evaluation—the **splinter**. There are numerous auctions in which it is possible for one bidder to show a fit for partner and also to locate shortness in his hand. When this is done partner has been given a complete picture. Partner knows that cards facing your shortness will be wasted for suit play but might be stoppers for notrump. When that hand has no wasted values facing the announced shortness partner knows that all of the honor cards in both hands will mesh to produce tricks. The inclusion of information on **splinters** at this early point in the text is vital to leading the student to accurate hand evaluation.

**CHAPTER TWO**—Opener must know how to describe. We address bidding to show shape. We emphasize opening with a planned rebid. We show the priorities of all auctions. Opener's rebids to show various value ranges are shown. The **reverse** and the **jump reverse** are explained. The problems of opening in third and fourth seat are discussed. Our first set of twenty exercises lets the reader tune in on how to use the principles just explained.

**CHAPTER THREE**—Critical to any auction is the ability to know what bids are forcing, invitational, or non-forcing. This chapter shows which auctions by both opener and responder are forcing, which invite, and which show minimum values and allow partner to pass if a viable contract has been reached. The primary presentation is responder's tool for making auctions forcing—**fourth suit forcing**. In older methods jumps were usually forcing but sometimes only invitational. No clear guidelines existed. Here the presentation clarifies the forcing, invitational or non-forcing nature of all auctions.

**CHAPTER FOUR**—Presentation of two-over-one auctions begins with responses in clubs after a one diamond opening bid. A two club responder's extended auctions are shown, then continuations by the one diamond opening bidder. **Fast arrival** first appears and is explained. Opener's rebids after a two-over-one response to a major suit opening bid are detailed. Responder's rebids with a three card fit for the major suit are shown. Forty exercises close this chapter

**CHAPTER FIVE**—All about the **forcing notrump**. Opener's rebids and responder's rebids with various strength ranges are shown. Twenty exercises appear.

**CHAPTER SIX**—Additional information on rebids by the responder appears, showing how responder continues with various strength ranges. Responder's rebids after opener has **reversed** are shown. Twenty exercises amplify this chapter.

**CHAPTER SEVEN**—The most extensive chapter in this text details auctions in which opener has shown a balanced hand in any of several specific ranges. Conventional presentations include **New minor forcing, Stayman, Jacoby and Texas Transfers, Gerber,** and other sequences after opener's description of a balanced hand. Forty exercises amplify these bidding sequences.

**CHAPTER EIGHT**—Modern suit raises are presented. Limit jump raises, **splinter** raises, and the **Jacoby two notrump** appear, as well as **Drury,** and game tries after a major suit raise. Twenty exercises conclude this chapter.

**CHAPTER NINE**—Opening bids at the two level and higher are shown. Some are presented as preemptive—others as descriptive. Weak two bids and two club auctions are presented in detail. Forty exercises amplify the presentations.

**CHAPTER TEN**—Entering an auction begun by the opposition is presented from all points of view. Overcalls of all varieties appear with continuing auctions. Balancing in various auctions is presented. Takeout doubles and continuing auctions are shown. Michaels cue bids precede another forty exercises.

**CHAPTER ELEVEN**—Combating intrusion shows how to compete against over-calls, takeout doubles, Michaels cue bids and the **unusual notrump**. Action doubles, **negative doubles**, free bids and redoubles are described. Another forty exercises give the reader a good workout.

**CHAPTER TWELVE**—Slam bidding presentations show how good slam auctions begin below the level of game. Determination of trick sources by the finding of fits at low levels is followed by various methods of determining whether adequate controls exist. **Blackwood, Gerber**, and cue bidding of controls are detailed. A description of the meanings of jumps to major suits at the five level and the grand slam force complete this presentation.

**FINAL EXERCISES**—The student is given a final workout on exercise hands of all varieties. One hundred seventy two individual problems are presented which allow the student to see how much he has been able to retain.

# TABLE OF CONTENTS

FOREWORD.................................................................................................1

**CHAPTER I**
**HAND EVALUATION**.........................................................................8
    The numbers game..........................................................................9
    Splinter bids....................................................................................13

**CHAPTER II**
**OPENER BIDS TO DESCRIBE**........................................................16
    Bidding to show shape...................................................................16
    Notrump? Or a five card major?....................................................18
    Planning a rebid.............................................................................19
    Priorities.........................................................................................20
    Opener rebids to show minimum opening bid values (12+ to 15 HCP).........21
    Opener rebids to show game invitational values (15+ to 18 HCP)................23
    The reverse....................................................................................24
    The jump reverse...........................................................................25
    Problem distributions....................................................................27
    Opening in third seat.....................................................................28
    Opening in fourth seat...................................................................30
    Opening bid exercises...................................................................31
    Answers..........................................................................................32

**CHAPTER III**
**IS IT FORCING?**................................................................................35
    Opener's forcing auctions.............................................................35
    Responder's forcing auctions........................................................37
    Fourth suit forcing........................................................................41

**CHAPTER IV**
**RESPONDER'S TWO-OVER-ONE IS FORCING TO GAME**.......47
    Responder's jump to three clubs after a one diamond opening bid..........48
    Responder to one diamond (or one club) jumps in notrump..........48
    Rebids by a two club responder to a one diamond opening bid..........48

Fast arrival...........................................................................................50
Opener's rebids after a two club response to one diamond.......................51
The two-over-one response to a major suit opening bid............................54
The two-over-one responder holds a three card fit for opener's major suit......54
Opener jump rebids with a good suit after a two-over-one response...............57
Opener's jump shift rebid after a two-over-one response is a splinter............58
Opener raises responder's suit...........................................................59
Opener's rebid of two notrump............................................................59
A one heart opener rebids in spades......................................................60
Opener rebids a new suit at the two level...............................................61
Opener rebids naturally at the three level after a two-over-one
      response....................................................................................62
Summary of basic two-over-one auctions..................................................63
Two-over-one auction exercises............................................................65
Answers..........................................................................................67

## CHAPTER V
## RESPONDER'S FORCING NOTRUMP.....................................................**73**
Opener's rebids after the Forcing Notrump...............................................73
Responder's rebids with minimum values (5+ to 9- HCP).............................76
Responder's rebids with maximum values (9+ to 12- HCP)...........................79
Summary of Forcing Notrump Auctions....................................................83
Forcing notrump exercises..................................................................84
Answers..........................................................................................85

## CHAPTER VI
## REBIDS BY RESPONDER...................................................................**88**
Responder has fewer than 5+ HCP.........................................................88
Responder's rebids with 5+ to 9- HCP....................................................89
Responder's rebids with 9+ to 12- HCP...................................................91
A special auction..............................................................................92
Responder's rebids when opener has reversed............................................93
Summary of responder's rebids.............................................................97
Responder's rebid exercises.................................................................99
Answers..........................................................................................100

## CHAPTER VII
## AFTER OPENER BIDS NOTRUMP........................................................**103**
Opener has rebid one notrump..............................................................103
New Minor Forcing.............................................................................105
Summary.........................................................................................113
Opener rebids two notrump..................................................................114

Summary..............................................................................118
Opener opens one notrump...........................................119
Stayman Convention....................................................121
Jacoby Transfer...........................................................125
Texas Transfer.............................................................130
Gerber Convention......................................................137
Summary......................................................................137
Opener bids two notrump.............................................140
Opener's notrump bid exercises...................................141
Answers........................................................................143

## CHAPTER VIII
## RAISING PARTNER'S SUIT..................................................**148**

Raising opener's minor suit...........................................148
Raising with minimum response values (5+ to 9- HCP)............149
Limit raises..................................................................149
Forcing raises..............................................................150
Splinters......................................................................151
Raising opener's major suit..........................................152
Responder jumps to game............................................152
Responder has a fit and poor values (less than 5+ HCP)............153
Responder has minimum response values (5+ to 9- HCP)............153
Limit raises..................................................................154
Splinters......................................................................155
The Jacoby Two Notrump.............................................156
Raises by a passed responder.......................................157
Game tries...................................................................161
Suit raise exercises......................................................164
Answers.......................................................................165

## CHAPTER IX
## HIGH LEVEL OPENING BIDS................................................**169**

Preemptive opening bids..............................................169
Responding to preemptive opening bids......................172
Descriptive opening bids..............................................172
Very high level opening bids........................................172
Weak two bids..............................................................173
Responding to weak two bids.......................................176
The opening bid of two clubs.......................................178
Responder's priorities..................................................179
Opener's rebids............................................................180
Responder's rebids.......................................................180

Summary......................................................................................................183
High level opening bid exercises.................................................................184
Answers......................................................................................................186

**CHAPTER X**
**INTRUDING WHEN THEY HAVE OPENED THE BIDDING....................190**
Overcalls....................................................................................................190
Simple overcalls in notrump.......................................................................191
Advancing an overcall in notrump..............................................................192
Jump overcalls in notrump..........................................................................192
Overcalls in suits........................................................................................194
Overcalls on four card suits........................................................................195
Overcalls at the two level............................................................................196
Advancing partner's overcall......................................................................197
Jump overcalls in suits................................................................................200
Balancing....................................................................................................202
Balancing in notrump..................................................................................202
Jumps in the balancing position.................................................................203
Balancing when the opponents have stopped at a low level........................204
Takeout doubles..........................................................................................206
Responding to takeout doubles...................................................................207
Rebidding after a takeout double................................................................209
Is it really for takeout?...............................................................................211
The numbers game—again..........................................................................212
Cue bids......................................................................................................212
Intruder's exercises.....................................................................................213
Answers......................................................................................................216

**CHAPTER XI**
**WHEN THEY INTRUDE...............................................................................219**
Defending against overcalls........................................................................219
Bidding at the one level..............................................................................219
Raising partner............................................................................................220
Free bids.....................................................................................................221
Action doubles............................................................................................222
Negative doubles........................................................................................223
Defending against overcalls in notrump......................................................227
Defending against the unusual notrump......................................................228
Defending against takeout doubles.............................................................229
Redoubles....................................................................................................231
Defending against Michaels cue bids.........................................................232
Exercises on combating intrusion...............................................................234

Answers...............................................................................................236

**CHAPTER XII**
**SLAM BIDDING**...........................................................................**240**
    Finding fits through game tries.....................................................240
    Slam invitations by not using fast arrival....................................241
    Slam invitations through fourth suit forcing................................242
    Slam invitations through New MinorForcing................................243
    Slam invitations after Stayman.....................................................244
    Slam invitations after a JacobyTransfer.......................................244
    Blackwood......................................................................................246
    Gerber............................................................................................247
    Cue bidding to show controls.......................................................248
    Jumps to Five of a Major Suit.....................................................249
    The Grand Slam Force..................................................................250
    Summary........................................................................................251

**FINAL EXERCISES**.......................................................................**253**

**ANSWERS**....................................................................................**263**

**INDEX**..........................................................................................**279**

# Standard Bridge Bidding
# for the Twenty-First Century

## Max Hardy

# FOREWORD

The Twentieth Century was truly amazing. It brought far more scientific progress than could possibly have been anticipated.

When the Century began, the common mode of transportation was horse and buggy. Early in the Century the internal combustion engine caused the common mode of travel to become the automobile.

When the Century began, man was bound to the surface of the Earth. Within one decade, flight had been attained, and within seven decades, man had set foot on the moon.

The Century led to the development of various power sources. Steam gave way to electricity and eventually atomic energy was unleashed. By the end of the Century computers had replaced paperwork and had completely reshaped common means of communication.

One of the marvels of the Twentieth Century was the creation and codification of the game of bridge as we know it. The early version, auction bridge, was replaced by a refined version, contract bridge, which captured the imagination of millions because of its beauty and the depth of possibilities it presented. The requirement that contracts be reached in the bidding if the bidders were to be rewarded with bonuses made the game far more challenging. It enjoyed great publicity in its early years, and most major newspapers contracted to carry daily bridge columns as regular features.

Early established bidding methods were very crude. The common thread was that strong hands were shown by jumps in the bidding while weaker hands bid cheaply. Opening two bids in all suits were strong. Jump raises were strong and forcing. Jump overcalls showed strong hands.

In Webster's New Twentieth Century Dictionary, Unabridged Second Edition, the word **standard** as an adjective has many definitions, a few of which are:

1. "having the quality or qualities of a model, gauge, pattern, or type; serving as a standard: hence, generally recognized as excellent and authoritative."
2. "having no special or unusual features; ordinary; regular; typical;"
3. "generally used, and regarded as proper for use, in books, periodicals, lectures, speeches, documents, literary compositions of various sorts, and the conduct of public affairs;"

Regarding bridge bidding, the word **standard** has been applied to the methods used and popularized by Charles Goren beginning with his first book which was published in 1936. During the 40's and 50's Goren achieved great popularity with the masses who read his daily syndicated bridge columns, devoured his books, and generally acclaimed him the guru of bridge in North America.

Organized competitive bridge in North America was the arena in which Goren competed, but his teachings became the standard for the world of social bridge players as well. Organized bridge activities in North America are conducted by the **American Contract Bridge League (ACBL),** which was born of the merger of several bridge organizations around 1948, and its membership, now about 185,000, once exceeded 200,000 members. Although it is not possible to determine the number of social bridge players in North America, that number has been estimated to be as great as 40,000,000.

The Goren methods have remained the standard for social bridge players throughout the years that have followed. Virtually no changes have been made in bidding structure or philosophy by the Goren organization throughout the balance of the Twentieth Century. What was standard for the social player in 1940 is still presented as standard for him in the 1990's. The only change in Goren's approach has been recognition that five card major suit opening bids have replaced his early allowance for opening major suit bids with only four cards in the suit.

Acceptance by the social player has always been facilitated by the fact that virtually everything in the Goren methods for bidding is natural. Very few artificial bidding "conventions" are included. Virtually all bids mean what they appear to mean, making bidding very natural and easy.

While almost nothing has changed in social bidding methods over the last five decades, exactly the opposite is true in the world of competitive organized bridge. Thinking players have created new ways to solve various bidding problems not adequately handled by the outdated Goren methods. Most particularly, Alvin Roth and Oswald Jacoby have created bidding practices that are now standard in the competitive bridge world. These methods require the use of artificial bids to a greater extent than the Goren methods did, but their inclusion in the standard repertoire serves players well and does not create a monster of artificiality.

The major improvements have not been attained through an increase of artificial conventions. The Goren approach relied heavily on consuming bidding space by using jumps in the bidding to show strong hands. Today's expert standards conserve bidding space with strong hands and use jumps preemptively, just the opposite in concept and practice from the Goren methods. Preemptive bidding has become so prevalent that showing fits early in most auctions has become critical.

The methods used by today's experienced players recognize that conservation of bidding space is important. They are geared to show strength while keeping the auction at low levels. When game appears to be the extent of the bidding hands, "fast arrival" is frequently used. Jumps to game in suits do not show extra strength or suggest that slam might be in the offing. They are used not to show strength, but rather to close auctions when it becomes clear that slam should not be sought.

Conversely, when extra strength is held and slam appears possible, today's expert makes the auction forcing and allows for the exchange of information about slam possibilities below the level of game. If the auction consumes less space, fits and controls can be shown below the game level. When the game level is reached slowly, far greater accuracy is the result. Goren's primitive jumps to show strength (which I call slam killers) have given way to far better methods that conserve bidding space and allow for greater exchange of information.

These natural bids are no longer standard:

1. Four card major suit opening bids in first and second seat.
2. Strong forcing jump raises (e.g. 1♠ - 3♠).
3. Strong natural opening two bids in all four suits.
4. Strong jump overcalls.
5. Two-over-one responses to show at least game invitational values (10 or more high card points (HCP).
6. A non-forcing response of one notrump to a major suit opening bid to show a value range of 5+ to 9 HCP.
7. Cue bids of the opponents' suit to show powerful hands (e.g. Opponent 1♣ - you 2♣).
8. Opening bids in notrump with ranges of 16 to 18 HCP, 22 to 24 HCP, and 25 to 27 HCP.
9. Natural two level suit responses to opening notrump bids (except in clubs).

Replacing the old standards listed above are these new standards:

1. Five card major suit opening bids in first and second seat.
2. Invitational (limit) jump raises - particularly in major suits (e.g. 1♥ - 3♥).
3. Opening weak two bids in spades, hearts and diamonds.
4. Preemptive jump overcalls (e.g. opponent 1♦ - you 2♠).
5. Two-over-one responses to show game forcing values (12+ or more HCP) (e.g. partner - 1♥ - you - 2♦).
6. A forcing response of one notrump to an opening bid of one of a major suit to show a value range of 5+ to 12- HCP.
7. Cue bids of the opponents' suit to show two suited hands with moderate values.
8. Opening bids in notrump with values of 15 to 17 HCP and 20 to 21 HCP.
9. Transfer responses to opening notrump bids (e.g. 1NT - 2♥ to show spades).

OK! Now the reasons for these changes:

1. The first goal of any auction is to find a major suit fit of eight cards or more and establish that suit as the trump suit. When responder holds three cards in opener's major suit and the values of a minimum response (5+ to 9- HCP) a simple raise is in order. When the opening bid in a major suit guarantees at least five cards, raising with three card support guarantees the desired fit of at least eight cards. If the opening bid can be on a major suit of only four cards, the auction is ambiguous.

The reason for this change is so clear that even social players have adopted five card majors as their preference. Seasoned tournament players know that in order for five card majors to function effectively certain adjuncts must be used. The social player may know nothing of these adjuncts, but still attempts to play five card major suit opening bids. Thus, five card major suit opening bids are the standard today.

2. The change from forcing jump raises to invitational (limit) jump raises interacts with many of the other new standards. Inviting game with a fit for opener's major suit has been simplified. The cumbersome approach of first making a forcing call in a new suit, then showing a fit for opener's major suit was often ambiguous. In certain auctions it was not clear whether a true fit was being shown or whether a simple preference had been taken. The use of the jump raise to both invite a game and show a fit simplifies auctions that otherwise have been tedious, and makes it diffi-

cult for opponents to enter the auction. Other means of making forcing raises have been established.

3. The change from strong, natural opening two bids to weak two bids added useful bidding tools. In spades, hearts and diamonds, the ability to make descriptive bids at the two level to show hands based on a reasonable suit and less than full opening bid values often makes the auction difficult for the opposition when the hand belongs to them, and at other times allows the bidding side the best way to reach its own best contract. The use of the opening bid of two clubs as an artificial force easily supplants the need for strong two bids.

4. A strong jump overcall required a hand that rarely occurred after an opponent had opened the bidding. Based on frequency, these bids have always had very little value. More frequently, after an opponent had opened the bidding the player next to call might hold a hand with a long suit—offensive strength, but little defense. The use of the jump overcall to preempt is tactically far superior, and the frequency factor makes this change clearly better than the old standard (and certainly more exciting).

5. The requirement that a new suit response at the two level show the values of an opening bid, and thereby force the auction to reach the game level, is the adjustment in bidding standards that is most significant. When the commitment to game is known by responder's first call, there is no reason to squander precious bidding space. When the Goren approach was standard and the two-over-one response promised only game invitational values, neither bidder knew whether partner would continue bidding or whether the next bid would be considered forcing. Distinguishing between the showing of fits and simple preferences was often not possible.

6. Because the two-over-one response shows a full opening bid, we need another approach when responder has only game invitational values. Instead of using one notrump as a non-forcing minimum response, responder bids one notrump to partner's opening major suit bid to show a much wider range of values. This response could be either minimum (5+ to 9- HCP) or invitational (9+ to 12- HCP). In order for responder to show the upper value range, it becomes necessary for the response of one notrump to be forcing for one round of bidding.

Making the notrump response to a major suit opening bid forcing for one round adds another benefit. Responder will often have a bad hand that includes a long suit. When the notrump response was not forcing, responder had no way to reach the best contract in the long suit because greater values were required to bid it at the two level. Whenever opener passed the non-forcing response in notrump, responder's suit had no chance to become something of value, and the notrump contract frequently failed when a contract in the long suit would have been comfortable.

When one notrump in response to a major suit opening bid is forcing, responder is able to rebid to show a suit and limited values. This makes it possible to get to superior contracts, which could not have been reached without the "Forcing Notrump" response.

These two changes in bidding standards—making the two-over-one response forcing to game, and making the one notrump response to a major suit opening bid forcing for one round—are the philosophical keys to better bidding. No more bashing, slam killing jumps just to show good hands. Slow auctions which facilitate the exchange of information with good hands, and the use of jumps preemptively allow more accuracy in bidding.

7. The use of a cue bid after an opponent's opening bid to show a monstrous hand in values and shortness in opener's suit never did make sense. Again, the frequency with which the opportunity arose made this application practically useless. In about 1965, Mike Michaels published a new approach to the use of the cue bid. His suggestion that the cue bid show a hand with two suits and moderate values took hold almost instantly. Today, almost all serious players use the cue bid to show a two suited hand with moderate values, giving the cue bid a far greater frequency, and a truly useful function.

8. The use of two clubs as an artificial forcing opening bid is necessary. It allows opener to establish a forcing auction. This replaces the need for strong natural two bids and opens the door to the use of weak two bids.

The artificial two club opening bid also allows for the change in notrump ranges from the early standards. Opener's rebid range of one notrump to show 12 to 15 HCP was simply too wide. It is unwieldy to guess whether to reach or stay out of game when opener's values have so great a span (no Tarot cards are included in the 52 card deck!). With the reduction of the range of the opening bid of one notrump to 15 to 17, opener's rebid is cut back to 12 to 14 HCP. This allows for greater accuracy.

Balanced hands with 22 or more in high card points can be shown after the artificial opening bid of two clubs. This changes other ranges of notrump bids. With 20 or 21 HCP, the current standard is to open by bidding two notrump. A jump to two notrump by opener after a simple one level opening bid now shows 18 or 19 HCP.

After opening with two clubs, opener's rebid of two notrump shows 22 to 24 HCP. A jump to three notrump instead shows 25 to 27 HCP.

Now, notrump ranges are reduced to at most a three point span (some to just a two point span). Greater accuracy is made easy.

9. Accuracy in responding to opening notrump bids was clearly gained when the **Stayman** convention was adopted as standard. Except in clubs, suit responses at the two level were natural and non-forcing; at the three level they were natural and forcing, and after **Stayman** major suit bids by responder were invitational. In each case, responder promised a five card suit, and became declarer whenever that suit was established as the trump suit.

The new standard (**Jacoby Transfers**) allows responder to use transfer responses to opening bids in notrump. This allows responder to control the auction, which ensues and allows the strong hand to remain concealed. Most tournament players have adopted these transfer bids, making them a clear standard today.

The purpose of this book is to make the new standard tools available so that either a beginner or a social or tournament player can understand them. I have attempted to present these new "standards" as simply as possible.

In addition, many refinements are widely used, but they are not necessary to the adoption of today's standards. The simplest version opens the door for social players, beginners, and tournament players who understand the need to update. The refinements are for those who not only wish to modernize, but also want superior bidding methods.

Presentation of the new standards will be made in stages. Two volumes are planned. The first Volume is in your hands. It shows the basic concepts and bidding agreements that allow comprehension of the methods that are now standard. It allows the reader to update on a simplified basis. The agreements that allow bidders to use expert methods are presented in Volume Two, which carries the title *Advanced Bridge Bidding for the Twenty First Century*.

This book is a complete textbook for anyone who needs today's standards in simplified form. When you have read it, we know you will agree that it has fulfilled that function. Farewell to crude and outdated bidding methods. Welcome to the Twenty-first Century!!!

# CHAPTER ONE

## HAND EVALUATION

Evaluating the trick taking potential of a hand requires some guidelines. Yard-sticks are available which will allow the bidder to have a feel for the hand before the auction begins. The earliest guideline was Ely Culbertson's system of honor count.

Culbertson assigned honor count points as follows: an ace equals one, a king equals one half, an ace-king combination equals two, an ace-queen combination equals one and one half, a king-queen combination equals one.

This is the table in chart form:

      A = 1
      K = ½
      A-K = 2
      A-Q = 1 ½
      K-Q = 1

Although honor count is not the primary method of evaluation today, it is still used. Instead of being called honor count, it is now called the table of "quick tricks", or "defensive tricks".

The 4-3-2-1 point count used today as a hand evaluation measure was first publicized by Milton Work in about 1915. It rose to prominence in the late 1940's when it was adopted and promoted by Fred Karpin and Charles Goren. It assigns four points to an ace, three points to a king, two points to a queen, and one point to a jack.

In chart form:

      A = 4
      K = 3
      Q = 2
      J = 1

This system overvalues queens and jacks, and undervalues aces. It also gives no due to tens and other high spot cards that are extremely valuable.

Goren also assigned points for short suits. One point for a doubleton, two points for a singleton, and three points for a void. It is clear that distribution affects hand evaluation. However, short suits do not take tricks. They provide controls. When a player runs out of a suit trumps can be used, but it is the trump cards which take the tricks, not the shortness. If your trumps have been drawn, your short suit will not take tricks.

Consider the value assigned to a singleton ace. This card will take one trick, but the holder has no control over the trick on which it will be played. The ace must be played on the first round of the suit or there would be a revoke. In fact, this ace will take one trick but it does nothing to help create extra tricks. Would not this ace would be far more valuable if it were in a long suit, where it would help small cards in that suit to become winning tricks?

Using the Goren method, bidders usually assign four points for the ace and two for the singleton, giving the singleton ace the value of six points. What a distortion! As a singleton, this ace actually loses value. It is truly worth about three points, rather than six. It is inflexible because it must be played immediately when the suit is led, and does nothing to contribute to the creation of additional tricks in any suit.

It makes far greater sense to add points for long suits. In the trump suit, in notrump, or if there is a trump suit and trumps have been drawn, the fifth, sixth and longer cards in a suit will become tricks when no other player can follow. In the evaluation process used by experts today, no points are assigned for shortness, but adding points for long suits is a common practice. To make it easy, after counting your high card points, add a point to your hand for every length card more than four in a suit. DO NOT ADD POINTS FOR SHORT SUIT HOLDINGS!!

## The Numbers Game

In using the point count, specific numbers have been established for certain actions. Minimum opening bids generally contain twelve or more high card points (HCP) with at least two quick tricks. If the hands of the partnership are to be able to make a game either in notrump or with a major suit as the trump suit, the partnership needs about twenty-six points. For a minor suit game, the assumed requirement is twenty-nine points; for a small slam it is thirty-three points, and for a grand slam the number is thirty-seven points.

The rationale for these numbers has to do with the defensive cards left for opponents to hold. When the bidding side has thirty-seven points, the opposition cannot have an ace. When the bidding side has thirty-three points, the opposition cannot have two aces. When the defenders cannot defeat the contract with fast tricks, the bidding side will usually be able to use its assets to fulfill the contract.

If it were always true that both hands were balanced, and all tricks would need to be generated by high cards, this scale would be reasonably accurate. However, the point count is not a panacea. Certain conceptions are necessary if one is to understand and use the point count with any accuracy. Look at three hands, all with the same distribution and high card content to understand how just counting points does not express uniform evaluation.

**Example 1:**

| a | b | c |
|---|---|---|
| ♠ Axx | ♠ AQx | ♠ xxx |
| ♥ Kxx | ♥ KJx | ♥ xxx |
| ♦ Qxx | ♦ xxx | ♦ xxx |
| ♣ Jxxx | ♣ xxxx | ♣ AKQJ |

**All three hands in Example One contain ten high card points—one ace, one king, one queen, and one jack. They all have exactly the same distributional pattern.**

**In hand 1a, the ace will win a trick, the king will win a trick about half of the time, and the queen and the jack are nebulous factors.**

**In hand 1b, when the queen is in the same suit with the ace, it will take a trick about half of the time, and when the jack joins the king, its potential for taking a trick changes from nebulous to real.**

**In hand 1c, the combination of all four honor cards presents four tricks. Despite the fact that the point count rates all three hands equally, the third hand has more than twice the trick taking potential of the first hand.**

Ergo, our first axiom for evaluation:

HONOR CARDS ARE WORTH MORE WHEN COMBINED THAN WHEN ISOLATED.

Just as important:

**Example 2:**

| a | b | c |
|---|---|---|
| ♠ 65432 | ♠ AQ432 | ♠ AQ1098 |
| ♥ 5432 | ♥ AK32 | ♥ AK109 |
| ♦ AK | ♦ 32 | ♦ 109 |
| ♣ AQ | ♣ 32 | ♣ 109 |

**All three hands in Example 2 have the same distributional pattern, and the same high card points. If the point count is at all accurate, these three hands should all have about the same trick taking value. Obviously, this is not true!**

**In 2a, the honor cards will take tricks, but do not help create additional tricks.**

**In 2b, the honor cards are working since they are in long suits, but the spot cards, for which there is no point count value, are terrible.**

**In 2c, the spot cards have been upgraded to usefulness.**

**It is clear that despite the fact that all three hands have the same distribution and high cards, and all count the same when the point count is applied, 2b is a far better hand than 2a, and 2c is better than either of the others.**

This leads to more axioms regarding evaluation:

HIGH CARDS ARE MORE VALUABLE IN LONG SUITS THAN IN SHORT SUITS.

GOOD SPOT CARDS ENHANCE TRICK TAKING POTENTIAL EVEN THOUGH NO POINT VALUE IS ASSIGNED TO THEM.

Throughout this text when reference is made to high card points, a plus or minus sign will accompany the number. The plus sign refers to a good hand for the number of HCP because of the location and combination of honor cards, the presence of good spot cards, and good shape for the hand. The minus sign refers to a bad hand for the number of HCP because of isolated honor cards, honors in short suits, bad spot cards and balanced distribution. Bear in mind that plus factors make a hand worth several more points than initially assigned, while minus factors can cause the HCP to be an overstatement of the value of the hand.

The numbers game has cast a completely wrong impression with players who rely only on counting their points to know whether or not to bid onward. The true secret of bidding is that of finding suit fits. FITS, NOT POINTS, TAKE TRICKS. Try this ultimate example of that fact.

**Example 3:**

|  | a | b |
|---|---|---|
| ♠ | AQ108642 | KJ9753 |
| ♥ | 853 | — |
| ♦ | — | 8765432 |
| ♣ | 762 | — |

**With spades as trumps, if these two hands are declarer and dummy, all thirteen tricks will be won on a cross ruff. Although they have only ten high card points, the ultimate fit produces all of the tricks. Note that the opposition holds thirty of the forty high card points and is powerless.**

Do you still feel that you should evaluate by counting points? Well, it is a starting point, but in order to evaluate your hand appropriately, you must listen to the auction. When you discover fits, you will have the wherewithall to take tricks. Fits take tricks. You may have lots of points, but when the two hands do not fit, taking tricks is difficult.

You are seeing the emphasis on finding fits, rather than counting points. Don't fall for the numbers game. Understand that often hands with few points will take a lot of tricks, while hands with lots of points and no fits will routinely disappoint the bidder who gets too high just because of points.

The best approach to accurate hand evaluation is to use both the Culbertson table of "defensive tricks" and the 4-3-2-1 point count. Begin by counting your high card points (HCP). If you are about to open the bidding or make a takeout double and you have the HCP requirement, then look to your defensive tricks. To either open or make a takeout double your hand should contain about 12+ HCP and at least two defensive tricks. Make a further assessment based on the axioms. Upgrade or downgrade your HCP holding based on placement of honor cards, combination of honor cards, absence or presence of good spot cards, and good or bad distribution.

Give attention to your distributional pattern. The more balanced your pattern is, the less value you should assign to your hand. If you have length in one or more suits, particularly when you have high cards in those suits, the value of your hand increases.

As the auction progresses, the value of your hand will increase or decrease based on what you can learn about fits in your partner's hand. Both you and partner will express your holdings. Listen and learn when you have fits. Upgrade hands with fits; downgrade hands that do not have fits. Most bidding errors are made by those who overbid hands with good values and underbid hands with meager values because they have not listened to the auction. Sometimes hands with lots of HCP lose value due to lack of fits, while hands with very few HCP grow astonishingly in value when fits are discovered.

Bidding by the opposition will also allow you to determine the value of the cards you hold. When you hold honor cards in a suit that is bid by the opponent in front of you, those honors increase in value because of their placement. If the opponent behind you bids a suit in which you hold honor cards, they decrease in value because of their placement.

## Splinter bids

One of the best of modern bidding tools which expresses a fit is the **splinter** bid.

The **splinter** is a bid that indicates two very important things:

1. A good fit for a suit that has been bid by partner.
2. Shortness (a singleton or void) in the suit identified as a splinter.

**Splinter** bids are made in one of two ways:

1. Conventional sequences which by agreement show shortness.
2. Unusual jumps that have not been assigned other specific meanings.

Of all modern bidding tools, none is as useful for hand evaluation as this one. When partner shows a fit for your suit, and indicates shortness in another, you have instant ability to know the value of every card in your hand.

The high cards you hold in partner's short suit lose value. Because partner is short in the indicated suit and has a fit for your suit, you would rather hold only small cards facing that shortness. You will be able to ruff those small cards in partner's hand and thereby eliminate your losers in that suit. But why should you want to ruff your honor cards?

It would be far better to have small cards in the suit where partner is short. Those small cards are losers that you will be happy to ruff. But, the payoff is that when you hold only small cards facing partner's short suit, the honor cards that you do have will face honors in partner's hand. This means that your honor cards will combine with partner's honor cards to produce tricks (remember—FITS TAKE TRICKS).

**Example 4:**

|  | a |  | b |  | c |
|---|---|---|---|---|---|
| ♠ | K5 | ♠ | AJ6 | ♠ | AJ6 |
| ♥ | 853 | ♥ | KJ92 | ♥ | 6 |
| ♦ | AQ65 | ♦ | 6 | ♦ | KJ92 |
| ♣ | K1094 | ♣ | AQ853 | ♣ | AQ853 |

|  | d |  | e |  | f |
|---|---|---|---|---|---|
| ♠ | AJ853 | ♠ | KQ96 | ♠ | KQ96 |
| ♥ | K95 | ♥ | 763 | ♥ | AQ8 |
| ♦ | 5 | ♦ | AQ8 | ♦ | 763 |
| ♣ | A1086 | ♣ | KQ4 | ♣ | KQ4 |

**Looking at Example 4, we see how the degree of fit determines the number of tricks that can be taken. When 4a faces 4b the diamond queen has no value, and there may be as many as three losers in hearts. But when 4a faces 4c shortness faces losers and the KJ92 holding faces fitting honor cards. With 4a facing 4c, a slam in either diamonds or clubs is a practical certainty.**

**The situation is similar with Example 4d facing 4e. The diamond queen is again wasted and there may be as many as three losers in hearts. But when 4d faces 4f, the singleton is opposite losers and the AQ8 in the heart suit solidifies the heart holding.**

**Note that both 4b and 4c are the same hand with suits switched, as are 4e and 4f. The point count and high card holdings are exactly the same. IT IS THE DEGREE OF FIT THAT DETERMINES THE NUMBER OF TRICKS THAT CAN BE WON.**

When you hold good high cards in partner's short suit and your fit is in a minor, it is likely that the best contract will be in notrump. If partner has made a **splinter** bid and then hears you bid in notrump, bad news, your high cards face shortness. This does not augur well for taking a lot of tricks as you probably do not hold high cards that mesh with partner's high cards. The good news is that you can assure partner that notrump will be a safe place to play because of your concentration of high cards opposite shortness.

We emphasize finding fits at every opportunity. The use of bids which show a fit for partner and specific shortness is a major bidding tool. You will see many examples in which those who live by the "numbers game" get it wrong. They will bid to the level indicated by the points that they hold. Point counters miss games and slams which make because of fits, and they bid games and slams which fail because of the lack of fits. By finding fits you will get it right more often than not.

Because the **splinter** is a modern tool you will not find it in most bidding texts that are intended for the relatively new player. Older texts do not refer to it at all. Newer texts present it for those who are considered advanced students. Rectification of this omission is necessary for the serious student. **Splinters** in action will be included in most of the following chapters.

The matter of hand evaluation is ongoing. In each chapter that follows reference is made to the principles outlined here. Let them guide you to more accurate appraisal of the value of your hand as the auction grows around you.

A wise man once said, "Good judgment comes from experience, and experience is often created by bad judgment." The more experience you acquire, the better your judgment will become. Learn from the errors you make and do not repeat them.

# CHAPTER TWO

## OPENER BIDS TO DESCRIBE

As opener, your goal is to describe your hand to your partner in an attempt to reach the best contract for your side. Various bids show hands of specific size and of specific shape.

## Bidding to show shape

Hands classified by shape are either balanced or unbalanced. The definition of a hand that is unbalanced is that it contains either a singleton or a void. Hands that do not contain a singleton or void are balanced.

There are exactly six hand patterns that do not contain a singleton or a void. The balanced patterns are 4-3-3-3, 4-4-3-2, and 5-3-3-2. The remaining three patterns are neither fish nor fowl - neither truly balanced nor unbalanced by definition. They are 5-4-2-2, 6-3-2-2, and 7-2-2-2 and are commonly called semi-balanced.

When bidding to describe a hand, try to convey to partner whether the hand is balanced, thereby oriented to notrump, or unbalanced, which makes a contract in a trump suit more likely to succeed. This task falls particularly to the opening bidder.

With a balanced hand opener will bid notrump as soon as possible. The point in the auction at which notrump is bid will describe the values of the hand. Here are the ranges of opening notrump bids and rebids:

1. Opener rebids one notrump with 12 to 14 HCP.
2. Opener begins with one notrump to show 15 to 17 HCP.
3. Opener makes a jump rebid of two notrump with 18 or 19 HCP.
4. Opener begins with two notrump to show 20 or 21 HCP.
5. Opener makes an artificial and forcing opening bid of two clubs and then rebids in notrump with 22 HCP or more.

What about those hands that are not truly balanced? When a hand has more than one doubleton, should it be treated as balanced, or should it be treated otherwise? The answer lies in the location of the honor cards.

When a semi-balanced hand has honor cards in its doubletons, it should be treated as balanced. With honor cards in short suits, the quality of the long suits will not be as good and bidding those long suits will not be as descriptive as when the long suits are better. When the short suit holdings are good, the hand will be better described by a bid in notrump rather than in a long suit that is relatively weak.

It follows that with powerful suits and bad doubletons, bidding in notrump would not be truly descriptive. Bidding powerful suits is far more descriptive. The bidder should treat this hand as though it were unbalanced when its doubletons are weak, even though the hand is not unbalanced by definition.

Do not let this deter you from bidding notrump when your balanced hand includes a worthless doubleton. If your hand is semibalanced you have choices in the descriptive process, but not when your hand is balanced. When your distribution is 4-4-3-2 you need to show your balanced pattern even when your doubleton is bad.

A voluntary bid in notrump describes a hand that is balanced. When the bidder has an unbalanced hand, description comes from bidding in suits, not in notrump.

**Example 5:**

| a | b | c | d |
|---|---|---|---|
| ♠ KJ6 | ♠ KJ6 | ♠ KJ6 | ♠ KJ6 |
| ♥ Q95 | ♥ AQ5 | ♥ AQ5 | ♥ A95 |
| ♦ A108 | ♦ A108 | ♦ AQ8 | ♦ AQ8 |
| ♣ Q1096 | ♣ Q1096 | ♣ Q1096 | ♣ AQ96 |

| e | f | g | h |
|---|---|---|---|
| ♠ KJ6 | ♠ K9 | ♠ 94 | ♠ K9 |
| ♥ AQ5 | ♥ Q1043 | ♥ AQJ3 | ♥ AQ4 |
| ♦ AQ8 | ♦ K8 | ♦ 98 | ♦ K8 |
| ♣ AQ96 | ♣ AJ942 | ♣ AKJ42 | ♣ K98432 |

**With Example 5a, open one club and when partner responds in a suit at the one level, rebid one notrump to show your balanced hand of 12 to 14 HCP.**

**With Example 5b, open one notrump to show your balanced hand in the range of 15 to 17 HCP.**

**With Example 5c, open one club. When partner responds in a suit at the one level, jump to two notrump to show your balanced hand of 18 or 19 HCP.**

**With Example 5d, open two notrump to describe your balanced hand in the range of 20 to 21 HCP.**

**With Example 5e, open two clubs (strong, artificial, and forcing). After your partner responds your rebid of two notrump will show your balanced hand in the range of 22 to 24 HCP.**

**With Example 5f, open one club. If partner responds by bidding one heart, raise to two hearts. If the response is one spade, rebid one notrump. Your semibalanced hand includes good doubletons and tenaces. You want to be declarer and have the lead come up to, rather than through your hand.**

**With Example 5g, open one club. Do not bid one notrump when you hold bad doubletons and good suits. You do not have an easy rebid. If partner responds one heart, make a jump raise to three hearts. If partner bids one diamond, rebid one heart. If partner responds, either one spade or one notrump rebid two clubs. Upgrade your values if partner responds in hearts, but facing any other response this hand should be rebid as a minimum.**

**With Example 5h, open one notrump. Your semibalanced hand has good doubletons and the lead should come up to it rather than through it at any contract. If partner makes a transfer bid, you will still be the declarer. If you open one club you will not be able to show your values with a rebid in notrump. And your hand should declare rather than become the dummy because of its tenace holdings.**

## Notrump? Or a five card major?

Sometimes opener's balanced hand will have a 5-3-3-2 pattern. When the five card suit is a minor suit opener has no decision to make, and with a hand of the right strength (14 to 16 HCP plus one point for the five card suit) opener easily bids one notrump. When the five card suit is a major suit, opener must decide whether to open in notrump or by bidding the major. Three factors determine this choice.

1. If opener is to bid one notrump, the hand should hold three cards in the other major. The reason for this is simple. If opener has only two cards in the other major suit and opens one notrump there is the risk that responder might **transfer** to that other major and then pass. If responder does this and also has three cards in opener's major, the contract will be in the two-five major fit rather than the five-three, and will probably take fewer tricks. This is opener's first test.

2. If opener has a bad doubleton, the hand will be more oriented to suit play and less to playing in notrump. Opener should have at least a jack in the doubleton suit in order to conceal the major suit in favor of an opening bid in notrump. This is opener's second test.

3. Hands that are "toppish"—mostly aces and kings—play better in suits. Hands that are "texturish"—mostly kings and queens—play better in notrump. This factor is opener's third test.

So, if opener has three cards in the other major, no empty doubleton, and a hand that is mostly texture, it is best to conceal the fact that the hand includes a five card major suit and open by bidding one notrump. If the hand fails any of the three tests, the opening bid should be in the major suit.

## Planning a rebid

When you are planning to open the bidding in first or second seat, be aware that when responder bids a new suit it will be forcing. This means that you must plan not only your first call, but a second descriptive call no matter what responder may bid. The opening bidder must be prepared for what will follow and have planned a rebid.

A balanced hand can be opened by bidding one or two notrump and this problem will not exist. The opening bid fully describes both the size and the shape of the hand. When the hand is balanced and in one of the other strength ranges, a planned rebid in notrump will again give a full description.

If the opening bidder holds an unbalanced hand the obligation is to make a descriptive rebid. Because of distribution, it will be either a repeat of the suit first bid, or in another suit, but not in notrump. Rebidding in a suit rather than in notrump usually describes a hand that is not balanced.

# Priorities

The first object of a good auction will be for the bidding side to find a fit of eight cards or more in a major suit. Contracts can be played in major suits, in notrump, or in minor suits. There is a clear pecking order. First choice goes to the major suit contract. If a fit is found in a major suit, it will almost always be right to play there. When no major suit fit is found, the second choice is notrump. When there is no major suit fit and an obvious problem in some suit that would scuttle a contract in notrump, playing in a minor suit is the last resort.

The reason for this pecking order is the scoring table. A game in notrump requires only nine tricks but is difficult unless all suits are under control. A game in a major suit requires ten tricks but when the bidding side has an adequate supply of trumps those trumps keep control (Think of trumps as super aces!). A game in a minor suit requires eleven tricks—difficult to judge since it is only one trick from slam.

With an opening bid and a five card or longer major, opener bids that major. With no five card major but the values to open the bidding, start with a minor of three or more cards. Playing minor suit contracts is the last priority. Opener need not fear that responder will become enthusiastic about making it the trump suit. This opening bid in a minor suit guarantees at least three cards. With three cards in each minor suit, opener will tend to open in clubs in order to give responder greater space to respond. However, with three excellent diamonds and three bad clubs an opening bid of one diamond may be better—particularly if the opening bidder's side defends.

A response in a major suit shows four or more cards. With a four card fit opener will raise to show that fit. With minimum opening bid values (12+ to 15- HCP) raise to the two level. With 15+ to 18- HCP, raise with a jump to the three level or **splinter**, and with 18+ or more raise to game in the major suit (or **splinter**).

After opener has begun with a minor suit and heard a one heart response, with fewer than four hearts but holding four spades, opener usually bids one spade. The only time opener will not show a four card spade suit is with a balanced hand in the range of 18 or 19 HCP. With that hand, a jump to two notrump will show size and shape.

Opener's rebid of one notrump after a response of one heart denies holding four cards in either major suit, but after a response of one heart if opener jumps to two notrump, that call does not deny four spades. The jump to two notrump describes a balanced hand with 18 or 19 HCP and takes priority over introducing spades at that point in the auction. When there is a four-four fit in spades, responder can still rebid so that the spade fit can be found. With a four card fit for responder's major and 18 or 19 HCP opener jump raises to game. Opener's failure to **splinter** will have promised a balanced hand.

Remember these bidding priorities:

1. The first goal in any auction is the finding of a major suit fit of eight or more cards.
2. Opener will describe a hand as balanced or unbalanced at the first opportunity.
3. The obligation to show a major suit fit may override opener's need to show distribution.
4. Opener must have a planned rebid when opening the bidding unless the opening bid has been one or two notrump.

## Opener rebids to show minimum opening bid values (12+ to 15 HCP)

Minimum opening bids in first and second seat usually begin with at least twelve high card points. Some hands with less in high card strength are opening bids when they have good distribution, but those hands need to meet the minimum defensive strength requirement - at least two tricks. This minimum opening bid range tops at a bad 15 HCP.

When opener's values are in this minimum range, the choice of rebids are these:

1. One notrump. Opener's hand will be balanced and no major suit fit will be available. This rebid severely limits both opener's values and distribution.
2. A suit at the one level higher ranking than the suit of the response. Although this rebid may be made with minimum values, opener may have extra values (up to as much as 18 HCP) which cannot be shown at this turn. When these extra values exist, opener will show them at the third turn to call.
3. A raise of the responder's suit to the two level. This raise definitely limits opener's values to the minimum range. In most auctions opener will have four card support for responder's (major) suit.
4. A repeat of the opening suit. When this rebid is clearly voluntary opener shows six or more cards. In some auctions opener may have no choice but to rebid a five card suit. It is rare to plan to rebid in a five card suit, and opener will do so only when no alternative exists.

5. A lower ranking suit at the two level. As with number two above, this rebid can be made with minimum values, but opener can have extras - as much as 18 HCP. In both such cases opener simply does not have sufficient values to make a jump shift rebid. The jump shift rebid shows the values of 19 or more HCP (or the playing strength equivalent) and is forcing to game.

**Example 6:**

|  | **a** | **b** | **c** |
|---|---|---|---|
| ♠ | K53 | AJ53 | K6 |
| ♥ | A6 | K6 | AJ53 |
| ♦ | KJ104 | 942 | 942 |
| ♣ | Q1065 | KQ73 | KQ73 |

|  | **d** | **e** |
|---|---|---|
| ♠ | K6 | K64 |
| ♥ | 853 | 9 |
| ♦ | AQJ965 | AJ532 |
| ♣ | K8 | KQ73 |

With Example 6a, most will open one diamond, although an opening bid of one club is advocated by some. After a response of either one heart or one spade, rebid one notrump to show your minimum balanced hand (12 to 14 HCP).

With Example 6b, open one club. If the response is either one diamond or one heart, your rebid will be one spade. If the response is one spade, raise to two spades.

With Example 6c, open one club. If the response is one heart, raise to two hearts. If the response is one diamond, rebid one heart. If the response is one spade, rebid one notrump, which will indicate that your hand is minimum (12 to 14 HCP) and balanced. Do not make the error of trotting out your heart suit. That rebid would be at the two level. It would be a reverse (description to follow in this Chapter) showing 16+ HCP and longer clubs than hearts.

With Example 6d, open one diamond. After a response at the one level make a rebid of two diamonds to show that you have minimum high card values (12 to 14 HCP), but that you also hold a six card diamond suit.

**With Example 6e, open one diamond. If partner responds one of either major suit, your rebid should be two clubs. Do not make the error of raising if partner bids one spade—partner will expect four card support. If partner bids again you can show three card support.**

When opener rebids one notrump, raises responder to the two level, or repeats the original suit as cheaply as possible, it shows the minimum range (12+ to 15- HCP). Rebidding in a new suit either at the one level or at the two level (2 and 5 above) shows values that can be minimum but they can also be in the next range of a good fifteen to eighteen HCP.

A new suit rebid by opener can be in either of two ranges (the minimum range of 12+ to 15- HCP or the game invitational range of 15+ to 18 HCP), and it may not be possible to complete a value description until opener's third call.

## Opener rebids to show game invitational values (15+ to 18 HCP)

Other ways that the opener can show values in this invitational range of 15+ to 18 HCP are:

1. Make another call as a try for game after a suit raise by responder. (Opener's game try auctions are detailed in Chapter Eight).
2. Make a jump rebid in the original suit. This guarantees that opener's suit is of good quality and at least six cards long.
3. Make a jump raise of responder's suit. This promises four card support for responder's (major) suit. A jump to game shows a balanced 18 or 19 HCP.
4. Make a **reverse** rebid (definition to follow).
5. Make a **jump reverse** rebid (also to be defined).

Example 7:

| a | b | c |
|---|---|---|
| ♠ AQJ85 | ♠ AQJ965 | ♠ KQ95 |
| ♥ 6 | ♥ 6 | ♥ AQ4 |
| ♦ KJ5 | ♦ KJ5 | ♦ AJ632 |
| ♣ AJ73 | ♣ AJ3 | ♣ 6 |

**With Example 7a, after you open one spade, your partner raises to two spades to show a minimum response with at least three cards in support of your suit. Game is possible if your partner's hand fits with yours, so make a try for game by bidding three clubs. If partner has club values a bid of**

four spades is correct and tricks will be available because of the fits in two suits. If partner next bids three diamonds it shows a response that is not minimum, has some club value but not enough to be sure that game will make, and is making a counter invitation to show some values in diamonds. You will accept this counter invitation by jumping to four spades, knowing that there is some fit in clubs and an honor fit in diamonds. If partner's counter invitation is in hearts, it denies diamond values and shows values in hearts which do not fit your hand. Bid only three spades and hope that you are not too high. A presentation on game tries appears in Chapter Eight.

With Example 7b, when your opening bid is one spade and there is a response of one notrump, make a jump rebid of three spades to show extra values and a very good spade suit. If partner has a good minimum response a raise to four spades without much spade support is fine since you have shown a good suit.

With Example 7c, open one diamond. If partner responds one heart, your rebid is an easy call of one spade. This rebid does not yet show your game invitational values. Partner knows that you could be either minimum (12+ to 15- HCP) or invitational (15+ to 18 HCP). If partner responds one spade, make a jump raise to three spades to show four card support and game invitational values.

## The reverse

It is possible to bid two suits and conserve bidding space, or to bid them and do the opposite—use up precious space. The economical order in which the two suits can be bid allows the bidder's partner to choose between them without increasing the level. However, if those suits are bid in **reverse** order, partner needs to go to the next higher level just to return to the bidder's first suit (economy has been defied).

Suppose opener wishes to bid both red suits. The economical auction will be as follows:

$$1♥ – pass – 1NT – pass, 2♦ – pass – ?.$$

Responder will be able to pass to prefer diamonds, or return to hearts and stay at the two level. However, if opener chooses to **reverse** the order in which these suits are bid, the auction will be:

$$1♦ – pass – 1NT – pass, 2♥ – pass – ?.$$

Note that opener's rebid is at the two level. Responder could pass to prefer hearts (but will not since the reverse is forcing for one round), but must go to the three level just to return to opener's first suit. Opener's **reverse** promises these things:

1. The first suit is longer than the second suit. The second suit is assumed to be at least four cards, therefore the first suit must be at least five cards long.
2. The values are enough to force a choice of suits at the three level. This means that when opener **reverses** the hand must have at least an ace more than a minimum opening bid. Specifically, the **reverse** promises at least a good 16 HCP in addition to the shape that is shown by the **reverse**.
3. Opener's values are not yet limited. Although a minimum of at least a good 16 HCP has been promised the values may be much greater. After opener **reverses** the auction is forcing for one round. Responder may not pass and must bid again (Partner would not be happy if we missed a game. Keep partner happy!).

**Example 8:**

|          a          |          b          |
|---------------------|---------------------|
| ♠ K5                | ♠ K54               |
| ♥ AQJ65             | ♥ AQJ6              |
| ♦ AK643             | ♦ AKQ43             |
| ♣ 2                 | ♣ 2                 |

**With Example 8a, opener starts with one heart and plans to rebid in diamonds. Although there is the required strength for a** reverse, **the suits are equal in length and a** reverse **would distort distribution. A rebid of only two diamonds will not show this extra strength, but that is what must be done. If responder attempts to sign off, opener has the right to bid again to show extra values.**

**With Example 8b, opener starts with one diamond. The planned rebid of two hearts—a** reverse—**will show values of more than a minimum opening bid, and also that diamonds are longer than hearts.**

## The jump reverse

The **jump reverse** is our first exposure to a **splinter** bid (many more will follow). Because the simple **reverse** is both natural and forcing, there is no need to both jump and **reverse** to show a good hand with two specific suits. Four **jump reverse** auctions exist:

1. 1♣ - pass - 1♠ - pass, 3♦
2. 1♣ - pass - 1♠ - pass, 3♥
3. 1♣ - pass - 1♥ - pass, 3♦
4. 1♦ - pass - 1♠ - pass, 3♥

Opener's **jump reverse** promises the values to invite a game (about 15 + HCP or more), a four card fit for responder's suit, and a singleton or void in the suit of the **jump reverse**.

> **Example 9:**
>
> |           a           |           b           |
> |-----------------------|-----------------------|
> | ♠ KQ95                | ♠ KQ95                |
> | ♥ 6                   | ♥ AQ4                 |
> | ♦ AJ632               | ♦ 6                   |
> | ♣ AQ4                 | ♣ AJ632               |

**With Example 9a, open one diamond. If partner responds one heart, continue to describe by bidding one spade. However, if partner responds one spade, rather than make a jump to three spades, which would invite game but not describe, jump to three hearts—a** jump reverse. **This shows four card support for spades, values enough to invite a game, and shortness in hearts.**

**With Example 9b, open one club. If partner responds one heart continue to describe by bidding one spade. However, if partner bids one spade, rather than make a jump to three spades which would invite a game but not describe, jump to three diamonds—a** jump reverse. **This call shows your four card support for partner's spades, values to invite a game, and shortness in diamonds.**

These **splinter** bids allow partner to evaluate high cards that are working and those that are not. Working high cards produce tricks, but high cards facing shortness do not.

When opener's values are nineteen plus HCP a descriptive rebid can be a **reverse** (forcing for one round), a **jump reverse** (clearly forcing), or a jump shift in a new suit (natural and forcing to game). With values so great that a game might be missed if an opening one bid is passed by responder, opener begins with the artificial and forcing call of two clubs (more discussion of this when we get into opening two bids).

## Problem distributions

With some few exceptions, when opener's rebid is in the same suit that was opened it promises at least six cards in that suit. When opener holds both a four card suit and a five card suit, the tendency is to open in the longer suit, hoping to be able to rebid in the four card suit. This may not be possible. Bidding both suits in this fashion may constitute a **reverse** (which opener cannot make with minimum opening bid values), and there is a choice of ways to solve this problem:

1. Start by bidding the four card suit and rebid in the five card suit. This is not a desired auction but may be necessary as the least of evils.
2. Start by bidding the five card suit, knowing that it may be necessary to repeat that suit as a rebid. This is not desired but might simply be the "least worst bad bid".
3. Rebid one notrump when semi-balanced and with a good doubleton in the unbid major suit. With a poor doubleton this rebid should not be made.
4. Opener may be forced to rebid in a three card minor suit. Although not completely descriptive, this may be best. Remember that partner will not rush to play a minor suit.

Here are some hands with which each of these rebids might be made.

1. ♠ A53 ♥ 7 ♦ KQ105 ♣ K8643. With twelve high card points, two and one half defensive tricks and good shape, this hand is a clear opening bid. Because it is unbalanced opener will plan to rebid in a suit. Open one diamond, planning a rebid of two clubs. Do this because the diamonds are reasonable and the clubs are poor.
2. ♠ AJ5 ♥ 7 ♦ K754 ♣ KQ1053. Opener here has the same distribution, but a different value placement. If opener begins with one diamond and rebids two clubs, responder may take a preference to opener's first suit when holding only two diamonds. This would clearly lead to a poor choice of contracts. With poor diamond quality, opener should start by bidding one club. If the response is one heart, opener rebids two clubs. If the response is one spade, opener has the choice of either rebidding the club suit, or raising spades (although responder will expect four card

support for the immediate raise opener does have excellent three card support). In situations where there is no right call, the secret of good bidding is to make "the least worst bad bid."

3. ♠ K6 ♥ 84 ♦ K954 ♣ AQ987. Opener now is semi-balanced. Begin with one club because the diamonds are poor. If the response is one heart, a rebid of one notrump will protect the spade king on opening lead and probably give the best description. If the response is one spade opener rebids two clubs because of the bad holding in hearts.

4. ♠ 7 ♥ AJ53 ♦ K8632 ♣ KJ6. Opener begins with one diamond, hoping for a response of one heart that would allow a gentle raise. If the response is one spade, a rebid of two clubs is better than a rebid of the bad five card diamond suit. A rebid of two hearts is out of the question. Opener has the shape, but does not have the values to **reverse**. After the two club rebid, with equal length in the minor suits, or even holding two diamonds and three clubs, responder should make a diamond preference.

Holding five-five in the black suits the old standard was to start with clubs, then bid spades twice. The auction promised at least five cards in each suit. This was necessary when responder could bid at the two level with only game invitational values. After an opening bid of one spade and a two level red suit response, in order to show the club suit at the three level opener needed at least game invitational values (15+ HCP). This auction was known as a "high reverse" even though the suit lengths were not those expected for an ordinary reverse.

Since the new standards require responder to hold game forcing values for a two-over-one response, the modern standard is for opener to start with one spade with this pattern. After a two-over-one red suit response clubs can be bid at the three level without more than minimum opening bid values since the response forces the auction to game.

It follows that when opener does bid clubs first and then bids spades twice, he now promises six clubs and five spades.

## Opening in third seat

After two passes opener's need for a planned rebid still exists but is not nearly so necessary. Partner has passed so a response in a new suit will not be forcing and opener has the option to pass. The strength requirement for an opening bid in third seat falls to about 10 HCP, and the defensive trick requirement can be lowered to about one and one-half. When opener does open light—a hand that would not have opened in first or second seat—opener must still be able to control the auction.

If the light opening bid is in a minor suit, opener must be prepared to pass any response. This means the hand must have at least three cards in each higher-ranking suit. When the light opening bid is in a major suit it might be only four cards long. If opener is light and holds four cards in each of the major suits, the opening bid should be one heart whenever the quality of the heart suit is such that a heart lead would be good if on defense. The one heart opening bid allows for finding a fit in either major suit. That would not be easy if the opening bid were one spade.

When responder is not a passed hand, one notrump in response to opener's major suit call is forcing (more about this convention when we deal with responses). When responder has passed, the bid of one notrump is natural and non-forcing. As a passed hand, responder will not bid one notrump with a fit for opener's major suit. Opener often will pass one notrump and a major suit fit might be missed.

**Example 10:**

| a | b | c |
|---|---|---|
| ♠ J985 | ♠ J95 | ♠ K6 |
| ♥ KQ106 | ♥ Q1063 | ♥ Q973 |
| ♦ A4 | ♦ K109 | ♦ KJ6 |
| ♣ 753 | ♣ AJ6 | ♣ Q1075 |

**With Example 10a, you have a perfect opening bid of one heart in third seat. You hold good hearts and want an opening lead in that suit if the opponents declare, and can easily pass a response of either one spade or one notrump.**

**With Example 10b, open one club in third seat. You would like a club lead if your side defends, and you are prepared to pass any response.**

**With Example 10c, you should pass in third seat. You would like to have a club lead, but you are not prepared for a response of one spade. Were you to open and hear a one spade response you could not pass, and your rebid of one notrump would promise a full opening hand.**

# Opening in fourth seat

If there have been three passes and it is your turn, you obviously have the option to pass and end the auction. If your hand is poor, opening the bidding may lead to a minus score, so your only reason to open the bidding is that you expect to achieve a plus score. This means that you will usually have full opening bid values when you open in fourth seat. In either third or fourth seat, do not open with a four card major suit when you would have opened the bidding in first or second seat. Your bidding should be structured just as it would have been in first or second seat.

If you have a reasonable hand and feel that to open the bidding might lead to a plus score, even though the hand would not have been an opening bid in first or second seat, you should be able to compete if and when the opponents enter the auction (which you might have ended with the fourth pass).

Since none of the four players holds a real opening bid, to be successful you need to have an edge over the other side. The edge that you need to have is control of the master suit—spades. If the auction becomes competitive, you need to be able either to bid spades, or to defend against spades in order to have that edge.

The formula that allows you to know when you have that edge is called "the rule of fifteen". Add the total of your high card points to the number of spades in your hand. When the total is fifteen or more, feel free to open the bidding even though you are a bit light, but be sure that you have the required two defensive tricks. This formula was devised by the late Don Pearson, a former regular partner of World Champion John Swanson. This evaluation method is frequently called "Pearson points".

### Example 11:

| a | b | c |
|---|---|---|
| ♠ KJ965 | ♠ AJ3 | ♠ KJ96 |
| ♥ AJ3 | ♥ Q94 | ♥ AJ3 |
| ♦ Q94 | ♦ J63 | ♦ 63 |
| ♣ 63 | ♣ K965 | ♣ Q954 |

**With Example 11a, in fourth seat count your eleven high card points and add five for your spade length. With sixteen "Pearson points" open one spade.**

With Example 11b, when you count your eleven high card points and can add only three for spade length, you should pass in fourth seat. However, in third seat you would open one club and pass any response.

With Example 11c, your eleven high card points and four spades allow you to open in fourth seat. Your choices are between one club and one spade, and one club is probably better since it allows a heart contract to be reached when partner has length there. In third seat, you could also open with one club, but would have a problem if partner should happen to respond by bidding one diamond. In that case a rebid of one spade by you would promise full opening bid values, so if partner did respond one diamond you would need to pass.

## Opening bid exercises

On each of the following hands, ask yourself these questions: Would I open the bidding in first or second seat? Would I open in third seat? Would I open in fourth seat? What opening bid would I make? If not opening with a bid in notrump, what rebid have I planned?

1.
♠ KQ8
♥ QJ95
♦ 83
♣ AQJ6

2.
♠ 6
♥ AQ984
♦ KQJ6
♣ 875

3.
♠ AKJ10
♥ 86
♦ 93
♣ AKJ95

4.
♠ AK104
♥ A95
♦ 6
♣ KQ1065

5.
♠ Q1076
♥ KQJ8
♦ 85
♣ K109

6.
♠ A10975
♥ AQ109
♦ 7
♣ 963

7.
♠ 7
♥ AQJ8
♦ AKJ108
♣ K65

8.
♠ KJ104
♥ AQ6
♦ QJ103
♣ AQ

9.
♠ J983
♥ AQ
♦ KQ1083
♣ K6

10.
♠ AQ8
♥ KJ5
♦ KQ103
♣ AJ6

11.
♠ Q105
♥ K874
♦ A6
♣ KJ93

12.
♠ KJ975
♥ 6
♦ AQ93
♣ 1075

13.
♠ QJ9
♥ K985
♦ J43
♣ KQ9

14.
♠ K9
♥ Q83
♦ K6
♣ AQ10953

15.
♠ AQJ763
♥ 5
♦ A1093
♣ 62

16.
♠ 5
♥ K54
♦ AQJ1086
♣ A43

|  | 17. | 18. | 19. | 20. |
|--|-----|-----|-----|-----|
| ♠ | J8643 | KQ105 | 5 | AJ1053 |
| ♥ | AJ6 | 106 | KQ1093 | 75 |
| ♦ | AQJ8 | 9543 | AJ1063 | 6 |
| ♣ | 6 | AJ6 | J6 | AK842 |

## Answers

1. Open one notrump in any seat. Do not let the weak doubleton bother you. One notrump describes both your shape and your strength.

2. One heart in any seat. This is a classic minimum opening bid. Rebid two diamonds.

3. Open one club in any seat, and rebid one spade if partner responds in a red suit, jump raise to the three level if partner responds by bidding one spade, or make a **reverse** of two spades if partner responds one notrump. Do not make the error of opening one notrump with this semi-balanced hand. The suits are good but the doubletons are poor.

4. A clear opening bid of one club in any seat. Rebid one spade if partner responds in either red suit. If partner responds one spade, make a **jump reverse** of three diamonds. This call promises a four card fit in spades, shortness in diamonds, and a hand good enough to play at the three level even if the response is on minimum values and includes wasted cards in the diamond suit.

5. Do not open this hand in first, second or fourth seat. In third seat you have minimum values to make a lead directing opening bid of one heart. Plan to pass any response partner makes except for a **Drury** response of two clubs (see Chapter Eight).

6. Open with one spade in any seat. Do not be deceived by the fact that you hold only 10 HCP. Your hand includes two and one half defensive tricks, good distribution, and useful spot cards. Rigid point counters will get this one wrong.

7. Open with one diamond in any seat. You are ready to **reverse** at your rebid by next bidding two hearts. If partner bids one heart, you are willing to play game in hearts. However, if you jump to four hearts you might easily miss a slam if partner's hand fits well. With as little as: ♠ 863 ♥ K10963 ♦ Q4 ♣ A83 six hearts will be cold and partner will not bid further. You should make a **splinter** bid of three spades. This double jump should not be confused as being natural—a jump to two spades would be natural and forcing to game. Unnecessary double jumps are always **splinter** bids. When partner hears your **splinter** in spades, knowing that there is a maximum of

one spade loser, and that honor cards in hearts, diamonds and clubs are all "working" cards, a slam should be sought.

8.  Another excellent hand. Start by bidding one diamond. If partner responds with one heart, jump to two notrump. If partner responds by bidding one spade, jump raise spades to game. Your failure to **splinter** will describe a hand that is balanced, and must be in the high card range of 18 or 19 HCP. If partner responds by bidding one notrump, raise to three notrump.

9.  Open in any seat by bidding one notrump. This semi-balanced hand has excellent doubletons, and regardless of the final contract, the lead should come up to these tenaces rather than through them. This hand may declare notrump at any level, spades after a **Stayman** auction, or either major after a **transfer** bid. Regardless of the contract reached, making this hand declarer is imperative. (**Stayman** and **transfer bids** are explained in Chapter Seven).

10. Regardless of seat, open by bidding two notrump. A complete description.

11. A clear opening bid of one club in any seat. Rebid one notrump if the response is one spade, or raise a response of one heart to the two level.

12. Another shapely ten count, like problem six. This time you have less defensive strength and fewer good spot cards. Pass in first or second seat, but open one spade in either third or fourth seat. You do have fifteen "Pearson points".

13. Pass this hand (a very bad twelve HCP) in first or second seat. Open with one club (lead direction) in third seat and pass any response. Open in fourth seat if you wish. You do have fifteen Pearson Points, but do not be pleased about it.

14. Open one notrump in any seat. What's that? You hold only 14 HCP? So what! Start adding for the fifth and sixth club and for the good spot cards. And as with problem nine, this hand's tenaces should be protected at any contract. Anyone who opens this hand one club has not been paying attention. We hope you understand the need not only to learn bidding techniques, but also to develop judgment.

15. Open with one spade in any of the first three seats. Plan to repeat spades at your rebid rather than introduce diamonds. Your spade suit is good enough to be the trump suit even when partner has no real fit. In fourth seat, open by bidding two spades (more about this when we discuss opening two bids).

16. Open in any seat by bidding one diamond. If the response is one spade, soft pedal this hand with a simple rebid of two diamonds. If the response is one heart, your fit for hearts upgrades this hand to a jump rebid of three diamonds.

17. Open in any seat by bidding one spade. I agree, it is a lousy suit, but if partner can show a spade fit we will both like it a lot better. If partner makes a forcing response, your rebid will be in diamonds.

18. Another hand to pass in any seat except third. In third seat make the lead directing opening call of one spade. Pass any natural response.

19. Just 11 HCP, but a clear opening bid in any seat because of its excellent distribution and spot cards. Open with one heart and rebid in diamonds.

20. Open one spade, not one club. You will be able to show clubs after a red suit response at the two level since that response shows game forcing values. This is a major change from older methods.

A relatively new player who had not yet studied bidding was asked to sit down and bid a hand. "I don't know how, " he said. "Just describe what you are looking at," he was advised. The auction began: "Four clubs," by our tyro. "double! – pass – pass, four diamonds – double!! – pass – pass, four hearts – double!!! – pass – pass, and the singleton jack of spades!!!! How descriptive can an auction be?

# CHAPTER THREE

It is imperative that when a bid is made it is understood as being forcing, invitational, or completely non-forcing. If it is forcing, the partner of the bidder knows to continue to keep the auction alive. If it is invitational, the partner of the bidder knows to either accept or reject the invitation. It is possible to move on and bid a game, or to sign off in a playable part score. If the bid is known to be non-forcing, bidding is natural. It may be right to quit in a part score, or continue to bid when values are adequate to do so. The important matter is that bids must be understood so that the partner of the bidder is able to know how to continue.

## Opener's forcing auctions

The opening bidder can make the auction forcing in one of three ways.

1. Start with a forcing opening bid of two clubs. This opening bid shows a very strong hand and requires the responder to bid regardless of strength. Auctions of this nature will be discussed thoroughly when we talk about the opening bid of two clubs.

2. After opening with a suit bid at the one level and receiving a response, opener can make a jump shift rebid. Knowing that responder has some values, the jump shift rebid makes the auction forcing to the game level. Since responder is expected to hold a minimum of about six points in high cards, opener's jump shift rebid shows a good 19 HCP or the playing strength equivalent. Responder is alerted to continue bidding until at least a game contract has been reached.

3. After opening with a suit bid at the one level opener can rebid by making a **reverse**. We know what a **reverse** is. It guarantees that opener has more cards in the suit opened than in the rebid suit; it shows at least an ace more than a minimum opening bid (at least about 16+ HCP); and it is forcing for one round.

When opener holds a hand with better than minimum opening bid values, it will often not be possible to show those values with a rebid. A simple rebid is in the minimum range of 12+ to 15- HCP. With values in the better range of 15+ to 18 HCP, if a **reverse** is not descriptive, a simple rebid in a new suit will not show those extra values. Opener will need to wait until the time to make a third call (which usually happens after responder has been able to show a specific value range) to show unknown extra values.

To summarize, opener can make the auction forcing in any of three ways.

1. When opener holds a balanced hand of 22+ HCP, or a hand which can produce at least nine tricks without help from responder, begin by making the forcing opening bid of two clubs.

2. When opener holds 19+ HCP or the playing strength equivalent, after opening one in a suit and receiving a simple response, a jump shift rebid by opener makes the auction forcing to game.

3. A **reverse** at opener's rebid is forcing for one round. The **reverse** shows 16+ HCP and that opener's first suit is longer than the second suit. This specialized auction is forcing for only one round and describes specific suit lengths in opener's hand.

**Example 12:**

| a | b | c |
|---|---|---|
| ♠ KJ6 | ♠ AKQJ975 | ♠ AKQJ97 |
| ♥ AQ5 | ♥ A4 | ♥ K6 |
| ♦ AQ8 | ♦ AK | ♦ AQJ4 |
| ♣ AQ96 | ♣ Q3 | ♣ 8 |

| d | e |
|---|---|
| ♠ AKQ6 | ♠ A5 |
| ♥ 4 | ♥ AQJ6 |
| ♦ A5 | ♦ 7 |
| ♣ KQJ1093 | ♣ KQJ953 |

**With Example 12a, opener holds 22 HCP. To describe this hand, begin by making the forcing opening bid of two clubs, planning to rebid two notrump. The two club bid is completely forcing. The rebid of two notrump is not. It describes a balanced hand of 22 to 24 HCP.**

With Example 12b, ten tricks are available with spades as the trump suit. Opener holds 23 HCP and anticipates that an opening bid of one spade might be followed by three passes. Opener forestalls that possibility by opening with a bid of two clubs. After a response opener plans to jump in spades, setting the trump suit and forcing the auction further.

With Example 12c, opener begins with one spade. When responder shows limited values by bidding one notrump, opener makes the auction game forcing by making a jump shift rebid of three diamonds.

With Example 12d, opener first bids one club. After a response in diamonds or hearts at the one level opener makes the game forcing jump shift rebid of two spades. If responder bids one notrump opener will reverse by bidding two spades. If responder bids one spade opener will make a jump reverse by bidding three hearts.

With Example 12e, opener again begins with one club. After a response of one spade, opener's rebid of two hearts is a reverse, which is forcing for one round. If the response is one heart opener makes a jump reverse by bidding three diamonds. If the response is one diamond, make a simple rebid of one heart. You will show your extra values later, given the chance.

## Responder's forcing auctions

We have seen how opener can make the auction forcing. How does responder do the same thing? There are two specific tools that responder may use.

1. If responder has not passed and first bids in a lower ranking suit at the two level, it is a two-over-one response. All two-over-one responses by an unpassed hand are forcing to game. They show that responder's values are sufficient to cause a game contract to be reached.

   Responder promises opening bid values, or a hand that is good enough to force game because of a fit for the opening bidder's first suit. This is a MAJOR CHANGE in standard bidding. The Goren methods only required that responder hold game invitational values of about 10 HCP or more to make a two-over-one response.

   The fact that two-over-one responses are forcing to game makes auctions decidedly easier. An auction that is known to be game forcing allows great exchange of information without unnecessary consumption of bidding space. In older methods, strength showing jumps ate up bidding space, and when responder had made a two-over-one, opener had no clue as to whether game should be reached or not. Chapter Four covers extended two-over-one auctions in depth.

2. If the opening bid is in a major suit, a response of one notrump is forcing for one round. Goren's range for a response of one notrump was the minimum range of 5+ to 9- HCP and was not forcing. Goren allowed two-over-one responses with as little as 9+ HCP, which correlated with the range for the response of one notrump as minimum and non-forcing.

Because the modern standard for the two-over-one response has been increased and requires game forcing values, it follows that when responder holds game invitational values and cannot bid at the two level, responder must be able to bid one notrump not only with the values of a minimum response, but also with game invitational values. Responder can no longer bid at the two level with less than game forcing values, which makes it necessary for the response of one notrump to be made with both minimum and game invitational hands.

Responder's values can be enough to invite a game. Therefore, the response of one notrump after an opening bid of one of a major suit must be forcing for one round. Having made the forcing response of one notrump to the major suit opening bid, responder's rebid will clarify the values held. Certain rebids will show minimum response values (5+ to 9- HCP), while other rebids will show game invitational values (9+ to 12- HCP). Chapter Five details the **Forcing Notrump** in depth.

Setting aside these two specific situations, for responder to make the auction forcing there exists a specific bidding axiom:

A NEW SUIT BY AN UNPASSED RESPONDER IS FORCING.

No axiom exists without its exceptions. There are four specific exceptions to this axiom.

1. A new suit by an unpassed responder is forcing, but not after opener has rebid one notrump. After opener has rebid one notrump, if responder wishes to force, either a jump in a new suit or a **reverse** must be used. This often makes for unwieldy auctions when responder needs to force. Modern bidding methods give us some special tools to apply in such auctions (see Chapter Seven).

2. A new suit by an unpassed responder is forcing, but not if responder's first call was one notrump. If opener's first bid is in a minor suit, when responder bids one notrump it denies a four card major suit and limits the hand's values to the minimum response range of 5+ to 9-HCP.

   However, if opener's first suit is a major, responder's call of one notrump is forcing and shows the wide range of 5+ to 12-HCP. If responder then rebids in a new suit, it shows minimum response values (5+ to 9- HCP) and is not forcing.

3. A new suit by an unpassed responder is forcing, but not after an opponent has overcalled by bidding one notrump. After the overcall, if responder holds a good hand the usual action will be to double for penalties. If the notrump contract can be beaten by two tricks, that result will be better than if responder's side had fulfilled some part score. When responder does bid, it will be because a part score in the suit named is likely to make, but one notrump was not likely to have been beaten by two or more tricks and the partscore will produce a better result than a penalty double.

   If responder holds a hand without many high card values, but has distributional values, which might produce a game even though an opponent holds the values of an opening notrump, a forcing call is needed. After the overcall of one notrump, responder has only one forcing bid.

   When it is necessary to force, responder makes the cue bid of two notrump. Can this be construed as natural? Well, that doesn't make much sense. If responder is bidding to win eight tricks for a score of 120, then a double would be better since the opposing contract of one notrump would take only five tricks and be set by two tricks for a score of 300 or 500. The cue bid of two notrump must be forcing.

Responder expects to reach some game contract and make more than would be made by penalizing the notrump overcall.

4. A new suit by an unpassed responder is forcing, but not if it is at the two level after there has been a takeout double of the opening bid. Let us assume that partner has opened one spade. After the opponent in turn doubles for takeout, responder has certain obligations. Usually, the doubler will be short in spades. If responder is also short in spades and passes, doubler's partner (the advancer) will often hold about six spades, and might pass, converting the takeout double for penalties. When this happens, your partner, the opener, needs to know what to do.

If you have passed after the takeout double, you should have at least two cards in your partner's suit. Except when you happen to hold 4-4-4-1 distribution with a singleton spade, you will have a five card suit to bid. After the takeout double, when you bid your five card or longer suit, partner will know that you are very short in the opened suit. You will have at least five cards in the suit you have introduced after the takeout double, and a weak hand. Note that the takeout double has changed the meaning of your response at the two level. Instead of being forcing, it is a weak escape.

The double also changes the meaning of a response of one notrump when the opening bid has been in a major suit. Because of the double, the response of one notrump shows scattered minimum response values (5+ to 9- HCP) and at most a doubleton in opener's major suit.

**Example 13:**

| a | b | c | d |
|---|---|---|---|
| ♠ KJ954 | ♠ 6 | ♠ 85 | ♠ 6 |
| ♥ QJ1062 | ♥ QJ9754 | ♥ KJ10964 | ♥ 973 |
| ♦ 64 | ♦ K62 | ♦ 76 | ♦ KQ1085 |
| ♣ 3 | ♣ 543 | ♣ Q84 | ♣ J943 |

**Responder with Example 13a bids one spade after an opening bid in a minor suit. When opener rebids one notrump, responder limits this hand's values by making the non-forcing rebid of two hearts. Opener's rebid of one notrump has caused this new suit by responder to become non-forcing.**

With Example 13b, responder bids one notrump when partner has opened one spade. After opener rebids two clubs responder continues by bidding two hearts. The fact that responder's first call was one notrump causes the second call of two hearts to become non-forcing even though it is a new suit and responder has not passed.

With Example 13c, responder has heard an opening bid of one club by partner and an overcall of one notrump by the opponent next in turn. Responder bids two hearts. The overcall in notrump has caused this new suit to be non-forcing.

With Example 13d, opener has bid one spade and there has been a double for takeout by the opponent next in turn. Responder bids two diamonds, which shows minimum values, denies a fit for spades, and is non-forcing because of the takeout double.

## Fourth suit forcing

Setting aside the four exceptions, in many auctions responder will be able to make the auction forcing only by bidding a new suit. When opener has started with a minor suit, responder's bid in a higher-ranking suit at the one level is forcing simply because it is a new suit. Responder may have values that are minimum, game invitational, game forcing, or enough to seek a slam. All that is known by opener is that responder has shown a suit of at least four cards and values enough to make a response.

If opener's rebid is in a third suit and responder needs to continue to make the auction forcing, there is only one suit left to bid. In this case, responder bids that **fourth suit** no matter what that suit holding might be. When this happens, responder guarantees at least game invitational values.

Because a rebid in a new suit by opener was not forcing, opener's values are known to be about 12+ to as much as 18 HCP. With a sound opening bid, when responder has made use of **fourth suit forcing,** opener knows that a game should be reached. In such auctions opener has specific responsibilities, which are:

> 1. The first priority is to show a three card fit for responder's (major) suit. Since responder's values are at least invitational, when opener does show three card support for responder it is necessary to also either accept or reject the implied invitation. Suppose the auction has been: 1♣ - pass - 1♥ - pass, 1♠ - pass - 2♦ - pass, ?? If opener next bids two hearts, that shows a three card fit for

responder's suit but rejects the implicit game invitation. Opener's values will be minimum (12 or 13 HCP). With values of 14 HCP or more, opener must accept the game invitation by jumping to three hearts.

**Example 14:**

| a | b |
|---|---|
| ♠ AQ94 | ♠ AQ94 |
| ♥ Q83 | ♥ Q83 |
| ♦ 64 | ♦ 64 |
| ♣ KJ105 | ♣ AQ105 |

**Opener with Example 14a begins by bidding one club and hears a response of one heart. After opener rebids one spade responder next bids two diamonds**—fourth suit forcing. **Opener shows minimum values and three card support for hearts by next bidding two hearts.**

**Opener with Example 14b begins by bidding one club and hears a response of one heart. After opener rebids one spades responder next bids two diamonds**—fourth suit forcing. **Opener accepts the implicit game invitation and shows a three card heart fit by jumping to three hearts.**

2. When opener does not have three card support for responder's suit, the second priority is to bid notrump when holding a stopper in the fourth suit. Again, with minimum values of 12 or 13 HCP opener will decline the game invitation by bidding only two notrump, but with greater values opener must accept the invitation and jump to three notrump.

   If responder's first call was one diamond after an opening bid of one club, these first two priorities are inverted. Seeking game in a major suit has good priority, but game in notrump is strongly preferred over game in a minor suit.

**Example 15:**

| a | b |
|---|---|
| ♠ AQ94 | ♠ AQ94 |
| ♥ 64 | ♥ 64 |
| ♦ Q106 | ♦ Q106 |
| ♣ KJ105 | ♣ AQ105 |

**Opener with Example 15a begins with one club and rebids one spade after a response of one heart. When responder next bids two diamonds**—fourth suit forcing—**opener bids two notrump. This shows minimum opening bid values, denies three hearts, and promises a stopper in diamonds**—the fourth suit.

**Opener with Example 15b begins with one club and rebids one spade after a response of one heart. When responder next bids two diamonds**—fourth suit forcing—**opener jumps to three notrump. This promises that opener has enough in extra values to accept the implicit game invitation (all hands with 14 HCP or more should accept when invited), denies three hearts, and promises a stopper in diamonds**—the fourth suit.

3. When opener can neither show a three card fit nor bid notrump, the most descriptive rebid will be sought. If opener's first suit is five cards or longer, that suit can be rebid next. Raising the **fourth suit** (with one exception) shows four card support for the **fourth suit** (this takes priority over bidding notrump to show a stopper in the **fourth suit**).

   **Example 16:**

   | a | b | c |
   |---|---|---|
   | ♠ AQ94 | ♠ AQ94 | ♠ 983 |
   | ♥ Q8 | ♥ — | ♥ 6 |
   | ♦ 64 | ♦ Q864 | ♦ AQ1094 |
   | ♣ KJ1095 | ♣ KQ1095 | ♣ AQJ6 |

**With Example 16a, opener starts with one club and rebids one spade after a response of one heart. When responder next bids two diamonds**—fourth suit forcing—**opener makes the best description by bidding three clubs to show a suit at least five cards long.**

**With Example 16b, opener again starts by bidding one club and rebids one spade after a response of one heart. When responder next bids two diamonds**—fourth suit forcing—**opener bids three diamonds, raising the** fourth suit **to show four cards in that suit.**

**With Example 16c, opener bids one diamond and after a response of one heart rebids two clubs. When responder next bids two spades**—fourth suit forcing—**opener raises to three spades. This is the sole exception to the fact that a raise of** the fourth suit **shows four cards in that suit. Opener denied holding four spades by rebidding two clubs. With a spade stopper, after** the fourth suit **opener would have**

bid notrump. Therefore, in this specific auction opener shows a pattern including three small spades and a singleton heart. If opener had been 3-0-5-5, the descriptive rebid would instead have been three clubs.

4. Opener can have one hand that cannot be expressed. With four-four in the two bid suits, a doubleton in responder's suit, and no stopper in the fourth suit, there is no call available that would be expressive. Improvisation is in order. If opener tells a "little lie" by showing three card support with a doubleton, or bids notrump with three cards to the ten in the **fourth suit**, partner will be completely misled, and the wrong contract will usually be reached.

Opener should instead tell a huge lie by rebidding the second suit. Of course, this auction shows that opener has six-five distribution, but responder should be aware that opener will have the unbidable hand far more often than the six-five hand which has been described. Responder should give opener one more chance to confirm which hand is held and the situation will be clarified. With Example 17a, opener could jump in spades to avoid confusion.

### Example 17:

| a | b |
|---|---|
| ♠ AQ965 | ♠ AQ94 |
| ♥ 7 | ♥ 85 |
| ♦ 4 | ♦ J74 |
| ♣ AQ10954 | ♣ AQ105 |

With Example 17a, opener bids one club. After a response of one heart opener rebids one spade. When responder next bids two diamonds—fourth suit forcing—opener completes the description of 6-5 distribution by rebidding spades. This rebid shows a hand pattern that includes six clubs and five spades.

With Example 17b, opener bids one club. After a response of one heart opener rebids one spade. When responder next bids two diamonds—fourth suit forcing—opener does not have a descriptive rebid. This hand does not have three card support for hearts, it has no stopper in diamonds, the first suit cannot be rebid as it is only four cards in length, and a raise of the fourth suit would not describe.

**This problem is solved when opener makes the most improbable rebid of two spades. This call actually describes the hand of Example 17a, but responder knows that opener could be faced with the inability to truly describe. Holding Example 17a, opener can jump to three spades to clarify.**

A jump in the **fourth suit** can be assigned one of several meanings. Some play that it is natural and forcing. Others play that when the **fourth suit** is a minor, this jump shows a weak hand with only four cards in responder's first suit and six or seven cards in the minor suit of responder's rebid. It is an attempt to play in the minor suit of the jump (see **New Minor Forcing** in Chapter Seven).

One auction deserves attention. When the auction has been: 1♣ - pass - 1♦ - pass, 1♥ - pass - ?, what does responder's bid of one spade mean? Is it natural, or is it **fourth suit forcing**. Since responder may wish to bid notrump but not have a stopper in spades, one spade should be **fourth suit forcing**, and a jump to two spades should be a natural call, showing both diamonds and spades and a hand with good values.

To summarize, responder has several tools that can be used to make the auction forcing:

1. If responder's first call is a two-over-one response, the auction is natural and forcing to game. Chapter Four deals in depth with two-over-one auctions.

2. If the opening bid has been in a major suit, responder's call of one notrump is forcing for one round. It shows the wide range of 5+ to 12- HCP. Chapter Five details the **Forcing Notrump**.

3. When three suits have been bid, responder can force by bidding the **fourth suit**, no matter what the holding in that suit might be. Responder may have game invitational values of 9+ to 12- or may have more. Responder cannot bid the **fourth suit** with less than game invitational values.

The function of this chapter has been to allow the reader to learn how to make an auction forcing, either as opening bidder or as responder. Responder's auctions have been given special attention. When the game to be bid is known, responder can bid it. When more information is needed, responder uses **fourth suit forcing**.

The next two chapters detail other tools which were mentioned but not elaborated upon—auctions that include a game forcing two-over-one response, and auctions which include use of the **forcing notrump**. In Chapter Six, which details responder's descriptive auctions, further explanation of the use of **fourth suit forcing** is included.

# CHAPTER FOUR

## RESPONDER'S TWO-OVER-ONE IS FORCING TO GAME

A major factor in the standard methods of today is: responder's first call at the two level in a suit which is lower ranking than the suit of the opening bid is forcing to game. This is a decided change from the old standard that required responder only to have game invitational values to make such a response.

Only six such auctions exist. In response to an opening bid of one diamond, responder can bid two clubs. In response to an opening bid of one heart, responder can bid either two clubs or two diamonds. In response to an opening bid of one spade, responder can bid two clubs, two diamonds, or two hearts.

All of these responses are natural, showing length in the suit bid. Only one of the six, however, guarantees a suit of five cards or more. The two heart response to the opening bid of one spade promises at least a five card suit. Other such auctions will frequently be made with a suit of five or more cards, but in minor suits four card length is frequent. In fact, if responder is 3-4-3-3 and must make a response at the two level after an opening bid of one spade, a bid of two clubs might be made on a three card holding when responder's values are too great for a **Forcing Notrump**.

There is one exception to the game force. If responder bids, rebids and rebids again in the same minor suit and opener has no fit, the auction can stop at four of the minor suit. With no apparent fit, the bidding side must have some place to play, and in this auction, four of responder's long minor is probably the best place.

When the opening bid is in a major suit and responder does not have the values to make a game forcing two-over-one response, the **Forcing Notrump** is available (read all about this in Chapter Five). However, in response to the opening bid of one diamond the **Forcing notrump** does not apply. Responder must know how to describe a hand with game invitational values (9+ to 12- HCP).

## Responder's jump to three clubs after a one diamond opening bid

After an opening bid of one diamond, when responder's club suit is six or seven cards long and the hand has the invitational values of 9+ to 12- HCP, responder makes an immediate jump to three clubs. When opener has a bare minimum in values, pass is an option, as this response is not forcing.

Holding greater values, particularly with a club fit, opener can accept the invitation and bid three notrump. With a very good hand, opener can search for a slam.

## Responder to one diamond (or one club) jumps in notrump.

With fewer than six clubs, responder's hand will frequently be balanced. A balanced hand with game invitational values and no four card major suit is described by an immediate jump to two notrump. (Note: In ACBL sanctioned tournament or club play both of these calls require alerts because they are weaker than they sound and are not forcing.)

**Example 18:**

| a | b |
|---|---|
| ♠ K5 | ♠ K53 |
| ♥ Q62 | ♥ Q62 |
| ♦ 95 | ♦ K95 |
| ♣ KQJ953 | ♣ QJ53 |

**When opener bids one diamond, responder with Example 18a responds three clubs. This call shows game invitational values (9+ to 12- HCP) and a six card club suit. With excellent suit quality, this auction has described responder's hand perfectly.**

**With Example 18b, when opener has bid either one club or one diamond, responder jumps to two notrump. This call denies a four card major and promises game invitational values in the range of 9+ to 12- HCP. This example is near perfect as responder also holds tenace positions in every suit.**

## Rebids by a two club responder to a one diamond opening bid

When opener bids one diamond and responder bids two clubs, the auction is always natural and forcing to game. If responder bids two game forcing clubs, then bids two notrump at the next turn, the values shown will either be in the minimum range of 12+ to 15- HCP, or they will be in the range of 18 to 19 HCP. When responder is balanced and in the range of 15+ to 18- HCP, the rebid after a two club response will be a jump to three notrump.

**Example 19:**

|  | a | b | c |
|---|---|---|---|
| ♠ | K9 | AQ5 | AQ5 |
| ♥ | Q62 | KQ6 | Q62 |
| ♦ | K54 | K52 | K52 |
| ♣ | KQ873 | KQ73 | KQ73 |

**With Example 19a, after an opening bid of one diamond responder has bid two clubs. If opener next bids two hearts responder bids two notrump. This protects the spade king and announces a range of either 12+ to 15- HCP or 18 or 19 HCP.**

**With Example 19b, responder again bids two clubs after an opening bid of one diamond. When opener continues by bidding two of a major suit, responder next bids two notrump. If opener raises to three notrump (likely) this responder will continue by bidding four notrump (invitational to 6NT - not Blackwood) to show a range of 18 or 19 HCP rather than minimum values. If after three notrump responder wished to ask for aces, a jump to five clubs would be** Gerber.

**With Example 19c, responder again bids two clubs after an opening bid of one diamond. If opener continues by bidding two diamonds or two of a major suit, responder jumps to three notrump to show the values of 15+ to 18- HCP.**

If responder bids two clubs, then rebids three clubs, it promises a very good suit of at least six cards which could be a source of tricks for a contract in notrump, or an excellent trump suit for a possible slam, but puts no top limit on the values held.

**Example 20:**

|  | a | b |
|---|---|---|
| ♠ | 63 | 6 |
| ♥ | K104 | AJ4 |
| ♦ | Q9 | K9 |
| ♣ | AKJ1083 | AKQ10832 |

**With each of the hands in Example 20, responder to an opening bid of one diamond will bid two clubs. If opener rebids two of a major suit both of these responders will rebid three clubs to show that the essence of the hand is an excellent club suit. If opener instead rebids two notrump, 20a will raise to three notrump, but 20b will bid three clubs because the extra values and solid suit still suggest that a slam in clubs is probable.**

Responder's rebid in a major suit does not put a top limit on the values held, but promises that this game forcing hand has more length in clubs than in the major suit. The minor suit will be at least five cards long and the major usually only four cards.

Example 21:

|  a |  b |
|---|---|
| ♠ AQ95 | ♠ K3 |
| ♥ K3 | ♥ AQ95 |
| ♦ 62 | ♦ A2 |
| ♣ KQ973 | ♣ KQ973 |

**With Example 21a, responder to an opening bid of one diamond bids two clubs. If opener's rebid is two notrump responder bids three spades. Opener has not denied holding a four card major and a four-four fit in spades still may exist. If opener rebids two hearts, responder next bids two spades. Opener could be 4-4-4-1 and may still have a four card fit for spades.**

**With Example 21b, responder to an opening bid of one diamond will bid two clubs. If opener next bids two notrump responder bids three hearts as there could still be a four-four fit in hearts. If opener's rebid is two hearts, this responder raises hearts to three - not four. The three heart call suggests a slam while a bid of four hearts at this point would be** fast arrival, **showing much less high card strength.**

## Fast arrival

After the two-over-one response a raise of opener's major suit rebid at the two level promises four card support for the major as well as longer clubs. If the raise is to the four level responder has used **fast arrival**, which limits the values of the hand to the range of 12+ to 15- HCP. With greater values, responder raises only to the three level. This gentle raise is still forcing. The initial two-over-one response made the auction forcing to game. Responder suggests a slam while conserving bidding space.

The principle of **fast arrival** needs explanation. When either partner knows the major suit that should be the trump suit, faces a hand that has limited its values to the minimum range of 12+ to 15- HCP, and knows that the combined values are not adequate for slam, a jump to game in the known major suit fit is used to end the auction. These jumps sound strong, but make no mistake, it is conceptually wrong to jump to show a strong hand when the auction is already forcing. (Note: the principle of **fast arrival** applies to major suit auctions only—not to notrump or minor suit auctions).

Conversely, when such an auction is forcing and the bidder still believes that slam is possible, rather than use bidding space by jumping, the fit is shown cheaply and space is conserved.

When responder has shown extra values by not using **fast arrival**, opener can reject the slam suggestion by simply continuing to game in the agreed major suit, or can show interest in slam by making a cue bid to show a control in a side suit. This auction allows for a slam search below the level of game. The old approach to standard bidding required jumps to show strength and did not allow for this exchange of information at such a low level. Often, when slam tries consumed too much bidding space the eventual contract was in jeopardy at the five level.

**Look again at Example 21. With 21a, after an opening bid of one diamond and a response of two clubs, if opener's rebid is two spades, responder will use** fast arrival **and raise to four spades. This shows minimum game forcing values in the range of 12+ to 15- HCP. However, with Example 21b, if in the same auction opener's rebid is two hearts, responder bids only three hearts to show extra values and invite a slam. This leaves room for opener to cue bid to show a control in a side suit below the level of game when opener shares responder's slam interest.**

## Opener's rebids after a two club response to one diamond

The first obligation of a one diamond opener after a game forcing two club response is to affirm or deny diamond length. Holding five or more diamonds, most hands will bid two diamonds to show that length. These exceptions exist:

1.  With 15+ HCP and six or more diamonds, responder shows extra length and good values by jump rebidding three diamonds.

2.  With a 5-3-3-2 pattern (or any balanced hand which should open one diamond) and 18 or 19 HCP, opener jump rebids three notrump.

3. When opener has a natural club raise, it is best to suppress diamond length in favor of the more descriptive raise. With minimum opening bid values, the raise requires four card club support. A three card raise requires a sound opening hand, usually 14+ HCP, and a high club honor. With four card support and good values opener can raise by making a **splinter**, jumping in an unbid suit to show shortness (a singleton or void).

**Example 22:**

|  | a | b | c |
|---|---|---|---|
| ♠ | A83 | AQ3 | 7 |
| ♥ | 7 | KQ4 | A53 |
| ♦ | AQJ1094 | QJ962 | Q9642 |
| ♣ | A103 | A9 | AQ62 |

|  | d | e |
|---|---|---|
| ♠ | AJ3 | A108 |
| ♥ | 85 | 6 |
| ♦ | Q9642 | A9543 |
| ♣ | AQ9 | AQJ6 |

**With Example 22a, opener bids one diamond and hears a response of two clubs. Opener's rebid to describe is a jump to three diamonds, which shows extra values (15+ to 18 HCP) and a good suit at least six cards long.**

**With Example 22b, opener bids one diamond and hears a response of two clubs. Opener makes a jump rebid of three notrump which shows a balanced hand in the range of 18 to 19 HCP.**

**With Example 22c, opener starts by bidding one diamond. When responder bids two clubs opener can see that a club raise is more descriptive although there are five diamonds. This hand is not strong enough to** splinter **in support of clubs.**

**With Example 22d, opener has a close choice after opening one diamond and receiving a response of two clubs. With a five card diamond suit and three clubs there is a choice between showing diamond length and raising responder's club suit. Either call may work on a given occasion.**

**With Example 22e, after opener bids one diamond and hears a response of two clubs, the best description is clearly a jump to three hearts. This is a**

splinter **bid which shows shortness in hearts, a four card fit for clubs, and a better than minimum hand for the auction.**

Opener's rebid in a major suit nearly always shows four cards in the major, no more than four diamonds, and does not promise any extra values. The two-over-one response has guaranteed game values. Opener needs no extra strength for this auction, which should not be mistaken as a **reverse**.

When opener rebids in a major suit, the auction sounds like a **reverse**, but it usually is not. Opener tends to deny as many as five diamonds since there was no rebid in that suit. The expected distribution is four diamonds and four of the major suit. Opener will not have a true **reverse** unless there are five cards in the major suit, and therefore at least six diamonds. That hand will be shown by a rebid of the major at opener's third turn.

**Example 23:**

|  | a | b | c |
|---|---|---|---|
| ♠ | 63 | K63 | 7 |
| ♥ | AQ94 | AQ43 | AKJ62 |
| ♦ | AQ62 | KJ102 | AQJ1085 |
| ♣ | J43 | 95 | 3 |

**With Example 23a, opener bids one diamond. After a response of two clubs opener's rebid of two hearts shows fewer than five diamonds, a four card holding in hearts, and a hand not suitable to the rebid of two notrump. Since responder has shown game forcing values, opener's rebid is not deemed a** reverse.

**With Example 23b, opener again starts with one diamond. When the response is two clubs, opener next bids two notrump to show stoppers and tenaces in both major suits. This call does not deny a four card major suit. If a four-four fit in hearts exists it will be discovered when responder next bids hearts.**

**With Example 23c, opener again starts with one diamond. When the response is two clubs opener next bids two hearts. Responder will believe that opener's hand is that of Example 23a—the usual hand on this auction. However, opener will next rebid the heart suit, promising five card length and thereby showing that the diamonds are six long. The auction shows that opener has the values to** reverse.

If opener instead rebids two notrump, it does not deny a four card major. The rebid shows minimum (12+ to 15- HCP) values, and promises stoppers in both majors. The hand should include tenaces that would furnish an advantage if the opening lead comes up to it rather than through it.

Knowing that opener has not denied a four card major with the two notrump rebid, when responder holds a four card major in addition to a longer club suit, the auction must continue to describe. Responder's rebid in a four card major shows at least five-four distribution. When the four-four fit in a major suit exists, a sensitive auction will discover it (See Examples 21 and 23).

## The two-over-one response to a major suit opening bid

When responder has made a two-over-one response to a major suit opening bid, a descriptive rebid must follow. A repeat of the suit in which the two-over-one response was made shows a six card or longer suit and the auction is still game forcing. If responder next bids a new suit, that choice will be the most descriptive call available at that turn to bid. If responder next bids in notrump the auction will show a somewhat balanced hand with interest in declaring at notrump and indicate the values of the hand.

Responder's jump to three notrump after a two-over-one response and a two level rebid by opener shows a value range of 15 to 17 HCP. When responder's rebid is only two notrump the values shown will be either less or more. With 12+ to 15- HCP, responder rebids two notrump. This rebid usually shows minimum values for the two-over-one response and announces stoppers in any unbid suits. With values of 18+ this same rebid will be made, but responder plans to show greater values if the auction continues with a three notrump raise from opener. Responder plans to next bid four notrump to show the extra values of 18+ HCP rather than the minimum of 12+ to 15- HCP.

Whatever responder's rebid might be after a two-over-one response, it is always the call that responder feels best describes the hand.

## The two-over-one responder holds a three card fit for opener's major suit

When the opening bid has been in a major suit, responder who makes a two level game forcing call will often hold a three card fit for that major. Responder's rebid will show that fit. If opener's rebid is either a repeat of the original major suit at the two level, or a call of two notrump, a value limit of the minimum (12+ to 15- HCP) opening bid range has been shown. (Note: A rebid that repeats opener's first suit does not promise more than five card length. There may be no other options). When opener's hand has been limited by either of these two auctions, responder can show a three card fit for opener's major in either of two ways.

1. If responder's values are also limited (12+ to 15- HCP), realizing that the combined values of the two hands are adequate for game, but insufficient for slam, responder jumps to game in the major suit, utilizing the principle of **fast arrival**.

2. When responder's values are greater (15+ HCP), the three card fit for opener's major suit is shown at the three level, thereby suggesting interest in a slam. Opener is able to reject this slam invitation by continuing to four of the agreed major suit, or can show similar slam interest by making a cue bid to show a side suit control. Again, we see an auction in which a slam try is generated below the level of game.

**Example 24:**

| a | b |
|---|---|
| ♠ K93 | ♠ K93 |
| ♥ A6 | ♥ A6 |
| ♦ 732 | ♦ K32 |
| ♣ AQ952 | ♣ AK952 |

**With Example 24a, responder bids two clubs in response to an opening bid of one spade. If opener's rebid is either two spades or two notrump, (both of these calls limit opener's values to the minimum of 12+ to 15- HCP), responder next jumps to four spades. The known values in the two hands are not likely to produce a slam, so responder invokes the principle of** fast arrival.

**With Example 24b, responder again bids two clubs after an opening bid of one spade. If opener's rebid is either two spades or two notrump, this responder next bids only three spades. This rebid shows responder's three card fit as well as extra values and slam interest.**

When opener rebids in a lower ranking suit, responder can show a three card fit for the opening bid at the two level with values that are minimum for the two-over-one response (12+ to 15- HCP), but can jump to the three level with greater values (15+ HCP).

**After a one spade opening bid and a two club response, if opener rebids either two diamonds or two hearts, responder with Example 24a bids two spades to show three card support with minimum two-over-one response values (12+ to 15- HCP).**

**After a one spade opening bid and a two club response, if opener rebids either two diamonds or two hearts, holding Example 24b responder will jump to three spades to show three card support with values enough to suggest a slam.**

When responder has made a two-over-one and opener has rebid in a new suit, that does not limit opener's values to the minimum range of 12+ to 15- HCP. Opener's values are virtually unlimited in this auction. In this case, if responder jumps to game in opener's major suit the jump does not constitute **fast arrival**. Instead, it is a descriptive rebid designed to show values concentrated in the suit of the response and in opener's major. It also denies any control either by high card or shortness in either of the unbid suits.

### Example 25:

♠ KQ6
♥ 74
♦ 932
♣ AKJ42

**After an opening bid of one spade and a response of two clubs, if opener's rebid is two diamonds or two hearts, with Example 25 responder next jumps to four spades. This auction says that responder holds good values in clubs and spades, but no control for a possible slam either by shortness or high card in diamonds or in hearts. The jump is completely expressive of responder's hand.**

When responder shows a three card fit by returning to opener's major suit at the two level, opener has the option to use **fast arrival** by jumping to game in the now agreed major suit holding values that are also minimum (12+ to 15- HCP), or to simply reraise the agreed major suit to the three level or to cue bid in a new suit to suggest interest in a slam. This time the responder can reject the invitation by going to game in the agreed major suit, or can show interest in slam by making a cue bid.

**Example 26:**

|  | **a** | **b** | **c** |
|---|---|---|---|
| ♠ | AQ864 | AQ864 | K93 |
| ♥ | K3 | K3 | A6 |
| ♦ | A863 | AJ63 | K54 |
| ♣ | 83 | K3 | A9762 |

With Example 26a, opener bids one spade. After a response of two clubs opener rebids two diamonds. If responder next bids two spades, this opener knows that both hands hold limited values and utilizes fast arrival **by jumping to four spades.**

With Example 26b, the auction is similar. Opener first bids one spade, then rebids two diamonds after a two club response. When responder continues by bidding two spades to show minimum (12+ to 15- HCP) values for the game forcing response, this opener realizes that slam is still possible, and continues by bidding two notrump to show extra values in a semibalanced hand and suggest the possibility of slam.

With a hand such as Example 26c, which includes controls, responder cooperates in the slam search by next bidding three clubs to show a control. Opener then bids three diamonds and responder continues by bidding three hearts. This series of cue bids shows the controls necessary for a spade slam, which now can easily be bid.

## Opener jump rebids with a good suit after a two-over-one response

If after the two-over-one response opener's rebid is a jump in the original suit, it promises that the suit is of excellent quality, at least six cards long, and that the hand has values are greater than those of a minimum opening bid (15+ HCP). Some modern bidders insist that this jump show a completely solid suit, but that restriction does not allow opener to show good values when the suit is good but not solid. The distortion of rebidding only two of the major, concealing those extra values just because the suit is not solid makes little sense.

**Example 27:**

| a | b |
|---|---|
| ♠ AKQJ92 | ♠ AQJ1093 |
| ♥ KJ2 | ♥ KQ2 |
| ♦ K84 | ♦ A54 |
| ♣ 6 | ♣ 6 |

**With both hands of Example 27, opener begins by bidding one spade. After a response of two clubs, both of these hands should describe by jumping to three spades as a rebid. Those who advocate that opener must hold a solid suit will be happy with Example 27a, but not with Example 27b. However, the requirement that this rebid must show a solid suit should be set aside and not interfere with opener's ability to describe both the good suit and extra values that are held.**

## Opener's jump shift rebid after a two-over-one response is a splinter

After a two-over-one response, if opener's rebid is a jump in any new suit, this jump is a **splinter** raise of responder's suit. Opener will have sound values, a singleton or void in the suit of the jump rebid, and four card support for responder. Since the two-over-one response has made the auction forcing to game, a natural jump shift by opener to show super values would take up bidding space unnecessarily. A slow auction makes more sense since it allows both bidders to describe more easily.

**Example 28:**

| a | b |
|---|---|
| ♠ AQ1094 | ♠ AQ1094 |
| ♥ KQ63 | ♥ 5 |
| ♦ 5 | ♦ K63 |
| ♣ K63 | ♣ KQ63 |

**With both hands of Example 28, opener begins by bidding one spade. If responder bids two hearts, opener with Example 28a should jump to four diamonds to show a sound hand, four card support for hearts, and a singleton or void in diamonds.**

If responder to the opening bid of one spade bids two clubs, with Example hand 28b opener should next jump to three hearts to show a sound opening bid, four card support for clubs, and a singleton or void in hearts.

## Opener raises responder's suit

If opener's rebid is a simple raise of responder's suit, with only 12 or 13 HCP, the hand will have four card support. If the raise is made with three card support for responder's suit, that will be because opener has no rebid that is more descriptive, and the hand shown will include 14+ HCP as well as a high honor card in responder's suit.

**Example 29:**

|  a  |  b  |
|-----|-----|
| ♠ KQ963 | ♠ KJ863 |
| ♥ A5 | ♥ AQ |
| ♦ J984 | ♦ KJ4 |
| ♣ K2 | ♣ 832 |

**With Example 29a, opener bids one spade. If responder bids two diamonds, opener can raise. This hand's values are minimum, but there is four card diamond support.**

**With Example 29b, opener bids one spade. If responder bids two diamonds, opener must find the most expressive rebid. Two notrump with no stopper in clubs is not acceptable, and showing a good three card holding in diamonds is better than a rebid of the five card spade suit. Opener rebids by raising to three diamonds. If responder had bid two clubs, opener would have had an expressive rebid of two notrump with stoppers in both unbid suits.**

## Opener's rebid of two notrump

When opener rebids two notrump, the auction does not promise any extra values. It shows a hand that is balanced (usually 5-3-3-2), and promises stoppers in both of the unbid suits. The values for this rebid will be minimum (12+ to 15- HCP) or very good (18 or 19 HCP). With the very good hand, opener will take later action to show the additional values. With the values of an opening notrump, opener's rebid will instead be a jump to three notrump. There will be some reason that the opening bid was in the major suit rather than one notrump.

Example 30:

|  | a | b | c |
|---|---|---|---|
| ♠ | K86 | K85 | K8 |
| ♥ | AQ942 | AQ942 | AQ942 |
| ♦ | K83 | AQ3 | A93 |
| ♣ | 94 | K4 | K64 |

With Example 30a, opener bids one heart. When responder bids two clubs, opener next bids two notrump. This shows that both unbid suits are stopped and that opener's values are either minimum or very good. The auction is forcing to game and opener can show the difference at the next call.

With Example 30b, opener bids one heart. When responder bids two clubs, opener next bids two notrump. This shows that both unbid suits are stopped and that opener's values are either minimum or very good. With this hand, opener will show extra values at the next turn. The most common auction will be that responder will next bid three notrump. If that happens opener shows extra values by continuing to four notrump (again, invitational).

With Example 30c, opener might have started by bidding one notrump, but did not because the hand includes five hearts and only two spades (see Chapter Two). After a response of two clubs or two diamonds, opener shows this value range (15+ to 18- HCP) by jumping to three notrump. Note that fast arrival **does not apply to jumps in notrump**.

## A one heart opener rebids in spades

If opener bids one heart and rebids two spades after a minor suit response, it shows shape, but does not promise the values of a **reverse**. Because the auction is already game forcing, the extra values of a **reverse** are not needed, and it behooves opener to complete the shape description.

Example 31:

|  | a | b |
|---|---|---|
| ♠ | AQ94 | AQ94 |
| ♥ | KQ963 | AKJ63 |
| ♦ | 84 | 84 |
| ♣ | 63 | A3 |

With Example 31a, opener bids one heart and hears responder bid two in either minor suit. Opener next bids two spades to show distribution. This bid does not show any extra values after the two-over-one response so responder must alert.

With Example 31b, opener again bids one heart. If responder bids two of either minor suit, opener bids two spades to show distribution. Opener has substantial extra values and will need to show them later in the auction, as the rebid of two spades has not shown more than minimum values.

If responder bids one notrump (forcing), rather than at the two level, opener with Example 31b would still bid two spades, which shows the values for a true reverse. With Example 31a, opener would not be able to rebid to show spades, since that requires the values of a reverse. Opener's rebid in that auction is discussed in Chapter Five.

## Opener rebids a new suit at the two level

By opening one spade and rebidding two hearts after a minor suit response, opener does not show anything extra in values, but does show at least four hearts. However, if the response has been two clubs and opener rebids two diamonds, this rebid might be on a suit of as few as three cards. The suit is a minor and not a true candidate to be the trump suit. Opener can rebid to show diamond values and deny a stopper in hearts.

Temporizing in a minor suit will rarely create problems and may be the best available description, but if any bidder temporizes in a major suit of less than four cards the auction may suddenly get out of control.

Example 32:

| a | b | c |
|---|---|---|
| ♠ KJ1094 | ♠ KJ1094 | ♠ KJ1094 |
| ♥ AQ83 | ♥ 963 | ♥ AK6 |
| ♦ A4 | ♦ AK6 | ♦ 963 |
| ♣ 92 | ♣ Q8 | ♣ Q8 |

With Example 32a, opener bids one spade. After a response in either minor suit, there is an easy and natural rebid of two hearts.

With Example 32b, opener again starts with one spade. If responder bids two clubs, opener's best description is to bid two diamonds. It cannot be right to rebid two notrump without a stopper in hearts. Although this rebid may convey the impression of length in diamonds, it is understood that responder will not reach out to play in a minor suit. Holding heart cards, responder will know to bid notrump.

With Example 32c, opener again starts with one spade. If responder bids two clubs, opener is somewhat strapped. Temporizing in hearts is dangerous, since if responder also holds four cards in hearts, a raise to game would be possible. Being unable to bid to show heart values, opener has no choice but to rebid two spades, even though the suit is only the five cards that have already been described. Responder must expect that this rebid of a five card suit is possible.

## Opener rebids naturally at the three level after a two-over-one response

If opener's rebid after a two-over-one response is in a new suit at the three level, it promises one of two things. Either the hand's values are sound (14+ HCP) or the shape is at least five-five. Opener will tend not to use up so much bidding space unless it is necessary in order to best describe the hand.

Example 33:

| a | b | c |
|---|---|---|
| ♠ KJ974 | ♠ KJ974 | ♠KJ974 |
| ♥ AQ3 | ♥ AQ3 | ♥A3 |
| ♦ 6 | ♦ 6 | ♦ 6 |
| ♣ Q1094 | ♣ KQ109 | ♣ KJ1094 |

With Example 33a, opener bids one spade. If responder bids two hearts, opener utilizes fast arrival and raises hearts to game. If responder bids two clubs, opener raises clubs to the three level. If responder bids two diamonds, opener does not have the values required to show the four card club suit at the three level. A rebid of two spades is fine, or opener might even rebid two notrump, despite holding an unbalanced hand.

With Example 33b, opener bids one spade. If responder bids two hearts, opener raises only to three, showing good values and a three card fit. If responder bids two clubs, opener can jump to three diamonds, a splinter to show four card support for clubs, good values, and shortness in diamonds. If responder bids two diamonds, opener can next bid three clubs. Good values (14+ HCP) make it easy to show a second suit at the three level.

**With Example 33c, opener bids one spade. If responder bids two of either red suit, opener rebids three clubs. Good distribution allows a continuance to the three level even though the high card values are minimum. If responder bids two clubs, the fifth club makes this hand good enough for a** splinter **jump to three diamonds.**

There is a false belief in the minds of many that if opener rebids at the two level in the major suit that was opened, that rebid promises a six card or longer suit. When opener has no other way to describe, the rebid of the five card suit may be necessary. Responder should never jump to the conclusion that opener's rebid has promised six or more cards—it simply may have been a last resort, when any other rebid would have created a greater distortion.

## Summary of basic two-over-one auctions

After the opening bid of one diamond:

1. The response of three clubs promises a six card club suit and game invitational values (9+ to 12- HCP). (Alert in tournament play. This sounds strong but is not even forcing.)
2. The response of two notrump after an opening bid in either minor suit shows a balanced hand with no four card major suit and game invitational values (9+ to 12- HCP). (Alert in tournament play. This sounds strong but is not forcing)
3. The response of two clubs is natural and forcing to game.
4. Opener's rebids:
    A. A rebid of two diamonds promises five or more cards in the suit. This is a priority call to show that opener does hold at least five diamonds. Other auctions tend to deny that opener holds as many as five diamonds.
    B. A jump to three notrump shows a balanced hand with 18 or 19 HCP. (With 15 to 17 HCP, this hand would have opened one notrump instead of one diamond).
    C. A jump rebid of three diamonds promises six or more in the suit and 15+ HCP.
    D. A jump in a new suit is a **splinter** promising four card support for clubs, good values, and shortness in the suit of the jump.
    E. A major suit rebid denies as many as five diamonds, unless opener has five cards in the major suit and six diamonds.
    F. A major suit rebid tends to deny a hand that could bid two notrump.
    G. A rebid of two notrump may conceal four card major suits.

5. Responder's rebids:

    A. Responder's rebid of three clubs shows a good suit of at least six cards.

    B. Responder's rebid of two notrump denies a four card major. The values of the hand will be either minimum (12+ to 15- HCP) or very good (18+ HCP).

    C. Responder's jump rebid to three notrump shows values of 15+ to 18- HCP.

    D. Responder's rebid in a major suit shows four of that major but promises more length in clubs than in the major—usually 5-4 or 6-4, possibly 6-5.

    E. If opener has rebid in a major suit and responder has a four card fit:

        1) Responder jumps to game to show minimum values (12+ to 15- HCP).

        2) Responder shows the four card fit and greater values (15+ HCP) by raising the major to the three level.

        3) Responder can show this fit and good values by making a **splinter** jump in the remaining suit to show a singleton or void.

In response to a one heart opening:

1. A response of two in either minor suit is natural and forcing to game.
2. Opener's rebids:

    A. A rebid of two spades shows shape but does not require the values of a **reverse**.

    B. Other rebids are the same as when the opening bid has been one spade.

In response to a one spade opening:

1. A response of two clubs, diamonds or hearts is natural and forcing to game.
2. The response of two hearts promises at least five cards.

Opener's rebids after a two-over-one response to either major suit:

1. A raise of the response usually shows four card support

    A. A raise by opener with three card support requires 14+ HCP and a high honor in responder's suit.

B. Opener can jump in a new suit to make a **splinter** raise of responder's suit. This promises sound values, four card support and a singleton or void in the suit of the jump.

2. Opener's non jump rebid in a lower ranking suit at the three level promises sound values (14+ HCP) or at least five-five distribution with minimum opening bid values.

3. If opener rebids in a higher-ranking suit at the two level.
   A. If that suit is hearts, opener promises at least four cards in the suit.
   B. If that suit is diamonds, opener might have only three good cards in the suit.

4. Opener's rebid of two notrump promises stoppers in both unbid suits and usually a balanced hand (probably 5-3-3-2). The values for this rebid will be minimum (12+ to 15- HCP), or very strong (18+ HCP). On rare occasions, this rebid will be made on a hand that has a singleton in responder's suit.

5. Opener's jump rebid of three notrump shows the values of an opening notrump (15+ to 18- HCP).

6. Opener's jump rebid of the original major suit shows six or more cards, 15+ HCP, and that the suit is of excellent quality.

7. Opener's rebid of the original major suit at the two level does not promise more than five cards. This rebid may be necessary when no better description can be made.

## Two-over-one auction exercises

Responding to an opening bid of one diamond, what do you bid with each of these hands?

| 1. | 2. | 3. | 4. |
|---|---|---|---|
| ♠ K62 | ♠ K62 | ♠ KJ10 | ♠ AQ4 |
| ♥ 42 | ♥ 42 | ♥ AJ5 | ♥ KJ7 |
| ♦ A8 | ♦ 108 | ♦ 984 | ♦ J52 |
| ♣ AQJ974 | ♣ AQJ974 | ♣ Q1093 | ♣ Q1093 |

You have opened one diamond and partner has responded two clubs. What do you rebid with each of these hands?

| 5. | 6. | 7. | 8. |
|---|---|---|---|
| ♠ A53 | ♠ A73 | ♠ QJ84 | ♠ AQJ6 |
| ♥ KJ86 | ♥ 5 | ♥ KJ7 | ♥ 983 |
| ♦ KQ1084 | ♦ AK874 | ♦ AQ52 | ♦ A1083 |
| ♣ 6 | ♣ KQ95 | ♣ 94 | ♣ Q7 |

9.
- ♠ A53
- ♥ J
- ♦ AKJ973
- ♣ K74

10.
- ♠ 7
- ♥ Q94
- ♦ AQ532
- ♣ KJ85

11.
- ♠ AQ4
- ♥ KJ7
- ♦ KQJ5
- ♣ Q93

12.
- ♠ KJ93
- ♥ AQ84
- ♦ A53
- ♣ 86

13.
- ♠ 3
- ♥ AK974
- ♦ AQJ863
- ♣ 8

14.
- ♠ K2
- ♥ AJ93
- ♦ KJ72
- ♣ J94

You have opened with one spade and partner has responded two clubs. What do you do with each of these hands?

15.
- ♠ KQ843
- ♥ 1095
- ♦ AQJ2
- ♣ 4

16.
- ♠ KQ843
- ♥ Q105
- ♦ AJ6
- ♣ J3

17.
- ♠ AQ742
- ♥ 6
- ♦ A82
- ♣ KQ63

18.
- ♠ KQ1094
- ♥ AJ3
- ♦ 965
- ♣ K4

With each of these hands, you have responded two clubs after an opening bid of one spade and opener has rebid two diamonds. What is your rebid?

19.
- ♠ K64
- ♥ 952
- ♦ A10
- ♣ AQ953

20.
- ♠ KQ6
- ♥ 952
- ♦ 104
- ♣ AKJ53

21.
- ♠ KQ6
- ♥ A4
- ♦ 962
- ♣ AKJ53

22.
- ♠ 83
- ♥ AQ10
- ♦ J62
- ♣ AQ1074

With each of these hands, you have responded two clubs after an opening bid of one spade and opener has rebid either two spades or two notrump. What is your rebid?

23.
- ♠ Q103
- ♥ A7
- ♦ J95
- ♣ KQJ84

24.
- ♠ Q5
- ♥ AQ7
- ♦ K104
- ♣ KJ1072

25.
- ♠ AQ4
- ♥ 95
- ♦ K43
- ♣ AKJ83

26.
- ♠ 84
- ♥ K94
- ♦ AQ32
- ♣ KQ104

With each of these hands, you have opened one spade and partner has responded two hearts. What is your rebid?

| 27. | 28. | 29. | 30. |
|---|---|---|---|
| ♠ KJ954 | ♠ AQJ974 | ♠ AK753 | ♠ AK753 |
| ♥ 63 | ♥ 6 | ♥ K1083 | ♥ K83 |
| ♦ AJ8 | ♦ A95 | ♦ 6 | ♦ 64 |
| ♣ KJ6 | ♣ KQ3 | ♣ A94 | ♣ AQ8 |

| 31. | 32. |
|---|---|
| ♠ AQ953 | ♠ AQ1095 |
| ♥ 4 | ♥ 64 |
| ♦ A5 | ♦ 954 |
| ♣ K10962 | ♣ AK6 |

With each of these hands, you have opened one heart and partner has responded two clubs. What is your rebid?

| 33. | 34. | 35. | 36. |
|---|---|---|---|
| ♠ AJ54 | ♠ 53 | ♠ 64 | ♠ KJ4 |
| ♥ AQJ96 | ♥ AQJ96 | ♥ AJ954 | ♥ Q9763 |
| ♦ 84 | ♦ J43 | ♦ AQ106 | ♦ AQ2 |
| ♣ 53 | ♣ AQ4 | ♣ Q3 | ♣ J4 |

| 37. | 38. | 39. | 40. |
|---|---|---|---|
| ♠ 5 | ♠ AJ4 | ♠ K6 | ♠ KJ8 |
| ♥ AK964 | ♥ KQ942 | ♥ AKJ973 | ♥ KJ953 |
| ♦ K4 | ♦ 853 | ♦ AJ4 | ♦ AQJ |
| ♣ AJ843 | ♣ K8 | ♣ 62 | ♣ 62 |

## Answers

1. Respond two clubs. Your call is forcing to game and you intend to show a wonderful club suit by bidding three clubs at your next turn. Remember that two clubs was forcing to game. The three club rebid does not say that you have changed your mind. It suggests that if partner has an appropriate hand, with a fit for clubs and control cards, a slam in clubs (or in notrump) is to be considered.

2. Respond by jumping to three clubs. This call is not forcing, but is invitational to game. It promises game invitational values (9+ to 12- HCP) and a reasonable club suit that is at least six cards long. When partner has a fit for your suit and scattered stoppers in the other suits, it is reasonable to bid three notrump, expecting your club suit to

be a source of tricks. Without a club fit or with a wide-open suit, pass is in order, and three clubs will become the contract.

3. Respond by jumping to two notrump. This describes a hand with game invitational values (9+ to 12- HCP), no four card major, and the desire to become declarer. If your values were aces rather than tenaces, you would not try to become the notrump declarer. But, this hand should be concealed and have the lead come up to it if notrump is to be played. With two honors and tenaces in both major suits your hand is classic for this auction. Partner must alert because your call is not forcing.

4. Respond by jumping to three notrump. Again, you have a hand with tenaces and want to declare at a notrump contract. This time your values are enough for game. Again, your partner must alert, as the new standards for this auction (and the previous one) have not yet been accepted by the masses. Any departure from what is deemed to be standard must be alerted in tournament play, even though those who are experienced expect that improved modern methods will usually be used by thinking players. The old standard was that this jump showed 16 to 18 HCP. But, with such good values, you should generate a slower, forcing auction to learn more about partner's hand.

5. Rebid two diamonds. Your first priority in this auction is to affirm or deny that you hold as many as five diamonds. The auction is forcing to game and there is plenty of time to find a four-four fit in hearts if it exists. After your rebid of two diamonds, partner will describe. With four cards in either major suit, that suit will be responder's rebid. After a rebid of two spades, you will bid two notrump. After a rebid of two hearts, you will raise to game, utilizing **fast arrival**. If partner rebids in notrump, you will raise to game there.

6. Your rebid should be a jump to three hearts—a **splinter** in support of partner's club suit. You have described a better than minimum hand which includes four card support for clubs and shortness (a singleton or void) in hearts. If partner next bids three notrump, that will show lots of values in hearts which will be stoppers for notrump, and you will know that a hand with such values in hearts will not be likely to also hold fitting values for your high cards in the other suits. Three notrump should play well when partner makes that rebid.

However, when partner's values are in the other suits and include weakness in hearts, it will be clear that secondary honor cards fit well in all of the side suits and that a slam in clubs is likely to be a good undertaking. If partner's hand is ♠KQ4 ♥862 ♦Q3 ♣AJ1073, a contract of six clubs will be a virtual laydown.

7. Rebid two notrump. Your call shows some opening bid with minimum values that is reasonably balanced and contains stoppers in both major suits. Do not worry about missing a four-four fit in spades. If partner holds four spades in addition to a longer club suit, it will be shown at the next call and you will show four card support at that time. The rebid of two notrump describes your hand well and protects your tenace holding in hearts.

8. Rebid two spades. After partner has made a two-over-one response, this call simply shows that you have a four card spade suit and fewer than five diamonds. It is not a **reverse**. The two-over-one response has committed your side to game. It also suggests that a call of two notrump was not appropriate with your hand, and partner will believe that you have few values in the heart suit.

9. Rebid by jumping to three diamonds. This shows a reasonably good suit at least six cards long and extra values in the range of 15+ to 18- HCP.

10. Rebid by raising to three clubs. This is a more descriptive call than repeating your five card diamond suit. Although you have the shape to **splinter** with a jump to three spades at your rebid, you do not have the values for that action.

11. Rebid by jumping to three notrump. This shows the values of a hand which planned to make a jump rebid of two notrump after an expected response at the one level (18 or 19 HCP). Your hand not only has the values expressed by the auction, but it also has good tenaces in both of the unbid (major) suits.

12. Rebid two notrump. You were prepared to raise to show four card support if partner had responded in either major suit. Your hand is well constructed to declare if partner does not have a four card major, but if partner has one and names it as a rebid, you will raise. Your rebid of two notrump does not deny that you have a four card major.

13. Rebid two hearts. Partner will not expect the hand that you have at this point in the auction. Despite only fourteen HCP, your excellent distribution and concentrated high cards caused you to open one diamond planning to **reverse** into hearts, then bid hearts again to show your six-five distribution. Continue with that plan. Bid two hearts now and partner will expect that you have only four cards in each of your suits. But, when you bid hearts again, you will have shown an excellent hand with six diamonds and five hearts.

14. Rebid two notrump. It is important that if notrump is to be played, you protect your spade king against the opening lead. You will raise if partner rebids to show four hearts, but the likely contract is in notrump and you need to be the declarer.

15. Rebid two diamonds. This is as natural as it gets.

16. Rebid two notrump. You have a balanced minimum with stoppers in both of the unbid suits. You also hold tenaces in both of those suits. A perfect description.

17. Rebid by jumping to three hearts, a **splinter** in support of partner's clubs. Partner will know to play clubs at game or slam with weak hearts, or bid three notrump with excellent hearts to warn of wasted values facing your short suit.

18. Rebid two spades. Yes, we can see that you do not hold six of them, but what other rebid will do? You cannot rebid two notrump with bad diamonds, and you cannot rebid in hearts with only three of them. It will often be necessary for the opener to repeat a five card suit after a two-over-one response for just these reasons.

19. Rebid two spades. Opener's values are not yet limited since there was no natural jump shift rebid available after your two-over-one response. Opener might have a hand with twenty HCP that could not be opened with two notrump. Your rebid shows three card support for spades and a minimum for your two-over-one response (12+ to 15- HCP). Partner will know what to do next.

20. Rebid by jumping to four spades. This rebid shows minimum values for your two-over-one response (12+ to 15- HCP), but also shows that all of your values are in the two suits and that you do not have a high card or a shortness control in either of the other suits. A very specialized auction, not to be confused with an auction in which **fast arrival** has been used.

21. Rebid by jumping to three spades. This shows that your two-over-one response was not minimum (12+ to 15- HCP), but had extra values (15+ HCP), as well as three card support for spades. You cannot hold more than three spades. You would have made a conventional spade raise at your first turn if that had been true.

22. Rebid two notrump. No spade fit and stoppers in hearts. A perfect description. Partner will not pass. We are in a game forcing auction. Your rebid limits your values to minimum (12+ to 15- HCP) unless you bid on later to show more than 18- HCP. A jump to three notrump at this turn would have shown 15+ to 18- HCP.

23. Rebid by jumping to four spades. This is **fast arrival**. Partner's rebid of either two spades or two notrump has shown values in the minimum range of 12+ to 15- HCP. Since you know that slam is not to be sought, show your three card fit for spades by closing out at game.

24. Rebid by jumping to three notrump if partner rebids two spades. Do not bid game in spades, making the error of believing that partner has six. The rebid of two spades will often be necessary with only a five card suit. Your jump to three notrump shows extra values (15+ to 18- HCP) after a rebid of two spades. If the rebid was two notrump, it also shows minimum values. There should not be enough extra to produce a slam so you should just bid three notrump.

25. Rebid three spades. Your failure to jump to game after partner's limited rebid will show that, in addition to a three card fit for spades, you have extra values. If partner's minimum has controls and possible trick sources a cue bid in a side suit will show that good minimum. If partner does not cue bid, your slam suggestion has been rejected.

26. Rebid two notrump if partner rebids two spades. Raise a rebid of two notrump to game. You have the expected values to make game with nothing extra.

27. Rebid two notrump. Your hand is minimum without a fit in hearts and stoppers in both of the unbid suits.

28. Rebid by jumping to three spades. This shows an excellent suit at least six cards long and the extra values of 15+ or more HCP.

29. Rebid by jumping to four diamonds. This is a **splinter** in support of the heart response. It promises four card support for hearts and a singleton or void in diamonds. No extra values are required in this auction.

30. Rebid by raising to three hearts. This shows at least three card support for partner's heart suit and more than minimum values for your opening bid. If your values had been minimum, you could have used **fast arrival** and jumped to four hearts.

31. Rebid three clubs. A natural auction. If the old standards were in effect and the two heart response could have shown only game invitational values, this rebid would have been known as a "high reverse" and would have promised more than minimum opening bid values. The new standards require game going values for the two-over-one response and opener can bid naturally in both black suits, starting with spades, with just minimum values.

32. Rebid two spades. Here is another instance in which you must rebid in your original five card major suit. No other rebid would describe.

33. Rebid two spades. After the two-over-one response, this is not a **reverse**. It simply describes your shape. You do not need extra strength after partner has shown

the values to make a game. If the response had been one notrump instead of at the two level, you would not have been able to make this natural rebid.

34. Raise to three clubs. You would rather have four card support for this raise, but no other call describes your hand.

35. Rebid two diamonds. A natural description of what you have.

36. Rebid two notrump. Another good description of what you hold.

37. Rebid by jumping to three spades. This is a **splinter** in support of partner's club suit. Your hand could not be better described.

38. Rebid two hearts. Another case where the five card suit must be rebid, since no other call will suffice. Lack of a diamond stopper precludes a rebid of two notrump even though your spades would be good for that call.

39. Rebid by jumping to three hearts. You show an excellent suit at least six cards long and values in the range of 15+ or more HCP.

40. Rebid by jumping to three notrump. This shows that your hand is balanced and in the range of an opening notrump (15 to 17 or 18-HCP), but that it was not appropriate for an opening bid of one notrump. Now that responder has shown clubs, this rebid shows stoppers in the unbid suits, as well as extra values.

# CHAPTER FIVE

## RESPONDER'S FORCING NOTRUMP

When the opening bid has been in a major suit and responder is not a passed hand, the one notrump response is conventional. It has the wide value range of 5+ to 12- HCP and it is forcing for one round. The older standard was that this response was not forcing and showed only the lower half of the new range (5+ to 9- HCP). When responder bid a suit at the two level it showed 9+ or more HCP. Since the new standard requires responder to hold game forcing values to bid at the two level (12+ HCP), both the range and nature of the one notrump response have been given new meaning.

## Opener's rebids after the Forcing Notrump

Rebids by the opening bidder are as described in Chapter Two. If opener's rebid is in the same major at the two level, it promises six card length and shows values in the minimum range of 12+ to 15- HCP. A jump to the three level in the original suit shows a good suit of six or more cards and the values of 15+ HCP, but not enough to insist on playing game. A jump to four in the major suit shows a good enough suit to need no support, and that facing minimum response values ten tricks appear probable.

### Example 34:

| a | b | c |
|---|---|---|
| ♠ AKJ963 | ♠ AKJ963 | ♠ AKJ10653 |
| ♥ 63 | ♥ 63 | ♥ 6 |
| ♦ K105 | ♦ K105 | ♦ KQ10 |
| ♣ QJ | ♣ AJ | ♣ A6 |

With Example 34a, opener bids one spade. After a forcing notrump **response, a rebid of two spades shows six card length and values of 12+ to 15- HCP.**

With Example 34b, opener bids one spade. After a forcing notrump **response a rebid of three spades shows both at least six cards in the suit and values that are better than minimum (15+ to 18 HCP).**

**With Example 34c, opener bids one spade. After a** forcing notrump **response, a rebid of four spades shows a self-sufficient suit, probably of seven cards, and that ten tricks are probable because responder has shown some values.**

If the opening bid has been one heart and opener's rebid is two spades, this is a true **reverse**. Opener has more hearts than spades with at least a good 16 HCP and the auction is forcing for one round.

**Example 35:**

♠ AKJ8
♥ AQ1085
♦ K102
♣ 5

**With Example 35, opener bids one heart. When the response is a** forcing notrump**, opener has the values to show shape by making a** reverse **rebid. This rebid of two spades shows longer hearts than spades, at least 16 HCP, and it is forcing for one round. If responder has bid two of a minor suit, opener does not need these values for a rebid of two spades, but makes that call to show shape.**

If the opening bid has been one spade and opener's rebid is two hearts it promises at least four hearts, but the hand's values have not been severely limited. Failure to make a jump shift rebid indicates values that are not enough to force a game, but opener may have anything from a minimum (12+ HCP) to a very good hand (about 18 HCP).

**Example 36:**

| a | b |
|---|---|
| ♠ AK953 | ♠ AK953 |
| ♥ KQ75 | ♥ KQ75 |
| ♦ 4 | ♦ 4 |
| ♣ 843 | ♣ AJ8 |

**With both hands in Example 36, opener bids one spade. After a** forcing notrump **response (or a response in either minor suit) opener rebids two hearts with both hands. Although 36a has minimum values and 36b has values that are much greater, opener has no way to distinguish between these possible value ranges at this rebid. Opener's third call will show those extra values when 36b is held).**

When opener rebids in a minor suit after a forcing notrump response, that suit will frequently be only three cards long. When opener's distribution is 5-3-3-2 there is no real suit to rebid. A rebid in the lowest ranking minor suit of at least three cards is normal. This rebid can be in a four card suit, but four is not promised.

In fact, if the opening bid has been one heart and opener's distribution is 4-5-2-2, the standard rebid will be in the two card club suit. This sounds dangerous, but responder will almost never pass with fewer than five clubs and will have only one or no hearts.

**Example 37:**

|  | a | b | c |
|---|---|---|---|
| ♠ | AQ1085 | AJ963 | A642 |
| ♥ | KJ3 | K8 | AJ963 |
| ♦ | Q1064 | A62 | 105 |
| ♣ | 5 | 1054 | K3 |

**With Example 37a, opener bids one spade. After a** forcing notrump **response there is an easy rebid of two diamonds on the four card suit.**

**With Example 37b, opener bids one spade. After a** forcing notrump **response the expected rebid is two clubs—the lower ranking of the three card minor suits.**

**With Example 37c, opener bids one heart. After a** forcing notrump **response, it is not possible to rebid two spades because the hand does not hold the values to** reverse. **The rebid of two clubs, a minor suit that is only two cards in length is correct. This is a rare auction but should not be a problem. Responder will pass only with five clubs and a singleton or void in hearts.**

If opener makes a jump shift rebid, the auction promises values enough that a game should be reached. Opener will hold 19 HCP or a hand with equivalent playing strength.

**Example 38:**

|  | a | b |
|---|---|---|
| ♠ | AKJ96 | AKJ10963 |
| ♥ | 63 | 6 |
| ♦ | AQJ7 | A5 |
| ♣ | A5 | AK4 |

**With both hands of Example 38, opener would bid one spade. After a** forcing notrump **response, both want to be sure that game is reached.**

**With Example 38a, opener would make a jump shift rebid of three diamonds. This would be a natural auction, which is forcing to game.**

**With Example 38b, opener might rebid four spades, but fears missing a slam. The jump shift rebid of three clubs seeks information although opener knows that the eventual contract will be in spades. After the jump shift opener might get information from responder which would allow a further probe for a spade slam.**

A raise of the **forcing notrump** response shows that opener has an excellent balanced hand. Opener shows 18 or 19 HCP plus the five card suit, and will usually be 5-3-3-2. This rebid by the opening bidder is almost forcing to game. Only when responder has stretched to bid will this call be passed.

**Example 39:**

♠ A9
♥ KQJ95
♦ AQ6
♣ Q105

**With Example 39, opener would bid one heart. If responder uses the** forcing notrump, **opener's expressive rebid is to raise to two notrump. This raise shows a hand that is balanced (5-3-3-2) and holds 18 or 19 HCP.**

## Responder's rebids with minimum values (5+ to 9- HCP)

When responder's values are minimum for the **forcing notrump** response (5+ to 9- HCP) the rebid must show this value range. These are the things that responder can do:

1. Take a preference to opener's major suit at the two level to show a doubleton in support. If opener has first bid spades and has rebid in hearts, responder will take a "false preference" and return to spades with exactly two spades and three hearts, but can pass with three hearts and fewer spades.

**Example 40:**

|  | a | b |
|---|---|---|
| ♠ | J7 | 6 |
| ♥ | K74 | K74 |
| ♦ | 10954 | 109754 |
| ♣ | Q984 | Q984 |

**With both hands of Example 40, responder would use a** forcing notrump **response to an opening bid of one spade.**

**With Example 40a, if opener's rebid is two clubs or two diamonds, responder takes a preference to two spades. If opener rebids two hearts, responder should take the false preference by bidding two spades. This will produce a 5-2 trump suit rather than a 4-3, which would be likely if responder made the error of passing. But, it also could lead to a 6-2 rather than a 4-3, and it allows opener to bid again with a hand which includes extra values.**

**With Example 40b, if opener's rebid is two clubs, responder will bid the five card diamond suit. If opener's rebid is two hearts, responder will pass.**

2. With minimum values (5+ to 9- HCP) and no fit for opener's major suit, responder can pass the suit of opener's rebid. When opener has rebid in a minor suit and responder does pass, unless responder is 4-4-4-1 with shortness in opener's major suit, the pass will show five card support for the (minor) suit of opener's rebid. Responder is aware that opener's rebid will often be in a three card minor suit, and in one specific auction the rebid of clubs after an opening bid in hearts could be on a doubleton.

**Example 41:**

|  | a | b |
|---|---|---|
| ♠ | 5 | 5 |
| ♥ | K1084 | K1084 |
| ♦ | J65 | J654 |
| ♣ | Q9543 | Q953 |

**With either hand of Example 41, responder has first bid a** forcing notrump **in response to an opening bid of one spade and opener has rebid two clubs. With Example 41a, responder is happy to pass. With Example 41b, responder is not so happy but has no alternative but to pass.**

3. Responder may introduce a new suit at the two level. This guarantees at least five cards as well as minimum response values (5+ to 9- HCP).

**Example 42:**

|     | a        |     | b        |
|-----|----------|-----|----------|
| ♠   | K54      | ♠   | 6        |
| ♥   | 6        | ♥   | QJ9754   |
| ♦   | QJ9754   | ♦   | K54      |
| ♣   | 1098     | ♣   | 1098     |

**With Example 42a, responder bids a** forcing notrump **in response to an opening bid of one heart. When opener rebids two clubs, responder bids two diamonds, which shows minimum response values (5+ to 9- HCP) and five or more diamonds. The introduction of a minor suit tends to deny as many as two cards in opener's major.**

**With Example 42b, responder has bid a** forcing notrump **in response to an opening bid of one spade. When opener rebids either two clubs or two diamonds, responder bids two hearts to show minimum response values (5+ to 9- HCP) and five or more hearts. Responder may also hold a doubleton spade and be looking for the best major suit fit.**

4. If responder introduces a new suit at the three level without jumping, this hand can be in the minimum range. The suit will be at least a good six cards and responder knows that if this suit is not the trump suit the hand will have little or no value.

**Example 43:**

| ♠ | 8        |
|---|----------|
| ♥ | 1075     |
| ♦ | 854      |
| ♣ | KQJ976   |

**This responder has bid a** forcing notrump **after an opening bid of one spade. If opener rebids two hearts, this hand can pass since the three card fit for hearts and spade shortness will have value. If opener rebids two diamonds, which could be on a three card suit, bid three clubs. With clubs as trumps this hand will probably take five tricks. When either a heart or club contract is played this hand will have value, but not if the contract is spades, diamonds or notrump.**

# Responder's rebids with maximum values (9+ to 12- HCP)

Responder may instead have the values to make a rebid that invites a game (9+ to 12- HCP). When responder's values are in this range a rebid will be chosen that shows game invitational values.

When invited to game, opener's rule of thumb is that when the opening bid has been made with a weak 13 HCP or less, the invitation to game should be rejected. When the opening bid has been with a hand of a good 13 HCP or more, the game invitation should be accepted.

1. Responder who has used the **forcing notrump** has not denied a fit for opener's major suit. With a hand that is balanced and has a three card fit for opener, responder will bid one notrump, planning to jump to the three level in opener's suit as a rebid. This is known as a "bad limit raise". When responder has a limit raise with a better hand, a different auction will be used.

   Holding this bad limit raise there are two rebids that opener might make which will cause a change in the planned auction.

   A. If opener's suit is repeated at the two level, responder's fit and values must be shown by a raise to game. If the raise is only to the three level responder indicates game invitational values (9+ to 12- HCP) but shows only a doubleton in support of the known six card suit. When this true fit exists and responder learns of opener's six card holding, a raise of the major suit to the four level is necessary.
   B. When opener's rebid is a jump shift, responder shows this balanced limit raise by jumping to four in the major. Bidding opener's major at the three level does not show a true fit, but shows a preference, indicating a doubleton in support. The jump to game is necessary so that the fit can be shown.

   **Example 44:**

   ♠ Q104
   ♥ A6
   ♦ KJ87
   ♣ 10943

**With Example 44, responder to an opening bid of one spade starts with a** forcing notrump, **planning to jump in spades at his rebid to show a balanced**

three card raise. If opener rebids at the two level in any of the lower ranking suits, responder will next jump to three spades. This auction shows a three card fit for spades, game invitational values, and no void or singleton. This hand is called a "bad limit raise" (9+ to 12- HCP).

However, if opener rebids two spades, this responder must raise to four rather than bid only three spades. A bid of three spades would show game invitational values (9+ to 12- HCP) but deny a true spade fit. It would show a doubleton spade.

If opener's rebid is a jump shift to three clubs, diamonds or hearts, re-sponder must again take action that describes this holding. A bid of only three spades would be a preference, showing a doubleton in support of spades and minimum values (5+ to 9- HCP). To show a true fit for spades and the values that had intended to invite a game (9+ to 12- HCP), responder next jumps to four spades. The distinction is imperative.

2. When responder does not have a fit for opener's major suit but has the values to invite a game (9+ to 12- HCP) a rebid of two notrump may describe. This rebid promises no more than two cards in opener's major suit and stoppers in both unbid suits.

**Example 45:**

♠ 95
♥ AQ84
♦ KQ105
♣ 1073

With Example 45) responder has used the forcing notrump in response to an opening bid of one spade. If opener rebids two clubs, responder next bids two notrump. This rebid promises no fit for spades, values to invite a game (9+ to 12- HCP), and that both unbid suits are stopped.

3. When responder does not fit opener's first suit but has a good fit for the suit of opener's rebid, with game invitational values (9+ to 12- HCP) responder raises the suit of opener's rebid. Responder defines a hand that has no fit for opener's major suit, the values to invite a game, and a good fit for the suit of opener's rebid.

Example 46:

♠ 7
♥ Q85
♦ A963
♣ KJ1084

**Opener bids one spade and this responder uses the** forcing notrump. **If opener rebids two spades, two hearts or two diamonds, responder bids two notrump to invite game. When opener's rebid is two clubs responder can choose between two notrump and a raise to three clubs as a rebid. If there were not stoppers in both red suits the rebid choices would narrow, and three clubs would be the only description.**

4. When responder holds a good suit as well as game invitational values, after using the **forcing notrump,** responder rebids to show this good suit. When opener's rebid is in a lower ranking suit at the two level, responder can jump to the three level to show this good suit and game invitational values. When responder cannot jump and rebids this suit at the three level, the extra values will not be known. Responder would bid similarly with lesser values (see Example 43).

Example 47:

|  a  |  b  |
|-----|-----|
| ♠ J6 | ♠ 6 |
| ♥ KQ10864 | ♥ A85 |
| ♦ A852 | ♦ KQ10864 |
| ♣ 6 | ♣ J62 |

**After an opening bid of one spade, responder with Example 47a will use the** forcing notrump. **If opener rebids either two clubs or two diamonds responder jumps to three hearts to show a good suit with game invitational (9+ to 12- HCP) values.**

**With Example 47b, after an opening bid of one spade, responder uses the** forcing notrump. **When opener rebids two clubs responder jumps to three diamonds to show game invitational values (9+ to 12- HCP) and a good suit of at least six cards.**

5. When the opening bid has been one heart and opener rebids in a minor suit after responder uses the **forcing notrump**, an interesting auction is available. Responder is able to rebid two spades. It is clear that responder cannot hold a spade suit because one spade, rather than one notrump would have been the initial response. This unusual rebid carries a special message. Responder shows game invitational values and promises a fit for the minor suit in which opener has rebid, but denies a stopper in spades. If responder rebids two notrump, that promises a spade stopper. This unusual rebid shows game invitational values (9+ to 12- HCP) while denying a spade stopper.

**Example 48:**

| a | b |
|---|---|
| ♠ QJ4 | ♠ 954 |
| ♥ J6 | ♥ J6 |
| ♦ K1063 | ♦ K1063 |
| ♣ QJ85 | ♣ AQJ8 |

**After an opening bid of one heart and a** forcing notrump **response opener rebids two of a minor suit. With Example 48a, responder next bids two notrump. This call invites a game and promises a stopper in spades.**

**With Example 48b, responder bids a** forcing notrump **after a one heart opening bid. When opener rebids in a minor suit, responder next bids two spades. This call invites a game (9+ to 12- HCP) and denies a stopper in spades. It suggests that responder also has a good holding in the minor suit of opener's rebid, which will be a satisfactory place to play when there is no spade stopper.**

One notrump by a passed responder after a major suit opening bid is not forcing. It still has the same wide range of 5+ to 12- HCP, but denies a fit for opener's major suit. When the response of one notrump is forcing (facing an opening major suit bid in first or second seat) responder might have a balanced limit raise - a hand with 9+ to 12- HCP and three card support for opener's major suit, but when responder is a passed hand that possibility no longer exists. If responder has a fit for opener's major suit in third or fourth seat, the **Drury** convention will be used (read about this when we discuss raises in Chapter Eight). When responder has passed, a major suit opener knows that a response of one notrump denies a fit for the major suit and is not forcing.

# Summary of Forcing Notrump auctions

Opener's rebids are standard except for two new situations:

1. Opener will frequently rebid in a three card minor suit.
2. If opener has first bid one heart, after a **forcing notrump** response, with 4-5-2-2 distribution, the expected rebid will be two clubs on a doubleton when the values held are not adequate for a **reverse** of two spades.

Responder's rebids:

1. Responder can show minimum values (5+ to 9- HCP) in any of four ways:
   A. Take a preference to opener's major suit to show a doubleton.
   B. Pass the suit of opener's rebid. Responder will have a singleton or void in opener's major suit and usually five cards in the suit of opener's rebid. If opener has rebid in hearts, responder can pass with as few as three, but will take a false preference to spades holding three hearts and two spades.
   C. Introduce a new suit at the two level with length of five or more cards.
   D. Introduce a new suit at the three level (must be at least six cards) without jumping when it is necessary for that suit to be the trump suit so that the hand will have value.
2. Responder can show game invitational values (9+ to 12- HCP) in several ways:
   A. Holding a balanced limit raise for opener's major suit:
      1. Jump to three in opener's major after a rebid by opener at the two level in a lower ranking suit.
      2. After a repeat of opener's first suit at the two level showing six or more cards, responder next jumps to game in the major to show a balanced limit raise.
      3. If opener's rebid is a jump shift, responder must not simply take a preference to opener's suit at the three level. Again, a jump to game in opener's major will show a balanced limit raise.
   B. Responder can next bid two notrump, promising stoppers in the two unbid suits, after opener has rebid in a second suit.
   C. Responder can jump to the three level in a new suit, promising six or more cards.

D. Responder can raise the suit of opener's rebid to deny a fit for opener's major suit and to promise length in the suit of opener's rebid. If opener has first bid spades and rebids in hearts responder should hold four card support to raise. If opener has rebid in a minor suit which might be only three cards long, responder should have five card support for this raise.

E. Responder can introduce a lower ranking suit at the three level with lesser values. The extra values will not be known in this auction so responder should bid two notrump with a stopper in the unbid suit as well.

F. When the opening bid has been one heart, after opener rebids in a minor suit responder can rebid two spades. This shows the values to invite a game but denies a stopper in spades and suggests a fit for the minor suit of opener's rebid.

## Forcing notrump exercises

With each of these hands, you have opened one spade and partner has responded with a **forcing notrump**. What is your rebid?

| 1. | 2. | 3. | 4. |
|---|---|---|---|
| ♠ AQ1073 | ♠ AK1097 | ♠ KQJ642 | ♠ KQ10874 |
| ♥ Q84 | ♥ AQ | ♥ AQJ7 | ♥ Q85 |
| ♦ AQ | ♦ AQ1054 | ♦ 8 | ♦ AJ6 |
| ♣ KJ6 | ♣ 2 | ♣ 53 | ♣ 4 |

5.
♠ KQ843
♥ KJ10
♦ A83
♣ 92

With each of these hands you have opened one heart and partner has responded with a **forcing notrump**. What is your rebid?

| 6. | 7. | 8. |
|---|---|---|
| ♠ AKJ9 | ♠ KJ84 | ♠ AQ74 |
| ♥ AQ1084 | ♥ AK753 | ♥ KQJ62 |
| ♦ K107 | ♦ Q86 | ♦ 95 |
| ♣ 3 | ♣ 7 | ♣ J3 |

With each of these hands you have responded with a **forcing notrump** to your partner's opening bid of one spade. On 9 through 14 opener has rebid two clubs. On 15 and 16 opener has rebid two diamonds. What is your rebid?

9.
♠ Q4
♥ J95
♦ K10864
♣ Q82

10.
♠ K95
♥ AJ32
♦ 8542
♣ K6

11.
♠ 6
♥ K105
♦ Q864
♣ J10853

12.
♠ Q4
♥ K10864
♦ J95
♣ Q82

13.
♠ 5
♥ A103
♦ AQ10974
♣ 842

14.
♠ J3
♥ AQ95
♦ KJ108
♣ 1064

15.
♠ 7
♥ Q84
♦ 653
♣ KQJ973

16.
♠ 94
♥ K72
♦ AQ953
♣ Q62

With each of the following hands, you have responded with a **forcing notrump** after your partner has opened with one heart. On 17 and 18 opener rebids two clubs. On 19 opener rebids either two hearts or makes a jump shift rebid in a minor suit. On 20 opener raises your response to two notrump. What is your rebid?

17.
♠ A43
♥ 5
♦ Q8764
♣ 10762

18.
♠ 1083
♥ K6
♦ KQ5
♣ K10974

19.
♠ A4
♥ K103
♦ 9542
♣ KJ63

20.
♠ K83
♥ J4
♦ K1087
♣ Q862

## Answers

1. Raise to two notrump. This is a very strong call showing a balanced eighteen or nineteen HCP as well as your five card spade suit. It is almost forcing to game.

2. Jump shift to three diamonds. This shows 19 or more HCP and is forcing to game.

3. Your rebid should be two hearts. Your spade suit is very good, but your four card heart suit is also good. The rule of thumb when you hold six spades and four hearts is to rebid in hearts when that suit has as many or more HCP as the six card spade suit.

4. Rebid two spades. This promises that your spade suit is six or more cards long and that you have no other rebid that would be more descriptive.

5. Rebid two diamonds. When your major suit is five cards long, you must not rebid it even though you do not hold another four card suit. When your shape is 5-3-3-2 and your values are minimum (12+ to 15- HCP) rebid in your lowest ranking three card minor suit.

6. Rebid two spades. This is a **reverse** promising longer hearts than spades and at least a good sixteen HCP. With minimum values, you would not be able to make this natural rebid. With less in high cards, your rebid would be in your three card diamond suit.

7. Rebid two diamonds. Your do not have sufficient values to **reverse** by bidding two spades. A rebid in a three card minor suit is not unexpected.

8. Rebid two clubs. Yes it is a bit scary to bid in a two card minor suit. However you cannot rebid your five card heart suit and you do not have the values to **reverse** to two spades at your rebid. Do not fear - partner will not pass with fewer than five clubs and will have only one heart (or none).

9. Rebid two spades. This is a preference that shows minimum response values (5+ to 9- HCP) and exactly two card support for spades. With only one spade you would have bid your diamond suit but showing a doubleton for opener's major takes priority over showing a five card minor suit when responder has minimum values.

10. Rebid by jumping to three spades. This shows a limit raise for spades with three card support and no ruffing value in a side suit. If opener's rebid had been two spades, or a jump shift rebid, this hand would have to show its true fit and limit raise values (9+ to 12- HCP) by jumping to four spades. In either of those auctions, responder's rebid of only three spades would be a preference showing a doubleton spade.

11. Pass. This shows minimum values (5+ to 9- HCP), short spades and long clubs.

12. Rebid two hearts. Although you have minimum values and a doubleton spade, a rebid in hearts may find a better fit than if you take a spade preference. If opener has a singleton or void in hearts the auction will continue on to two spades and that will be the best fit, but if opener has two or more hearts a pass will leave you in the best contract.

13. Rebid by jumping to three diamonds. This shows game invitational values (9+ to 12- HCP) and a six card diamond suit.

14. Rebid two notrump. This shows game invitational values (9+ to 12- HCP) and that both unbid suits are stopped.

15. Rebid three clubs. This does not promise more than minimum response values (5+ to 9- HCP) but indicates a very playable trump suit. It says that if clubs is not the trump suit your hand will have little or no value.

16. Raise to three diamonds. This shows game invitational values (9+ to 12- HCP), denies as many as three spades, and should contain five or more diamonds.

17. Rebid two diamonds. Partner will frequently have rebid two clubs on a three card holding, and with a shape of 4-5-2-2 will have only two clubs (see problem 8). You are trying to find the best available fit.

18. Rebid two spades. This shows game invitational values (9+ to 12- HCP) and denies a stopper in spades. It also shows a fit for the suit of opener's rebid. If opener has a spade stopper notrump will be bid, but when partner also lacks a stopper in spades you have shown a fit for clubs which can be a happy home.

19. Rebid by jumping to four hearts in either auction. You must show that you have a true heart fit and game invitational values (9+ to 12- HCP). If you bid only three hearts in either auction you will show a different hand. If opener has rebid two hearts and you raise to three you will show game invitational values (9+ to 12- HCP) but only a doubleton in hearts. If opener has made a jump shift rebid in a minor suit and you bid only three hearts you will show only a doubleton heart and minimum response values (5+ to 9- HCP).

20. Rebid three notrump. Partner's rebid has shown a balanced 18 or 19 HCP along with a  five card heart suit.

# CHAPTER SIX

## REBIDS BY RESPONDER

We have covered auctions in which responder's first call was a game forcing two-over-one response and auctions in which responder has used the **forcing notrump**. We have shown how responder can create a forcing auction by using **fourth suit forcing**. Responder's rebid usually defines the values of the responding hand. It remains to show the rest of responder's auctions in detail.

## Responder has fewer than 5+ HCP

1. Zero to 5- HCP. In this range, responder's first call will usually be a pass. Having passed initially, with a fit for partner or having a long suit, responder can show this asset at the next turn without leading partner to believe that the hand has the values normally shown by a response. However, when responder is distributional, it may be best to respond without the expected minimum strength. Here are three hands that have less than expected response values, but if responder passes the contract may be unplayable.

   ♠ KJ10853 ♥ 764 ♦ 532 ♣ 6. If the opening bid is one heart, a pass is acceptable; but if the opening bid is one club, responder should bid one spade although the values are less than those expected for a response.

   ♠ Q9864 ♥ Q10853 ♦ 74 ♣ 4. If the opening bid is in a minor suit, responder should bid one spade with the plan to show hearts later if a spade fit is not found, and if this can be done without showing better values.

   ♠ K1095 ♥ 76 ♦ J109754 ♣ 5. Responder has no problem when the opening bid is in spades, hearts or diamonds. However, when the opening bid is one club, responder has two possible places to play and should not pass. Using standard responses, responder will bid one diamond and hope to be able to pass if opener bids one spade, or to repeat the diamond suit as cheaply as possible. Some sophisticates will bypass diamonds to bid one spade. This response is not a bizarre as it looks. See "Walsh Responses" in our second planned volume, *Advanced Bridge Bidding for the Twenty First Century.*

## Responder's rebids with 5+ to 9- HCP

2. Responder's usual minimum response hand is in the value range of 5+ to 9- HCP. There are four different rebids that limit responder's values to this range:

A. A preference made cheaply to opener's first suit. In the auction: 1♣ - pass - 1♥ - pass, 1♠ - pass - ??, responder can bid two clubs. This limits responder's values to the minimum range of 5+ to 9- HCP. As the opening bid of one club is often on a three card suit, when responder returns to clubs that shows five card support.

B. Repeat the suit of the original response. This rebid not only limits responder's values to the minimum range; it also promises a six card or longer suit. In the auction above, if responder rebids two hearts, the suit is six cards or longer and the values are minimum.

C. Take a preference to opener's second suit. Responder can pass opener's rebid, or can raise that suit to the two level. Using the same start, the auction can go: 1♣ - pass - 1♥ - pass, 1♠ - pass -?? If responder passes at this point that shows three or four card support for spades, and values so minimum that the auction should not get any higher (5+ to 7- HCP). If responder does raise to two spades, that promises four card support and shows 7+ to 9- HCP which is the top half of the minimum response range. Remember - opener can hold as many as 18 HCP and game might be missed if responder does not raise with a fit holding this maximum minimum.

D. Responder's catchall is to rebid one notrump. Ideally the hand shown will be somewhat balanced with a stopper in the unbid suit. But, it's an imperfect world. Responder might be 2-5-5-1 with a seven count. Not only are the three previous bids shown above not possible, responder also cannot next bid two

diamonds. Why? Because a bid of two diamonds would not show
diamonds. It would be **fourth suit forcing.** Remember that
when responder uses **fourth suit forcing** the values promised
are at least the values to invite a game (9+ HCP).

**Example 49:**

|  | a | b | c |
|---|---|---|---|
| ♠ | 62 | 62 | J983 |
| ♥ | KJ85 | KQ10942 | KJ94 |
| ♦ | 94 | 832 | 763 |
| ♣ | Q10853 | Q4 | 54 |

|  | d | e | f |
|---|---|---|---|
| ♠ | Q1083 | 953 | 95 |
| ♥ | KJ94 | KJ64 | KJ643 |
| ♦ | Q63 | Q105 | Q10852 |
| ♣ | 54 | 983 | 6 |

With Example 49 hands, responder rebids to show minimum response values.
All auctions begin with a one club opening bid and a response of one heart.
Opener rebids one spade.

With Example 49a, responder shows limited values (5+ to 9- HCP) with a
simple preference to opener's first suit. Responder bids two clubs.

With Example 49b, responder's rebid of two hearts promises six or more
cards as well as minimum response values (5+ to 9- HCP).

With Example 49c, after the opening bid and one heart response, when
opener rebids one spade responder shows a fit and puny values (5+ to 7-
HCP) by passing. This pass can also be made when responder holds only
three spades but cannot visualize a better contract than one spade.

With Example 49d, when responder has first bid one heart and hears a
rebid of one spade it is known that opener could hold as much as 18 HCP.
With the idea that game is still possible responder shows this spade fit and
raises to two spades (7+ to 9- HCP) so that when opener does have those
excellent values game will be bid.

With Example 49e, responder shows limited values (5+ to 9- HCP) and attempts to place the contract with a rebid of one notrump. This hand is a classic minimum.

With Example 49f, responder would like to try to play in a red suit, but minimum response values and shape do not allow either repeat of hearts or a bid in diamonds. These values (5+ to 9- HCP) require responder to bid one notrump despite the unbalanced hand pattern.

## Responder's rebids with 9+ to 12- HCP

3. When responder holds the values to invite a game (9+ to 12- HCP), the above-mentioned rebids can be made one level higher. These will all be jumps, which announce that responder's values are invitational.

   A. When the auction is: 1♣ - pass - 1♥ - pass, 1♠ - pass - 3♣, this jump preference promises five card club support as before, but the values shown are in the invitational (9+ to 12- HCP) range.

   B. When the auction is: 1♣ - pass - 1♥ - pass, 1♠ - pass - 3♥, responder shows a six card heart suit with invitational values (9+ to 12- HCP).

   C. When the auction is: 1♣ - pass - 1♥ - pass, 1♠ - pass - 3♠, responder shows four card spade support and invitational values (9+ to 12- HCP).

   D. When the auction is: 1♣ - pass - 1♥ - pass, 1♠ - pass - 2NT, responder shows invitational values (9+ to 12- HCP) and promises that the unbid suit (diamonds) is stopped.

   **Example 50:**

   |  | a | b | c |
   |---|---|---|---|
   | ♠ | 6 | 62 | KJ83 |
   | ♥ | KJ85 | AQJ954 | KJ94 |
   | ♦ | A94 | K32 | Q63 |
   | ♣ | Q10853 | 84 | 54 |

|   | d | e | f |
|---|---|---|---|
| ♠ | 953 | 983 | Q83 |
| ♥ | KJ64 | KJ1064 | KJ106 |
| ♦ | AQ10 | AQ10 | 1093 |
| ♣ | 983 | 84 | AJ4 |

With Example 50 hands, responder holds game invitational values (9+ to 12- HCP). All rebids are designed to show those values while indicating a hand type.

With Example 50a, after an opening bid of one club, a response of one heart and a rebid by opener of one spade, responder describes by jumping to three clubs.

With Example 50b, after responder bids one heart and opener rebids one spade, responder describes by jumping to three hearts.

With Example 50c, after responder bids one heart and opener rebids one spade, responder invites a spade game by jumping to three spades.

With Example 50d, after responder bids one heart and opener rebids one spade, responder describes by jumping to two notrump.

With Example 50e, responder has a problem after the response of one heart and opener's rebid of one spade. Responder cannot jump to two notrump because opener might pass and a five-three heart fit might be missed. Responder must use fourth suit forcing with this invitational hand to try for the heart fit that might exist.

With Example 50f, responder again has a problem after the one heart response and a rebid of one spade by opener. Responder needs to show game invitational values, but cannot jump to two notrump for lack of a stopper in diamonds. The only option again is to use fourth suit forcing.

From these examples, you can see our simple observation—responder's second round jumps are invitational. There is a single exception.

## A special auction

In the auction: 1♣ - pass - 1♦ - pass, any rebid - pass - 3♣, responder's jump preference is forcing. The reason is that minor suit contracts are not sought. Rather than try to reach a contract in a minor suit, experienced bidders will first search for a major suit fit, then turn to a possible contract in notrump. Only when neither of these searches proves fruitful will good bidders stress their minor suit holdings.

**Example 51:**

♠ 93
♥ 7
♦ KQ9765
♣ AQJ6

**With Example 51, responder hears an opening bid of one club. After a response of one diamond, when opener rebids in any higher denomination at the one level, responder can next make a jump to three clubs. This is the only jump preference responder can make which is forcing rather than invitational.**

## Responder's rebids when opener has reversed

When opener's rebid has been a **reverse**, holding the normal values of a game invitation (9+ to 12- HCP) it is clear that game should be reached. Opener has guaranteed at least a good 16 HCP as well as certain suit lengths. However, responder might also hold minimum response values and not know whether game should be reached or not. There is a bidding tool available to solve this problem.

When responder's values are minimum (5+ to 9- HCP), the rebid selected must sound an alarm to the opener. If responder's first suit is five or more cards, a rebid in that suit will show minimum response values (5+ to 9- HCP). (This is one of very few instances in which a five card suit will be rebid voluntarily.) With a suit of only four cards, responder must instead bid two notrump with values that are minimum. This call is not natural. It is conventional and asks opener to bid three clubs regardless of the suit of the opening bid.

In the auction: 1♣ - pass - 1♠ - pass, 2♥, opener can bid two spades with a minimum hand that includes five or more spades, but must otherwise bid two notrump with limited values. This auction warns opener of probable minimum values.

When opener holds game forcing values of 19+ HCP there is no problem. The knowledge that responder has at least enough to make a response insures that game should be reached. Opener will not bid three clubs as asked because responder might pass.

But, when opener's values are in the range of 16 to 18 and responder's values might be minimum, there is no such assurance about reaching a game contract. Opener will bid three clubs as requested.

If opener's values are not enough to assure game and responder's rebid is two notrump, opener shows limited values by bidding three clubs as responder has asked. Responder can then pass or correct and the auction will be non-forcing. Keeping in mind the availability of the two notrump tool, look at several auctions to see what is forcing and what is not.

1. 1♣ - pass - 1♠ - pass, 2♥ - pass - 2♠. Responder has shown five or six spades and minimum response values (5+ to 9- HCP).

**Example 52:**

| a | b |
|---|---|
| ♠ AQ853 | ♠ KJ9862 |
| ♥ 962 | ♥ 92 |
| ♦ J54 | ♦ Q54 |
| ♣ 72 | ♣ 72 |

**With both hands of Example 52, responder has bid one spade after an opening bid of one club. When opener reverses by bidding two hearts, each of these responders will bid two spades, which shows minimum response values, and five or more spades.**

2. 1♣ - pass - 1♠ - pass, 2♥ - pass - 2NT. Responder has denied five spades and has asked opener to next bid three clubs. Responder's values will usually be minimum, but there are some auctions in which responder will show greater values.

3. 1♣ - pass - 1♠ - pass, 2♥ - pass - 3♣. Responder has club support and the auction is forcing. If responder were weak, two notrump would have been used to get to three clubs.

**Example 53:**

| a | b |
|---|---|
| ♠ AJ84 | ♠ AJ84 |
| ♥ 9 | ♥ 92 |
| ♦ Q854 | ♦ 8542 |
| ♣ KJ63 | ♣ Q86 |

With Example 53a, responder would bid one spade after an opening bid of one club. If opener bids two hearts, responder would bid three clubs. This direct show of support after opener has reversed is forcing, promising at least a good nine HCP.

With Example 53b, in the same auction responder would rebid two notrump. This will allow responder to pass and play in the known club fit when opener bids three clubs as requested. Opener has shown a club suit of at least five cards, and a bid of three clubs as requested will show values that are minimum for the reverse (16+ to 18 HCP). The three club contract will be the best available place to play.

4. 1♣ - pass - 1♠ - pass, 2♥ - pass - 3♥, is a forcing auction. If responder held only minimum response values including a four card heart fit the two notrump relay would be the indicated rebid, and when opener then bid three clubs as requested responder would correct to three hearts.

**Example 54:**

|  a  |  b  |
| --- | --- |
| ♠ AQ853 | ♠ Q8753 |
| ♥ Q1062 | ♥ Q1062 |
| ♦ K84 | ♦ K84 |
| ♣ 2 | ♣ 2 |

With Example 54a, responder bids one spade after partner opens with one club. When opener rebids two hearts, responder next bids three hearts, which shows four card support and is forcing. It promises values enough (9+ HCP) to make a game facing opener's known extra values (16+ HCP).

With Example 54b, responder bids one spade in response to opener's call of one club. When opener next bids two hearts, responder knows to show four card support for that suit, but must limit values. A rebid of two spades does not suit the situation, despite the holding of five cards there. Responder should bid two notrump to ask opener to bid three clubs. If opener bids three clubs to show minimum values for the auction (16+ to 18 HCP), responder then shows four card support for hearts. By limiting the values held, responder does not allow the auction to get too high. The values shown in the combined hands are not enough for game, and the heart partscore is the best place to play.

5. 1♣ - pass - 1♠ - pass, 2♥ - pass - 3NT, Responder shows opening bid values of 12+ to 15- HCP.

6. 1♣ - pass - 1♠ - pass, 2♥ - pass - 2NT - pass, 3♣ - pass - 3NT,
Responder holds 9+ to 12- HCP.

**Example 55:**

| a | b |
|---|---|
| ♠ AQ83 | ♠ AQ83 |
| ♥ K4 | ♥ Q4 |
| ♦ KJ98 | ♦ K982 |
| ♣ J102 | ♣ 854 |

**With Example 55a, responder bids one spade after an opening bid of one
club. After opener** reverses **to two hearts, this responder jumps to three
notrump. This shows that responder's spade suit is only four cards, and his
hand has a value range of 12+ to 15- HCP.**

**With Example 55b, responder again bids one spade after an opening bid of
one club. When opener next bids two hearts, a** reverse, **responder knows
that the values for game are present, but must show the correct values as
the contract of three notrump is reached. Responder cannot jump to three
notrump, as that would show 12+ to 15- HCP, but instead bids two notrump
to ask opener to bid three clubs. Following opener's three club bid, responder then bids three notrump. This promises a diamond stopper and
shows that responder's values are 9+ to 12- HCP. The ability to show greater
or lesser values on the way to three notrump allows opener to know when to
continue towards a slam.**

7. 1♣ - pass - 1♠ - pass, 2♥ - pass - 3♠, shows that responder holds
six or more spades and values enough to play game (9+ HCP).
The auction is forcing.

8. 1♣ - pass - 1♠ - pass, 2♥ - pass - 2NT - pass, 3♣ - pass - 3♠
shows that responder holds values enough for game (9+ HCP)
and only five card spades.

**Example 56:**

|   a   |   b   |
|-------|-------|
| ♠ AQJ953 | ♠ AQJ93 |
| ♥ 82 | ♥ 82 |
| ♦ K63 | ♦ K63 |
| ♣ Q4 | ♣ Q74 |

**With Example 56a, responder bids one spade after an opening bid of one club. When opener next bids two hearts, a** reverse, **this responder jumps to three spades. This auction shows at least six spades and game forcing values of 9+ HCP.**

**With Example 56b, responder bids one spade after an opening bid of one club. When opener** reverses **to two hearts, this responder bids two notrump, asking opener to bid three clubs. When opener does bid three clubs as asked, responder bids three spades. This auction shows exactly five spades and game forcing values of 9+ HCP.**

In all of these auctions, when responder's rebid is two notrump (an effort to slow down the auction), opener bids three clubs with values that are less than game forcing but will bid otherwise with greater values (19+ HCP). The only exception occurs when opener's first suit has been diamonds and a diamond contract is more appealing than a contract of three clubs.

Opener may have a hand such as: ♠ Kx ♥ AQJx ♦ KQJ10xx ♣ x. After an opening bid of one diamond and a **reverse** to two hearts over one spade, if responder next bids two notrump this opener should bid three diamonds. A rebid of three clubs might be passed by responder. A diamond contract is clearly better than a contract in clubs. In this auction only, opener does not promise extra values by refusing to bid three clubs after responder's rebid of two notrump. In all other situations, opener's refusal to bid three clubs shows game forcing values (19+ HCP). Opener cannot rebid three clubs since responder might pass.

## Summary of responder's rebids

1. Responder's rebids after a two-over-one response are all forcing to game.
2. When responder uses a **forcing notrump,** all rebids are either minimum or invitational as shown in Chapter Five.
3. Responder can make the auction forcing by using **fourth suit forcing** as shown in Chapter Three.

4. Responder's rebids with minimum values (5+ to 9- HCP) are:
    A. A simple preference to opener's first suit.
    B. A repeat of responder's own suit (requires six cards).
    C. A preference to opener's second suit by pass or a raise to the two level.
    D. One notrump—a catchall.
5. Responder's rebids with invitational values (9+ to 12- HCP) are:
    A. A jump preference to opener's first suit.
    B. A jump rebid of responder's own suit (requires six cards).
    C. A raise of opener's second suit to the three level.
    D. A jump to two notrump (requires a stopper in the unbid suit).
    E. **Fourth suit forcing** may be necessary
        1. Responder may need to find a three card fit for a five card major.
        2. Responder may be unable to jump to 2NT without a stopper in the unbid suit.
6. Responder's only forcing jump preference is in the auction: 1♣ - pass - 1♦ - pass, any rebid - pass - 3♣.
7. Responder's rebids after opener has **reversed** are specialized.
    A. A rebid of two in the same suit shows five or more cards and minimum values.
    B. A rebid of two notrump asks opener to next bid three clubs.
    C. A rebid in any other suit is forcing showing 9+ or more HCP.
    D. A jump rebid of 3NT shows 12+ to 15- HCP.
    E. A rebid of 2NT then 3NT shows 9+ to 12- HCP.
    F. A jump rebid of responder's first suit shows six or more cards and is forcing.
    G. A rebid of 2NT by responder followed by a rebid in the suit of the original response shows five cards and is forcing.
    H. After opening one diamond and **reversing** to two hearts after a response of one spade, opener can rebid three diamonds to show an excellent suit without extra value after responder's 2NT slowdown.
    I. If responder bids two notrump as a rebid and opener otherwise declines to bid three clubs, opener's values are game forcing (19+ HCP).
    J. Generally, any bid by responder after he bids two notrump is weaker than the same bid made immediately.

# Responder's rebid exercises

With each of the following hands, you have responded one heart to an opening bid of one club and opener has rebid one spade. What is your rebid?

1.
- ♠ Q93
- ♥ K1064
- ♦ 8754
- ♣ J3

2.
- ♠ Q3
- ♥ K10764
- ♦ Q9872
- ♣ 8

3.
- ♠ Q3
- ♥ J874
- ♦ 95
- ♣ KJ873

4.
- ♠ 8
- ♥ AQJ9764
- ♦ 86
- ♣ K104

5.
- ♠ J8
- ♥ AQ1074
- ♦ K96
- ♣ J104

6.
- ♠ 108
- ♥ KQ95
- ♦ AQ104
- ♣ 852

7.
- ♠ KJ84
- ♥ Q1073
- ♦ 5
- ♣ J763

8.
- ♠ Q3
- ♥ KJ10964
- ♦ AJ5
- ♣ K4

9.
- ♠ 7
- ♥ AQ1085
- ♦ KJ1073
- ♣ J6

10.
- ♠ KJ105
- ♥ AK83
- ♦ AJ2
- ♣ 106

With the next hand, you have responded one diamond to an opening bid of one club. When opener makes any rebid at the one level, what rebid do you make and why?

11.
- ♠ 7
- ♥ 83
- ♦ AKJ954
- ♣ KQ106

With each of the following hands, you have responded one spade to an opening bid of one club. Opener has continued with a **reverse** of two hearts. What is your rebid?

12.
- ♠ KJ1075
- ♥ AJ93
- ♦ 86
- ♣ 73

13.
- ♠ AQ84
- ♥ Q6
- ♦ KJ94
- ♣ J82

14.
- ♠ K1074
- ♥ Q82
- ♦ 953
- ♣ Q72

15.
- ♠ KJ1075
- ♥ Q1074
- ♦ 85
- ♣ 93

16.
- ♠ AQ84
- ♥ QJ5
- ♦ Q1094
- ♣ 98

17.
- ♠ AQJ963
- ♥ K84
- ♦ 975
- ♣ 3

18.
- ♠ KQ95
- ♥ 83
- ♦ Q104
- ♣ K1076

19.
- ♠ KJ1075
- ♥ 964
- ♦ AQ9
- ♣ 86

20.
- ♠ KJ1075
- ♥ 964
- ♦ Q104
- ♣ 86

## Answers

1. Pass. You know that you have reached a four-three fit, but with your meager values, you don't want to get any higher. One spade will probably be as good a contract as any.

2. One notrump. Not the description that you would like to make, but no other call will show your limited values. Your cannot rebid hearts with only five and you do not have the values to bid two diamonds.

3. Two clubs. This shows your minimum response values (5+ to 9- HCP) and only four hearts with longer clubs.

4. Four hearts. Your heart suit is self-sufficient and your ten high card points grow up to be enough for game when you factor in your seven card suit.

5. Two diamonds. This is **fourth suit forcing**. It says nothing about the diamond suit but makes the auction forcing for one round. With your game invitational values, you want to know if partner has a three card fit for your five card heart suit.

6. Two notrump. You have game invitational values (9+ to 12- HCP) and hold a stopper in diamonds. Your heart suit is only four cards so you do not need to probe for a three card fit there.

7. Two spades. A courtesy raise since your minimum is maximum (7+ to 9- HCP) and you do have four card support (look again at problem one).

8. Two diamonds. This again is **fourth suit forcing**. You are building a forcing auction after which you intend to bid hearts again to show six cards or more. You know that

game should be reached but do not know what game. If partner holds two card support for hearts or a singleton honor, your game contract should be in hearts and partner will know to support you with either of those holdings. You cannot bid three hearts because that would be only invitational.

9. Two diamonds. This again is **fourth suit forcing**. Your hope that partner will show three card support for hearts in which case that will be the trump suit. If partner denies holding three hearts, you will next bid three diamonds. Your auction will show at least five cards in each of the suits that you have bid and game invitational values (9+ to 12- HCP).

10. Two diamonds. This again is **fourth suit forcing**. You hold four card support for spades but your values are too great to just jump raise spades to game. You intend to next bid three spades to show four card support with values too much to just bid game. You will have invited a slam in spades.

11. Three clubs. Although all other jump preferences are invitational, this one is the only jump preference that is forcing. It describes your hand perfectly, suggesting a slam in one of the minor suits.

12. Three hearts. This call is forcing and shows a four card fit for hearts. Your values facing opener's **reverse** are adequate for game and your auction shows that fact.

13. Three notrump. You show that diamonds are stopped and that you hold only four spades, and that your values are those of an opening bid (12+ to 15 HCP). If partner's **reverse** is better than minimum a slam may be reached, since you have described good values.

14. Two notrump. This asks opener to bid three clubs with **reverse** values that are minimum (16+ to 18 HCP). When this is the case, three clubs in the known fit (partner has promised at least five clubs) will be the best place to play.

15. Two notrump. Yes, we know that you hold five spades and a bid of two spades would show that fact. However you also know that a four-four fit in hearts exists and that hearts should be the trump suit. You intend to bid three hearts if partner bids three clubs as requested to show a minimum **reverse** (16+ to 18 HCP). When you then bid three hearts, you will have shown a four card fit with minimum response values (5+ to 9- HCP). If partner does not show minimum values by bidding something other than three clubs you intend to show your heart fit at whatever level is necessary. This slow heart raise limits your hand to minimum response values.

16. Two notrump. This asks partner to bid three clubs with minimum **reverse** values. You intend then to bid three notrump to show the values of 9+ to 12- HCP. If you jumped immediately to three notrump, you would have shown greater values (see problem 13). The "slow" three notrump bid limits your values.

17. Three spades. This call is forcing, showing at least 9+ HCP and at least six spades.

18. Three clubs. This call shows a club fit and is forcing. The auction promises that you hold at least game invitational values (9+ HCP), which is enough for game facing your partner's **reverse**. If your values were less, you would have bid two notrump (see problem 14) to try and escape to clubs without getting higher when opener's values were not game forcing (19 HCP or more).

19. Two notrump. You ask partner to bid three clubs with minimum **reverse** values after which you intend to bid three spades. This shows that your suit is only five cards long, but that your values are adequate to make a game facing a minimum **reverse** (9+ HCP facing at least 16+ HCP).

20. Two spades. This shows that you hold five or more spades, but that your values are minimum for a response (5+ to 9- HCP).

# CHAPTER SEVEN

## AFTER OPENER BIDS NOTRUMP

An opening bid in notrump or a rebid in notrump describes a hand that is balanced and in a certain strength range. When the opening bid is one notrump, the range is 15 to 17 HCP; if the opening bid is two notrump, the range is 20 or 21 HCP. Two other ranges are described by rebids in notrump. When opener rebids one notrump, the range is 12 to 14 HCP: if the rebid is a jump to 2NT, the range is 18 or 19 HCP. Hands stronger than 21 HCP begin with a two club opening bid as shown in Chapter Nine.

Once so complete a description has been made, opener yields complete control of the auction to responder. Any further action taken by opener will not be voluntary, but at the instigation of the responder. Responder may ask questions, may invite, or may decline to move higher, but whatever responder does, opener must respect that decision and do as partner asks. Responder knows what opener holds. Responder becomes the captain—opener the crew.

Having been designated the captain of the auction, responder must have bids that will control the auction. Responder must be able both to convey information and request information about opener's limited hand. The methods used will vary based on the hand. Responder must be able to make bids that are forcing, bids that are invitational, and bids that require opener to pass.

In the pages that follow, there are several situations in which opener has bid or rebid in notrump, indicating both the size and shape of the opening hand. Look to the bids available to responder that will facilitate an easy search for what appears to be the best contract.

## Opener has rebid one Notrump

When opener has rebid one notrump to show 12 to 14 HCP and a balanced hand, responder may also be balanced and will be happy to play in notrump. With minimum response values responder will pass and one notrump will become the contract. When responder has game invitational values (9+ to 12-), raise to two notrump.

Holding values that suggest game (12+ or more HCP) 3NT should be responder's choice.

Sometimes responder may believe that slam is possible if opener's values are maximum. A jump to 4NT by responder asks opener to bid that slam with maximum values for the limited hand. Because opener's values are limited to the 12 to 14 HCP range, if responder invitationally jumps to 4NT that shows about 19 HCP. All of this relates to the numbers usually required when notrump contracts are reached. When notrump contracts depend upon winning tricks with high cards, these numbers are reasonably accurate. It is different when the contract can be fulfilled with tricks that are produced by long suits.

### Example 57:

| a | b | c |
|---|---|---|
| ♠ K95 | ♠ KJ5 | ♠ KJ5 |
| ♥ Q1083 | ♥ AQ83 | ♥ AQJ4 |
| ♦ AJ4 | ♦ A84 | ♦ AQ107 |
| ♣ J106 | ♣ 1096 | ♣ Q3 |

**With Example 57a, after an opening bid of one club responder bids one heart. When opener rebids one notrump, responder raises to two notrump to invite game.**

**With Example 57b, responder again bids one heart after an opening bid of one club. When opener rebids one notrump, raise to three notrump.**

**With Example 57c, responder bids one heart after an opening bid of one club. When opener rebids one notrump, jump to four notrump to invite a slam.**

At times responder will hold values enough for game, but not know which game is best. When responder has bid a five card major suit, a game in the major suit will be best whenever opener holds a three card fit. Responder's try for game will need to seek more information about opener's hand.

Opener's rebid has guaranteed a balanced hand that must include either two or three cards in responder's major suit. With fewer, opener's hand would have been unbalanced and should not have rebid one notrump. With four card support for responder's major, opener would have raised the major rather than rebid one notrump. With minimum response values, responder repeats a five card major and plays the 5-2 or 5-3 fit.

Responder needs to be able to determine two things. Responder would like to know whether opener has a two or three card fit for the five card major suit of the response, and whether opener's values are the minimum 12 HCP or the maximum 14 HCP.

## New Minor Forcing

For years, standard bidding has severely limited responder. The only available invitation to a game was a bid of two notrump. When responder's major suit is only four cards long there is no problem with the use of this invitation.

But, when responder holds a five card major suit, if this invitation is used and opener passes, the contract of two notrump will be inferior to a contract in the five-three major fit when opener has that fit. In a game scored by match points, being plus 120 at a contract of two notrump will produce a very poor score when par is plus 140 in the five-three major suit fit. Responder needs a way to find the five-three major suit fit when it exists in order to get to a par contract, even when game is not reached. After **new minor forcing,** when opener has a three card fit and a minimum, the major can be played at the two level.

With only old standard methods available, after opener rebids one notrump, responder can make a forcing bid only by a jump in a new suit or by making a **reverse.** When that is what must be done to simply make the auction forcing, there will often be no choice but to distort and make bids that do nothing to describe the responding hand.

This approach has never been adequate. It is imperative that better bidding methods be available which allow complete exchange of information after opener's rebid of one notrump. Modern standard bidding presents a convention that solves these problems. It is called **New Minor Forcing.** Responder uses it with values that are game invitational or better (9+ or more HCP).

After responder has bid a major suit and has heard opener rebid one notrump, responder makes the auction forcing and seeks further information by bidding in a minor suit that is new to the auction. When this happens, opener knows that responder's rebid is conventional rather than natural. (When playing in organized competition opener must alert the opponents that a conventional call has occurred.)

When opener has bid one club, responder has bid one of a major suit, and opener has then rebid one notrump, if responder next bids two diamonds, this convention has been used. Responder's call is artificial and forcing, asking opener to describe further.

Similarly, if opener begins by bidding one diamond and rebids one notrump after responder bids one of a major suit, if responder next bids two clubs this is **New Minor Forcing**. This bid is not natural, but is a convention that asks opener for more information.

Understand that this is an exception to something written earlier. The bidding axiom you learned in Chapter Three was that a new suit by an unpassed responder was forcing, but not after opener had rebid one notrump. The addition of **New Minor Forcing** to our bidding overrides that axiom. Those who adhere to the old standards have always played that when responder rebids in a new minor suit after opener has rebid one notrump, it is natural and non-forcing. Of course, they will continue to have clumsy auctions when responder must invite or force after opener has rebid one notrump.

The modern standard, which includes **New Minor Forcing**, allows much more comfort in the auction and solves a previously unaddressed bidding problem.

If opener begins with a call of one heart and responder bids one spade, again opener can describe a balanced hand in the range of 12 to 14 HCP by bidding one notrump. In addition to the known five card heart suit, responder will have two three card holdings and a doubleton. In this auction, the convention known as **New Minor Forcing** is still available. Here we see that neither minor suit has been bid, and that either one can be used. Having a choice, responder bids the minor suit that is most natural. In all of these instances, opener is being asked to describe specific things about a limited hand, and responder's call is known not to be natural. Responder uses **New Minor Forcing** for one of these reasons:

1. Responder may be searching for a three card fit for a five card major as an exploration for game is initiated. This exploration will allow responder to find out whether opener holds a two or three card fit for the five card major suit, and also to find out whether opener is minimum (12 HCP) or maximum (14 HCP).

2. Responder may need to simply create an auction that is forcing for other purposes, such as inviting a slam in either opener's original minor suit, or in the unbid minor suit. **New Minor Forcing** can be used for either of these reasons.

When responder uses **New Minor Forcing,** opener is asked to describe further. After the auction has begun with a minor suit, responder has bid one heart and opener has rebid one notrump. If responder uses this convention, opener's requirement is to bid two hearts with three card heart support with minimum values (12 or a bad 13

HCP), or jump to three hearts with three card heart support and maximum values (14 or a good 13 HCP).

Holding only two hearts, opener bids two notrump with minimum values, but will jump to three notrump to show maximum values. An exception is that when opener's first suit was diamonds, and the **New Minor Forcing** call has been two clubs, when opener holds only two hearts but also has five diamonds, a rebid of two diamonds rather than two notrump is more descriptive.

Opener also has available a call of two spades. This cannot be showing a spade suit. Opener's rebid of one notrump after the one heart response denied holding as many as four spades. It follows that when opener does bid two notrump to show only two hearts and minimum values, it promises a stopper in spades. When opener does not hold a spade stopper, the "impossible" two spade bid can be used to express that fact. This call gives the additional information about the lack of a stopper in spades as it shows a doubleton in responder's heart suit.

**Example 58**:

|  | a | b | c |
|---|---|---|---|
| ♠ | AQ4 | AQ4 | AQ4 |
| ♥ | J8 | J8 | J83 |
| ♦ | K1082 | K1082 | K10842 |
| ♣ | Q874 | KJ104 | Q8 |

|  | d | e | f |
|---|---|---|---|
| ♠ | A104 | 1083 | J84 |
| ♥ | Q83 | Q8 | Q8 |
| ♦ | KJ108 | KJ108 | KJ1084 |
| ♣ | A83 | AQ97 | AQ3 |

**With Example 58a, opener bids one diamond and rebids one notrump after a response of one heart. When responder uses** New Minor Forcing **by bidding two clubs, opener bids two notrump. This denies either three hearts or five diamonds and shows minimum values with a stopper in spades.**

**With Example 58b, opener bids one diamond and rebids one notrump after a response of one heart. When responder uses** New Minor Forcing **by bidding two clubs, opener jumps to three notrump. This denies either three hearts or five diamonds and shows maximum values for the one notrump rebid.**

**With Example 58c, opener bids one diamond and after a response of one heart rebids one notrump. When responder next uses** New Minor Forcing **by bidding two clubs, opener bids two hearts to show three card heart support and minimum values.**

**With Example 58d, opener bids one diamond and after a response of one heart rebids one notrump. When responder uses** New Minor Forcing **by bidding two clubs, opener jumps to three hearts to show three card support with maximum values.**

**With Example 58e, opener bids one diamond and after a response of one heart rebids one notrump. When responder uses** New Minor Forcing **by bidding two clubs, opener bids two spades to deny holding either three hearts or five diamonds and to deny a stopper in spades.**

**With Example 58f, opener bids one diamond and after a response of one heart rebids one notrump. When responder uses** New Minor Forcing **by bidding two clubs, opener bids two diamonds. This denies three hearts and promises at least five diamonds.**

After a minor opener, when responder has bid one spade, there is another possibility. Responder may have bid one spade holding a five card spade suit and also have four hearts. When both a five-three major suit fit and a four-four major suit fit exist, the four-four fit should be the trump suit.

The reason is that with a four-four trump fit, a ruff in either hand will produce an extra trick, while with a five-three trump fit, extra tricks are only available when ruffs can be made in the three card holding. Also, the five-three fit as a side suit can be established as a place to discard losers from the other suits, and this cannot be done when the four-four fit is on the side rather than serving as the trump suit.

Therefore, when responder bids one spade and opener rebids one notrump, if responder uses **New Minor Forcing,** opener has a different priority order. Rather than show a three card fit for spades, opener will first show a four card heart holding when it exists. By showing a four card heart holding, opener does not deny holding three spades. Economy in the auction simply requires that the possibility of a four-four fit in hearts take precedence over the immediate discovery of a five-three spade fit.

Therefore, opener will bid two hearts after responder has first bid spades and then uses **New Minor Forcing,** since to show four hearts has priority. This neither affirms nor denies three card support for spades. Spade support can still be determined when responder has the need to know. When opener has neither four hearts nor three spades, if the first bid suit was diamonds, there is still the option to show a diamond holding of five cards by rebidding that suit after the **New Minor Forcing** call of two clubs.

**Example 59:**

|  a  |  b  |
|:---:|:---:|
| ♠ AQ4 | ♠ Q8 |
| ♥ K1082 | ♥ J84 |
| ♦ J8 | ♦ KJ1084 |
| ♣ Q874 | ♣ AQ3 |

**With Example 59a, opener bids one club and rebids one notrump after a response of one spade. When responder uses** New Minor Forcing **by bidding two diamonds, opener bids two hearts to show four in that suit. Despite also holding three spades, the first requirement is to show a four card heart holding rather than three card support for spades.**

**With Example 59b, opener bids one diamond and rebids one notrump after a response of one spade. When responder uses** New Minor Forcing **by bidding two clubs, opener bids two diamonds to deny holding either three spades or four hearts and to show five or more diamonds. If opener had one more spade, it would be right to conceal the five card diamond suit and show three card support for responder's spade suit.**

Let us assume that responder has bid spades and then uses **New Minor Forcing.** Opener then bids two hearts to show a four card holding, but this does not interest responder who is looking for a spade fit. If responder continues by bidding two spades, that shows a five card spade suit with game invitational values—opener may pass or continue having received this information.

If instead responder bids three notrump, that shows game going values and the reason for using **New Minor Forcing** must be a holding of five spades. Opener may again make an informed decision. Pass is right with a holding of only two spades, but correction to a contract of four spades is right with three card support if opener also has a ruffing value (some side doubleton).

A jump to three spades by responder shows a six card suit and interest in a slam. Responder could have jumped either to three spades (invitational) or four spades (just to play game) after the notrump rebid rather than use **New Minor Forcing.** So, in addition to a six card suit responder must have slam interest.

**Example 60:**

| a | b | c | d |
|---|---|---|---|
| ♠ KJ963 | ♠ KJ963 | ♠ KJ10853 | ♠ KJ10853 |
| ♥ Q93 | ♥ Q93 | ♥ Q93 | ♥ AQ3 |
| ♦ AJ6 | ♦ AJ3 | ♦ A106 | ♦ AQ6 |
| ♣ 93 | ♣ K9 | ♣ 3 | ♣ 3 |

With Example 60a, responder bids one spade after an opening bid of one club and opener rebids one notrump. Responder should use New Minor Forcing, by bidding two diamonds. If opener rebids two hearts to show a four card holding, this responder bids two spades to show five spades and invitational values. If opener bids two spades to deny four hearts and show three spades with minimum values, responder passes. If opener jumps to three spades to show three card spade support with a maximum, this responder continues to four spades.

With Example 60b, responder bids one spade after an opening bid of one club and opener rebids one notrump. Responder next uses New Minor Forcing, by bidding two diamonds. If opener bids two hearts to show a four card holding, this responder jumps to three notrump to show five spades and values enough for game. If opener also holds three spades, the next call will be a correction to four spades.

With Example 60c, responder bids one spade after an opening bid of one club and opener rebids one notrump. Responder does not use New Minor Forcing, but instead jumps to three spades to show invitational values with a six card suit.

With Example 60d, responder bids one spade after an opening bid of one club and opener rebids one notrump. Responder next uses New Minor Forcing, by bidding two diamonds. If opener bids two hearts to show a four card holding, this responder jumps to three spades to show a six card spade suit with slam interest.

Responder's second reason to use this convention occurs with a hand something like:

♠ 7
♥ AK64
♦ 86
♣ KQJ953

When opener begins by bidding one club, responder first bids one heart, hoping to hear a raise of hearts. However, opener next bids one notrump, describing a balanced hand with fewer than four hearts and fewer than four spades. Responder's thoughts then turn to the possibility of a slam in clubs. Responder's problem is that at this turn there is no available bid that both is forcing and shows support for clubs. A bid of two clubs shows club support with minimum response values, and opener must pass. Jumping to three clubs again shows club support, but the values shown are game invitational (9+ to 12- HCP). This is not adequate. Opener might accept such an invitation and bid three notrump, but also might pass. A jump to four clubs would be the **Gerber** convention, saying nothing about clubs and asking opener to show the number of aces held.

A modern responder solves this problem by bidding two diamonds, **New Minor Forcing**. When opener bids two or three hearts to show three card heart support, or bids two or three notrump to indicate exactly two hearts, responder can then bid clubs at the next level to show a fit and slam interest and the auction is forcing.

When opener hears this try for slam in clubs, it will be clear that responder does not care how many hearts opener holds, but has used **New Minor Forcing** to set the stage to try for a club slam. Opener will know that responder holds only four hearts but has long clubs and a very good hand.

Having heard responder's club slam try, opener will deny interest by returning to notrump as cheaply as possible, or will show interest in a club slam by making a cue bid. If opener shows interest and makes a cue bid in diamonds, a successful club slam is virtually assured. Opener will have a maximum with a good fit and controls in order to show slam interest. The balanced hand that rebid one notrump will look something like:

♠ A86
♥ Q7
♦ A95
♣ A10864

or like:

♠ A86
♥ J8
♦ A953
♣ A1087

With either of these hands as declarer we see an easy twelve tricks on a combined holding of only 26 or 27 HCP because of the fits in clubs and hearts and the controls in the remaining suits.

Or responder might have a hand like:

♠ 5
♥ AK972
♦ KQJ87
♣ A4

Opener bids one club and after responder bids one heart opener rebids one notrump. Responder next bids two diamonds, **New Minor Forcing** and discovers whether opener holds two or three hearts. If opener shows three hearts responder asks for controls using **Blackwood.** If opener has the perfect hand:

♠ A86
♥ Q63
♦ A94
♣ K1085

this can all be described and a grand slam can be bid even though the bidding side holds only 30 HCP between the two hands.

If opener denies holding three hearts when responder uses **New Minor Forcing**, responder continues by bidding three diamonds (or four diamonds if opener has jumped to three notrump to show maximum values). If opener then bids again in notrump, that denies interest in a diamond slam, but with a hand that includes controls and a diamond fit, opener will make a cue bid to show interest in reaching a slam in diamonds. That hand might be:

♠ A106
♥ J6
♦ A963
♣ KQ98

These two facing hands might easily take all thirteen tricks playing in diamonds.

Here is one last wrinkle relating to the **New Minor Forcing** convention. Responder might pick up a hand such as:

♠ **A965**
♥ **76**
♦ **3**
♣ **Q98642**

When opener starts with one diamond, responder bids one spade. This hand is too weak to show the club suit even though it is longer than the spade holding. Opener continues by bidding one notrump to show a balanced minimum hand, and responder knows that clubs should be the trump suit. Responder needs to be able to show clubs and make the auction non-forcing at the same time.

A bid of two clubs will not show clubs. That call would be **New Minor Forcing.** Even if two clubs is followed by a bid of three clubs which does, in fact, show clubs, the auction will be forcing and that is not what responder needs to convey.

Responder's message bid is to jump directly to three clubs after the opener bids one notrump. This direct jump by responder to the unbid minor suit at the three level after opener has rebid one notrump carries the message of a hand with minimum response values (5+ to 9-HCP), only four cards in the major suit which was bid at the first turn, and six or seven cards in the previously unbid minor suit in which the jump to the three level has been made. It places the contract and requires opener to pass.

To summarize:

When opener rebids one notrump, responder makes the auction forcing and seeks further information by **New Minor Forcing.**

1. Responder must have at least game invitational values.
   A. Responder may be seeking a three card fit for a five card major.
   B. Responder may be interested in opener's values in order to determine the appropriate level for play.
      1. Opener describes a minimum of 12 or bad 13 HCP.
      2. Opener describes a maximum of 14 or a good 13 HCP.
2. Opener will show one of these things:
   A. Minimum values with a three card fit for responder's major suit by bidding that suit at the two level.
   B. Maximum values with a three card fit for responder's major suit by bidding that suit at the three level.

> C. Minimum values with a two card fit for responder's major suit by bidding two notrump.
> D. Maximum values with a two card fit for responder's major suit by jumping to three notrump.
> E. When responder's major suit is spades, priority falls on opener to first show a holding of four hearts, rather than three card spade support.
> F. If responder's first suit was hearts, opener can show a doubleton heart with minimum values and either affirm or deny a spade stopper.
>> 1. Opener's next call of two notrump promises a stopper in spades.
>> 2. Opener's next call of two spades denies a stopper in spades.
> 3. After opener has first bid diamonds and responder makes the **New Minor Forcing** call of two clubs, if opener cannot show an appropriate major suit holding and holds five or more diamonds, a rebid in diamonds describes.
> 4. Responder's adjunct with a weak hand with only four cards in the major suit and six cards in the unbid minor suit is to jump to the three level in that minor suit. Opener is then required to pass and the auction ends.

## Opener's rebid is a jump to two notrump

If opener has bid a minor suit and after a response at the one level makes a jump rebid of two notrump, the auction shows a balanced hand in the range of 18 or 19 HCP. When responder's hand is balanced the auction continues with a pass or a notrump raise to the appropriate level (see summary).

After opener's jump rebid of two notrump, any call responder makes at the three level is forcing. It is assumed that the values of both hands are sufficient to produce a game.

If responder holds a six card or longer major suit and rebids that suit at the three level, it suggests the possibility of a slam. With no interest in a slam, responder jumps to the four level in the six card major, knowing that opener holds two or three cards in that suit.

Example 61:

|  | a |  | b |
|---|---|---|---|
| ♠ | K5 | ♠ | AKJ954 |
| ♥ | KQ10754 | ♥ | 7 |
| ♦ | 8642 | ♦ | KQ83 |
| ♣ | 7 | ♣ | 64 |

**With Example 61a, you have responded one heart to an opening bid of one club. When opener rebids by jumping to two notrump, you next bid four hearts to end the auction. You know opener holds two or three hearts, and you have no interest in trying for a slam.**

**With Example 61b, you have responded one spade to an opening bid of one club. When opener rebids by jumping to two notrump, you next bid only three spades. This call is forcing and promises a six card or longer suit. Since you did not use** fast arrival **by jumping to four spades, you indicate interest in a slam.**

If responder has first bid one spade and next bids three hearts after opener's jump rebid of two notrump, the distribution shown is five-five in the majors. When opener's shape is 2-3-4-4, a raise to four hearts is in order.

If responder's major suit is five cards, after the jump rebid by opener of two notrump, **New Minor Forcing** can be used to seek the five-three fit. When responder holds five spades and four hearts that convention should be used to seek either a four-four heart fit or a five-three spade fit. Opener's priorities remain the same, and showing four hearts has priority over showing a three card spade fit. Finding either a four-four fit in hearts or a five-three fit in spades is easily accomplished.

Responder, who has bid one heart, might also hold four-four in the major suits. In this case, the function of **New Minor Forcing** is to discover a four-four fit in spades. If opener shows a three card fit for hearts and responder retreats to three notrump, opener must understand that the use of **New Minor Forcing** was for the purpose of finding that four-four spades fit rather than a five-three fit in hearts.

**Example 62:**

|   | a | b | c | d |
|---|---|---|---|---|
| ♠ | KJ1074 | K54 | KJ1074 | KJ107 |
| ♥ | QJ987 | KQ1075 | QJ98 | QJ98 |
| ♦ | — | 862 | 7 | 73 |
| ♣ | 954 | 74 | 954 | 954 |

With Example 62a, you have responded one spade to an opening bid of one club. When opener next jumps to two notrump, you will continue by bidding three hearts. This promises five-five in the major suits.

With Example 62b, you have responded one heart to an opening bid of one club. When opener makes a jump rebid of two notrump, you use New Minor Forcing by bidding three diamonds. Opener will show or deny three card support for hearts and you know which game to play.

With Example 62c, you have responded one spade to an opening bid of one club. When opener makes a jump rebid of two notrump, you use New Minor Forcing, by bidding three diamonds. If opener bids hearts to show four cards, you can raise to game in hearts. If opener bids three spades to deny four hearts and show three card spade support, you can raise to game in spades. If opener bids three notrump to deny either four hearts or three spades, you will pass.

With Example 62d, You have responded one heart to an opening bid of one club. When opener makes a jump rebid of two notrump, you use New Minor Forcing by bidding three diamonds. Opener's jump rebid has not denied a holding of four spades and you are checking for a fit in that suit. If opener bids three hearts to show three card support, when you continue by bidding three notrump, it will be clear that you were not trying to find a five-three fit in hearts. Your reason for using New Minor Forcing was clearly an attempt to find a fit in spades, and if opener does hold four spades, a correction to four spades is clearly indicated.

If responder's rebid is in opener's minor suit at the three level, it is a slam suggestion. Opener can reject that suggestion by bidding three notrump, or can show interest by cue bidding in a new suit.

If responder is two suited and holds the unbid minor, a rebid in that suit will be conventional rather than natural. Responder will know after opener's next call if there is a fit in the major. If no fit in the major is found, responder will have the option of playing three notrump or rebidding the second suit as a natural slam try. Again, opener will be able to reject the slam suggestion by bidding notrump, or show interest in the suggested slam by cue bidding.

**Example 63:**

|  | a | b | c |
|---|---|---|---|
| ♠ | AQ108 | K4 | J4 |
| ♥ | 6 | A975 | KQJ5 |
| ♦ | KQ1096 | AJ84 | AJ84 |
| ♣ | 1095 | AQ3 | AQ3 |

|  | d | e |
|---|---|---|
| ♠ | KJ | K4 |
| ♥ | KQJ | A754 |
| ♦ | J43 | AJ8 |
| ♣ | AK1083 | AK72 |

**Example 63a has responded one spade to an opening bid of one diamond. When opener makes a jump rebid of two notrump responder suggests a slam in opener's first suit by bidding three diamonds.**

**Example 63b has opened with one diamond and rebid two notrump after a response of one spade. When responder next bids three diamonds to suggest a diamond slam, this opener who is rich in controls bids three hearts to show slam interest. Cue bids in both black suits should then cause the good slam to be reached.**

**Example 63c has opened with one diamond and rebid two notrump after a response of one spade. When responder next bids three diamonds to suggest a diamond slam, this opener rejects the invitation and bids three notrump.**

**Example 63d has opened one club and rebid two notrump after a response of one spade. Responder next bids three diamonds, which is** New Minor Forcing **and opener bids three notrump to deny four hearts or three spades. Responder next makes a natural slam try by bidding four diamonds. With soft values and poor diamonds opener rejects this slam try by signing off at four notrump.**

**Example 63e has opened with one club and rebid two notrump after a response of one spade. When responder uses** New Minor Forcing **by bidding**

**three diamonds opener bids three hearts to show a four card holding. Responder then makes a natural slam try by bidding four diamonds. Opener then can cue bid in hearts and clubs and responder can cue bid spades - then hearts. The excellent diamond slam is easily bid when adequate methods are available.**

To summarize:

When opener's rebid is a jump to two notrump to show a balanced hand with 18 or 19 HCP, these continuations are possible:

1. Responder may continue by raising notrump to an appropriate level.
   A. With 6 to 13 HCP and no five major card suit, raise to three notrump.
   B. With 14 HCP and no five card major suit, raise to four notrump to invite slam.
   C. With 15 to 17 HCP and no five card major suit, jump to six notrump
   D. With 18 HCP and no five card major suit, jump to five notrump to require a small slam and invite a grand slam.
   E. With 19 or more HCP, bid seven notrump
2. All of responder's rebids at the three level are forcing.
3. When responder holds a six card or longer major that should be the trump suit.
   A. With no interest in a slam responder uses **fast arrival** and jumps to four in the suit.
   B. With interest in a slam responder rebids the suit at the three level. Opener can deny slam interest by bidding game in the major, or may show slam interest by cue bidding an ace.
4. If responder has first bid one spade and continues by bidding three hearts that promises five-five in the two suits.
5. If responder needs to probe further there is **New Minor Forcing.** Responder may hold:
   A. Five cards in the major suit.
   B. Five spades and four hearts.
   C. Four spades and four hearts.
6. With five hearts and four spades, responder will first have bid hearts. After **New Minor Forcing,** when opener shows a three card heart fit, a four-four fit in spades cannot be reached. Responder instead rebids by making a **reverse,** to show four spades and longer hearts.

7. If responder rebids to show a fit for opener's minor suit, the auction
   is a natural slam try.
   A. Opener can reject this offer by bidding three notrump.
   B. Opener can accept this offer by cue bidding an ace.
8. If responder first uses **New Minor Forcing**, then repeats that suit,
   the auction is a natural slam try. Opener's options are as above.

In the early 70's, Richard Walsh was an expert panelist for the Master Solvers Club of the Bridge World Magazine. He responded to a problem, which asked for a continuation by responder after opener had rebid one notrump. His answer was in keeping with the accepted methods of the time, but he commented that he would actually use **New Minor Forcing,** which was not widely known at that time. The Editor of the Bridge World Magazine was Alphonse Moyse, who also was the director of the Master Solvers Club. Walsh's comment inspired him to call this suggestion a "petty little odious bid". Users of the method eagerly seized this comment and made an acronym of the comment by Moyse. They began to call this convention PLOB. Users of this convention proudly advanced the nickname in its early years.

## Opener begins by bidding one notrump

Opener begins by bidding one notrump with a balanced hand in the range of 15 to 17 HCP. Again, responder is in charge, since opener has given a narrow description with the opening bid. The old standards set by Goren used one artificial call—the **Stayman** convention. All other calls were natural with suits (other than clubs) at the two level non-forcing and suit jumps to the three level were natural and forcing. Invitational auctions required the use of **Stayman** followed by a suit bid in the majors, while a **Stayman** bid followed by three clubs was a signoff.

The modern standard for auctions after an opening of one notrump takes into account the change of range. Instead of showing 16 to 18 HCP, it now shows 15 to 17 HCP. The **Stayman** convention remains standard, as it is an effective method for finding major suit fits. Natural bids in major suits give way for the most part to **Jacoby Transfer Bids**, and **Texas Transfer Bids**. The **Gerber** convention remains standard. Modern notrump auctions follow.

When responder holds a hand that is balanced and hears the opening bid of one notrump, a notrump contract will be played at some level.

1. With minimum values of 0 to 7 HCP responder passes and hopes
   that one notrump will make.

2. With 8 or 9 HCP and shape other than 4-3-3-3, responder invites game in notrump by raising to two notrump. The completely balanced pattern does not offer suits that may produce length tricks, and should be downgraded in the evaluation process.

3. With values of about 10 to a bad 15 HCP, responder bids three notrump.

4. With a good 15 to 17 HCP, responder jumps to four notrump. This invites opener to bid a slam with a maximum, pass with a minimum, or reinvite with a hand in the middle.

5. With 18 or 19 HCP, responder jumps to six notrump, again, placing the contract, or uses **Gerber**.

6. With 20 or 21 HCP, responder jumps to five notrump. This is absolutely forcing. It requires opener to bid six notrump with minimum values, but invites seven when maximum values are held.

7. With 22 or more HCP, responder jumps all the way to seven notrump. The combined values of the two hands are at least 37 HCP.

All of these formulae are based on simple addition of numbers. When the two hands are known to hold 33 HCP, a small slam should be bid; when they are known to hold 37 or more HCP, the grand slam should be bid.

Look at a balanced responder's values and actions in chart form:

| Responder's HCP | Action | Description |
|---|---|---|
| 0-7 | Pass | Hope you make it, partner. |
| 8-9 | 2NT | Bid game if maximum—pass if minimum. |
| 10-15- | 3NT | This is usually enough to make game. |
| 15+-17 | 4NT | Bid six if maximum—pass if minimum—or return the invitation by raising to five NT. Respond as though this had been **Blackwood**, if you have fewer than three aces and are maximum. Maximum means either a good 17 HCP or a source of tricks. |
| 18-19 | 6NT | We should have enough to make this contract. |
| 20-21 | 5NT | This forces at least six, and invites seven. |
| 22 or more | 7NT | Very unlucky, if we can't make this. |

**Example 64:**

| a | b | c | d |
|---|---|---|---|
| ♠ J84 | ♠ J84 | ♠ K84 | ♠ AK4 |
| ♥ K93 | ♥ K9 | ♥ K93 | ♥ K93 |
| ♦ 10762 | ♦ K1072 | ♦ K1072 | ♦ K1072 |
| ♣ Q95 | ♣ Q952 | ♣ Q95 | ♣ QJ5 |

| e | f | g |
|---|---|---|
| ♠ AK4 | ♠ AK4 | ♠ AK4 |
| ♥ K93 | ♥ K93 | ♥ KQ3 |
| ♦ K102 | ♦ AJ2 | ♦ AJ2 |
| ♣ KQJ5 | ♣ KQJ5 | ♣ KQJ5 |

All hands of Example 64 are responding to an opening bid of one notrump.

With Example 64a, pass. Your combined maximum is 23 HCP.

With Example 64b, raise to two notrump to invite game.

With Example 64c, raise to three notrump. Enough for game, but not for slam.

With Example 64d, raise to four notrump. There is enough for slam if opener has maximum values.

With Example 64e, raise to six notrump. Values enough for a small slam.

With Example 64f, bid five notrump. This forces at least a small slam and invites a grand slam if partner has maximum values.

With Example 64g, raise to seven notrump. Your combined values are at least 38 HCP.

## The Stayman convention

**Stayman** is just about as perfect a convention as one could hope for. It gives up the chance to play a contract of two clubs when the opening bid has been one notrump, but it opens doors to many other possible auctions. Most importantly, it paves the way to finding four-four fits in major suits.

Responder's call of two clubs does not show a club suit. It is artificial and asks the opening bidder to show a four card major suit. Opener bids a four card major suit when possible (holding both majors—bid hearts; this a change from the old standards), or bids two diamonds to deny holding a four card major.

Responder does not need anything in values holding a hand with the right pattern. If responder has 4-4-5-0 distribution with no high cards at all, **Stayman** will be wonderful. Responder bids two clubs and passes any rebid from opener. If opener bids a major suit, a fit of eight cards is guaranteed.

If opener instead bids two diamonds to deny a four card major suit, diamonds becomes the trump suit, giving value to an otherwise useless hand.

Responder can also use **Stayman** with little in values and a major suit pattern of five-four. If opener happens to bid either major suit in response to **Stayman,** responder has struck gold and is happy to pass. But, if opener bids two diamonds to deny holding a four card major suit, responder next bids the five card major to sign off. In this way, responder gets a shot at finding a fit in either major suit. And, if this shot misses, responder can still stop and play in the longer major suit at the two level.

### Example 65:

|          | a          |          | b          |
|----------|------------|----------|------------|
| ♠        | J942       | ♠        | J942       |
| ♥        | 8763       | ♥        | Q10873     |
| ♦        | 109854     | ♦        | 632        |
| ♣        | —          | ♣        | 8          |

**Both hands of Example 65 are responding to an opening bid of one notrump. An otherwise worthless hand gains values when it holds trump cards.**

**With Example 65a, use** Stayman **by bidding two clubs. Pass any rebid by opener.**

**With Example 65b, use** Stayman **by bidding two clubs. Pass if opener rebids in either major suit. If opener bids two diamonds to deny a four card major, correct to two hearts and opener will pass. This usage is often called "Drop Dead** Stayman**" or "Garbage** Stayman**" for obvious reasons.**

Sometimes responder uses **Stayman** with values that are game invitational (about 8 or 9 HCP). In such an auction, when opener happens to bid the major suit in which responder holds four cards, responder continues by bidding three in that same major suit. Opener understands that this is an invitation to game and that an eight card fit has been found. With minimum values opener will pass, but with better values opener will bid on to game in the established major suit. If responder's pattern is 4-3-3-3, **Stayman** should not be used. Responder has no capacity to ruff, which means notrump will play better even when there is a four-four fit in a major suit.

If responder has used **Stayman,** when opener bids two diamonds to deny holding four cards in either major suit, responder next bids two notrump to show game invitational values. Opener either passes or continues to three notrump based on the values held.

When responder uses **Stayman** and opener bids two hearts, this shows a four card heart suit, but does not deny four spades. If responder has used **Stayman** with game invitational values and four spades, there is still a chance that a four-four spade fit exists. In order to find that fit, responder next bids two spades. This correction promises exactly four spades and game invitational values—a change from the older standard for this auction. **Transfer** bids are part of the new standard. Therefore holding a five card major suit responder would not have used this auction. Instead, there would have been a **transfer** bid to show the five card spade suit, and then responder would have bid two notrump to show game invitational values.

When opener hears the correction from two hearts to two spades, a further correction to two or three notrump is made depending on opener's values with fewer than four spades, or opener can pass or raise spades to the three or four level holding four spades.

**Example 66:**

| a | b |
|---|---|
| ♠ 85 | ♠ KJ94 |
| ♥ KJ94 | ♥ 85 |
| ♦ A1063 | ♦ A1063 |
| ♣ 954 | ♣ 954 |

**Both hands of Example 66 are responding to an opening bid of one notrump. Responder bids two clubs—the** Stayman **convention.**

**With Example 66a, if opener rebids two hearts, raise to three hearts to invite game in the fit that has been found. If opener rebids either two diamonds or two spades, your game invitation will be two notrump.**

**With Example 66b, if opener rebids two spades, raise to three spades to invite a game in the fit that has been found. If opener rebids two diamonds to deny a**

**four card major, you will invite game by bidding two notrump. If opener rebids two hearts, a four card heart holding has been shown, but a holding of four spades has not been denied. Your next call of two spades invites game and shows only four spades. If you had held five spades, you would have made a** Jacoby Transfer **rather than use** Stayman **(unless you held four hearts as well, in which case you would have raised hearts rather than show spades).**

After a two diamond response to **Stayman,** responder can jump in a major suit to show five cards and make the auction forcing. When responder uses **Stayman** and opener shows a major which responder fits, the next call can be a jump to game or to slam with values which indicate that course of action. A check for controls on the way may be in order to know whether the slam should be bid. A direct jump to four clubs after the response to **Stayman** is **Gerber**, agreeing that the major suit which opener has shown is the trump suit.

When **Stayman** and **Jacoby Transfer Bids** are agreed (which is the modern standard), and responder wishes to sign off cheaply and play in a minor suit, a **Transfer** to the minor suit will be used. Therefore, responder's means of trying to reach a minor suit slam is to first use **Stayman**, then bid the good minor suit at the three level. When opener hears this auction, the continuation will show opener's opinion of the idea of the minor suit slam which responder has suggested.

With a poor fit, minimum values and few controls opener will show dislike for a minor suit slam by bidding three notrump. However, with a reasonable fit for the minor suit, maximum values and control cards, opener cooperates in the search for a slam in responder's minor suit by cue bidding an ace. The cue bid says that opener likes the idea of slam, while a call of three notrump denies interest in the suggested slam.

**Example 67:**

| a | b | c |
|---|---|---|
| ♠ KQ95 | ♠ KQ95 | ♠ KQ9 |
| ♥ 86 | ♥ 6 | ♥ 6 |
| ♦ AQ83 | ♦ KQJ93 | ♦ KQJ932 |
| ♣ J104 | ♣ AJ4 | ♣ AJ4 |

| d | e |
|---|---|
| ♠ AJ4 | ♠ AQ4 |
| ♥ KQ82 | ♥ AJ96 |
| ♦ 64 | ♦ A1065 |
| ♣ KQ85 | ♣ K3 |

All hands in Example 67 are responding to an opening bid of one notrump. All responders use Stayman by bidding two clubs.

With Example 67a, if opener rebids two spades, raise to four. If opener bids either two diamonds or two hearts, jump to three notrump. Opener will correct to four spades having bid two hearts and holding four-four in the majors. Responder must hold four spades or would have not used Stayman.

With Example 67b, if opener bids two spades, jump to four clubs. This is Gerber with spades as the agreed trump suit. If opener rebids either two hearts or two diamonds, bid three diamonds as a natural slam try.

With Example 67c, make a slam try in diamonds by bidding three diamonds after any rebid from opener.

With Example 67d, if opener rebids two hearts the conservative continuation is to sign off at four hearts—the aggressive course would be to jump to four clubs, which is Gerber with hearts as the agreed suit. If opener rebids either two diamonds or two spades, jump to four notrump to invite a slam.

With Example 67e, if opener rebids two hearts, jump to four clubs as before. There may be a grand slam if opener has a maximum with fitting controls. If opener's rebid is either two diamonds or two spades, jump to six notrump.

## The Jacoby Transfer

Responder makes a **Jacoby Transfer Bid,** by bidding the suit that ranks below a major suit at the two level in order to transfer to that suit. A bid of two diamonds promises five or more hearts and asks opener to bid that suit. A bid of two hearts promises five or more spades and asks opener to bid that suit. This modern innovation does two things that improve the quality of the auction.

1. The transfer auction causes the opening notrump bidder to declare in most auctions. This means that the opening lead will be up to rather than through tenace holdings. The stronger hand (usually the opening notrump bidder) remains concealed during the play rather than on display as dummy.

2. The responder is given greater control of the auction. Responder's hand is not limited by the transfer bid. The available continuations allow responder to describe many different hands.

Transfers to minor suits are also possible. Two methods exist. Some use two spades as a transfer to show either minor suit. Opener is asked to bid three clubs. Responder will pass with clubs or correct to diamonds to show that suit.

The second method is to use two spades as a transfer promising clubs and two notrump as a transfer promising diamonds. When this approach has been agreed, responder need not have the desire to stop and play a partscore in the minor suit. Opener can show or deny a good fit for the minor suit, which has been shown by the transfer bid.

When responder bids two spades to show clubs, if opener has a bad hand for clubs, three clubs will be bid as requested, but if opener truly likes clubs the in between bid of two notrump shows that fact. Similarly, when responder bids two notrump to show diamonds, opener bids three diamonds with no strong desire to move the auction forward, but makes the in between call of three clubs with a hand that is good for a diamond contract. This use of the in between bid to show that (within the established limits) opener has a good hand to play in the suit responder has chosen is called a "super acceptance". When opener does not show a "super acceptance", responder knows to sign off in the minor suit part score by passing on most hands.

If responder's call of two notrump is a transfer to diamonds, that call can no longer be used as a natural invitation to game in notrump. With such an agreement, when responder wants to invite game in notrump, **Stayman** is used, even though responder does not have a four card major suit. Regardless of opener's response to **Stayman,** responder next bids two notrump to invite game (In tournament play, opener must alert at the time of responder's rebid of two notrump, because a four card major suit in responder's hand has not been promised). The "super acceptance" concept also extends to auctions where responder has transferred to a major suit.

### Example 68:

|   a   |   b   |   c   |
|-------|-------|-------|
| ♠ 83 | ♠ 83 | ♠ Q8 |
| ♥ 5 | ♥ 5 | ♥ J84 |
| ♦ J943 | ♦ Q108643 | ♦ 104 |
| ♣ Q108643 | ♣ J943 | ♣ KJ9643 |

|   d   |   e   |   f   |
|-------|-------|-------|
| ♠ Q8 | ♠ AQ8 | ♠ AQ93 |
| ♥ J84 | ♥ A9 | ♥ KQ74 |
| ♦ KJ9643 | ♦ K1093 | ♦ K9 |
| ♣ 104 | ♣ KJ74 | ♣ J86 |

Example 68a is responding to an opening bid of one notrump. Responder bids two spades as a transfer to clubs. If opener next bids three clubs, responder passes. If opener next bids two notrump to show a good hand for clubs, responder signs off at three clubs. Remember that Stayman followed by a minor suit from responder is a slam suggestion.

Example 68b is responding to an opening bid of one notrump. Depending on agreed methods, responder transfers to diamonds. If that transfer is bidding two spades for either minor, when opener bids three clubs responder corrects to diamonds and opener must pass. If responder transfers by bidding two notrump, it will be to pass, if opener bids three diamonds, or correct to diamonds, if opener bids three clubs to show a good hand for diamonds.

Example 68c is responding to an opening bid of one notrump. Responder bids two spades to transfer to clubs. If opener bids two notrump to show a good hand for clubs, responder knows a source of tricks is available and bids three notrump. If opener simply bids three clubs, responder passes.

Example 68d is responding to an opening bid of one notrump. Depending upon agreed methods, responder transfers to diamonds. If the transfer is two spades for either minor, when opener bids three clubs, responder must guess what to do. Either three diamonds or three notrump might be correct.

If responder bids two notrump to transfer to diamonds and opener bids three diamonds, responder should pass. However, if responder bids two notrump and opener bids three clubs to show a good hand for diamonds, responder should again recognize that a source of tricks exists and should bid three notrump.

Example 68e has opened one notrump. If responder transfers to either minor suit opener should make a "super acceptance". Over a two spade transfer to clubs, opener should bid two notrump to show a good hand for clubs. Over a two notrump transfer to diamonds, opener should bid three clubs to show a good hand for diamonds.

Example 68f has opened one notrump. If responder transfers to either minor suit, opener should accept the transfer and not make a call that shows a good hand for the auction.

After responder has made a **Jacoby Transfer** by bidding two diamonds to show hearts or two hearts to show spades, the next action may either be a pass or an advance of the auction based upon responder's values and suit length. When the suit length is only five cards, responder advances the auction by bidding two notrump with values that are game invitational. The bid of two notrump after the transfer bid shows a five card suit and values of 7+ to 9- HCP.

Opener can pass with minimum values and a doubleton in responder's known five card suit, or can bid three notrump with better values. When opener holds more than two cards in responder's announced five card major suit, it is correct to play in the major at the three level with values that are minimum, or jump to the four level with both a good fit and maximum values (but there may have already been a "super acceptance" with that hand).

When responder has made a **Jacoby Transfer** to a major suit with values that are enough for game (9+ to about 14 HCP) and a balanced hand, the next call will be three notrump. Opener will pass with only two cards in the transfer suit, but will correct to game in the major suit with a better fit.

If responder makes a **Jacoby Transfer** and then jumps to four notrump, it is natural and quantitative. It affirms that the suit is exactly five cards long as it shows values of about 15 or 16 HCP. This auction offers choices to the opening bidder.

**Example 69:**

| a | b | c | d |
|---|---|---|---|
| ♠ K10843 | ♠ K10843 | ♠ K10843 | ♠ KQJ83 |
| ♥ 964 | ♥ A64 | ♥ A64 | ♥ A64 |
| ♦ 52 | ♦ 52 | ♦ 52 | ♦ Q2 |
| ♣ 1062 | ♣ J102 | ♣ K102 | ♣ KJ10 |

**All Example 69 hands are responding to an opening bid of one notrump.**

**Example 69a should transfer to spades and pass.**

**Example 69b should transfer to spades and then invite game by bidding two notrump.**

**Example 69c should transfer to spades and then jump to three notrump to offer a choice of games.**

**Example 69d should transfer to spades and then jump to four notrump to invite a slam.**

If responder makes a **Jacoby Transfer** and then bids a new suit at the three level, the auction is forcing to game and often suggests that responder has interest in a slam. Responder's second suit must be at least four cards long, which means that opener knows where at least nine of responder's cards are—in the two suits. Opener can then return to the major suit shown by the transfer, holding three or four cards in that major. With no interest in slam, opener will jump to game in responder's major suit (**fast arrival**), but a bid of only three in the major shows some slam interest.

When opener holds only two cards in responder's major suit, the next call will affirm or deny interest in a slam in responder's second suit. When opener has no interest in slam that is shown by a call of three notrump. With interest in a slam in responder's second suit, opener continues by making a cue bid of an ace. After opener makes a cue bid, if responder bids three notrump, it indicates that responder was just bidding to show shape and did not have the values to suggest a possible slam.

When responder has transferred and then bid a second suit, showing at least nine cards in the two suits that have been indicated, opener may be aware of yet another problem. Opener knows that responder holds no more than four cards in the other two suits. If opener has no stopper in one of the suits in which responder has shown shortness, it may be clear that to play in responder's major suit with a fit of only seven cards will be better than to play three notrump. Maybe opener has a tenuous stopper in one of responder's short suits, and a game contract in a seven card major suit fit will be better than the expected contract in notrump.

**Example 70:**

|  a  |  b  |  c  |
|-----|-----|-----|
| ♠ 6 | ♠ AJ5 | ♠ AJ53 |
| ♥ AJ1085 | ♥ KQ6 | ♥ KQ6 |
| ♦ K93 | ♦ A1084 | ♦ A1084 |
| ♣ AQ94 | ♣ J83 | ♣ K3 |

|  d  |  e  |  f  |
|-----|-----|-----|
| ♠ AQ52 | ♠ AQJ4 | ♠ 985 |
| ♥ K5 | ♥ Q6 | ♥ KQ |
| ♦ A108 | ♦ A1084 | ♦ AQ104 |
| ♣ KJ83 | ♣ Q83 | ♣ KJ83 |

In response to an opening bid of one notrump, Example 70a transfers to hearts to show a five card suit and then bids three clubs.

The rest of the hands in Example 70 are one notrump openers who face a responder who has first transferred to hearts and then bid three clubs.

Example 70b shows three hearts and minimum values by jumping to four hearts. This use of fast arrival is intended to discourage any thoughts of slam.

Example 70c bids only three hearts. This shows a heart fit and maximum values, encouraging responder to consider a heart slam.

Example 70d cue bids the diamond ace to show a doubleton heart and interest in a club slam.

Example 70e bids three notrump to show a doubleton heart and deny interest in a club slam.

Example 70f has values too soft to suggest a club slam, but fears a contract of three notrump. Responder has at most four cards in spades and diamonds and there may be no spade stopper. Opener opts to show a heart fit with an excellent doubleton, and a heart contract plays very well. While a notrump contract would have been doomed.

When responder makes a **Jacoby Transfer** and then bids the same suit again, that promises that the suit is at least six cards long. A transfer and then a raise of the suit to the three level invites a game and promises a suit of six or more cards. Responder will have about seven points in high cards, which will be adequate for the invitation because of the extra suit length.

If responder transfers to a major suit at the two level and then raises to game, the auction is a mild try for slam. This is because there was also available a **Texas Transfer**. With a six card suit, responder has the option of making a transfer bid at the four level instead of at the two level. Responder may elect to make a **Texas Transfer,** by jumping to the four level to retain control of the auction. After the transfer at the four level responder can pass or can then instigate a search for slam. Opener has no say in what follows.

But, if responder instead makes a **Jacoby Transfer** at the two level and then jumps to game in that suit, control of the auction is given back to the opener. Opener has an opportunity to either pass or to bid on, and should understand that a slam invitation has been extended. The knowledge that responder has available either auction is the key to understanding why one auction invites a slam and the other does not give opener any options.

**Example 71:**

| a | b | c | d |
|---|---|---|---|
| ♠ KJ9642 | ♠ 3 | ♠ 3 | ♠ AQJ964 |
| ♥ 3 | ♥ KQ9642 | ♥ KQ9642 | ♥ 3 |
| ♦ K104 | ♦ AJ4 | ♦ AJ4 | ♦ KQ4 |
| ♣ 1098 | ♣ 1098 | ♣ K98 | ♣ K109 |

**All Example 71 hands are responding to an opening bid of one notrump.**

**Example 71a first transfers to spades, then invites game by raising to three spades.**

**Example 71b makes a** Texas Transfer **by jumping to four diamonds, then passes when opener bids four hearts.**

**Example 71c makes a** Jacoby Transfer **at the two level, then jumps to game in hearts to invite opener to consider a slam in hearts.**

**Example 71d makes a** Texas Transfer **by jumping to four hearts. After opener bids four spades, responder then bids four notrump seeking controls for a spade slam.**

After a **Jacoby Transfer,** opener can make a "super acceptance" for the responder's major suit. Opener makes a "super acceptance" by not bidding as expected when responder makes a transfer bid. When opener wants to make a "super acceptance" and holds four card support for the suit shown by the transfer, a jump response in the transfer suit shows that fact. After responder transfers by bidding two diamonds, opener jumps to three hearts to show maximum values and four card heart support. After responder transfers by bidding two hearts, opener jumps to three spades to show maximum values and four card spade support.

When opener holds a maximum in values and only three card support, the "super acceptance" is not a jump. Instead, it is a bid in one of the two remaining suits allowing for a repeat transfer.

When responder bids two diamonds to transfer to hearts, opener can bid either two spades or three clubs to show a good hand for play in hearts with only three card support and with a concentration of values in the suit bid. Never bid the transfer suit. That suit must be left available so that responder can repeat the transfer having heard the "super acceptance". Responder then will continue to bid descriptively.

Similarly, if responder bids two hearts to transfer to spades, opener with a maximum and four card support will jump to three spades. But, when opener has that same maximum and only three card support for spades, the "super acceptance" call will be either three clubs or three diamonds, bidding in the suit in which there is a concentration of values. Opener will not bid to show values in hearts. That is the transfer suit, which must be left available to responder. Responder will always repeat the transfer, and then will pass or bid on as indicated by the hand held.

**Example 72:**

|  a | b |
|---|---|
| ♠ KJ98 | ♠ A4 |
| ♥ A4 | ♥ AQ6 |
| ♦ AQ6 | ♦ KJ98 |
| ♣ K1073 | ♣ K1073 |

**Both Example 72 hands have opened by bidding one notrump.**

**Example 72a hears responder bid two hearts to transfer to spades. This opener shows a four card fit with maximum values by jumping to three spades.**

**Example 72b hears responder bid two diamonds as a transfer to hearts. This opener, who holds only a three card fit, can show this maximum by bidding either two spades or three clubs. Opener's preference would be to bid the best side suit—diamonds, but that is the transfer suit that must be left for responder to repeat. Three clubs shows the best side holding in the two suits available. Responder will next repeat the transfer by bidding three diamonds.**

When there is interference after the opening bid of one notrump, it nearly always takes away the use of **Jacoby transfers. Stayman** can still be used. A cue bid of the suit bid by the opponent assumes that role, asking the opening notrump bidder to show a four card major suit if possible.

When the interference is two clubs and that call is artificial and conventional, a double of that call becomes **Stayman**, and **Jacoby Transfers** still apply. But, if the interference is a natural bid of two clubs, or any other bid at the two level, in addition to using a cue bid as **Stayman**, suit bids at the two and three levels become natural rather than transfers.

Interference, however, does not usually hamper our ability to use **Texas Transfers**. It will still be possible for responder to make a transfer bid by jumping to the four level. A jump to four diamonds promises at least the values to make a game (about 7 HCP or more) and a six or seven card heart suit. A jump to four hearts promises the same values and a six or seven card spade suit.

When the interference is three clubs or less, there is no ambiguity to opener about the meaning of responder's call. Four diamonds shows long hearts, four hearts shows long spades, and a cue bid asks opener to show a four card major suit. But, what happens when the interference is three diamonds? Is responder's call of four diamonds **Stayman**? Or is it a **Texas Transfer**? It is obvious that we must have a way to solve this potential dilemma.

Logic tells us that when an opponent jumps to the three level after an opposing opening bid of one notrump, they will always have the safety of a good and long suit. It follows that it is virtually impossible for responder to hold a hand that wants to make a classic penalty double. This exercise in logic leads to the agreement that since responder will never have a hand that wishes to double for penalties, a double should be a **negative double** rather than a double for penalties. Since the **negative double** asks partner to bid a four card major suit, its use in this auction replaces the need for **Stayman**.

This agreement solves the problem of what to do when an opponent interferes after an opening bid of one notrump by jumping to some suit at the three level. Only after interference at the three level, double becomes **negative**, and if responder bids either four diamonds or four hearts, that call is still a **Texas Transfer**, even when it happens to be a cue bid.

### Example 73:

| a | b | c |
|---|---|---|
| ♠ KQ74 | ♠ 8 | ♠ AQ10864 |
| ♥ AJ95 | ♥ AQ10864 | ♥ 8 |
| ♦ 63 | ♦ K842 | ♦ J5 |
| ♣ J82 | ♣ J5 | ♣ K842 |

**All Example 73 hands are responding to an opening bid of one notrump.**

**Example 73a plans to use** Stayman. **With no interference it is easy to bid two clubs. If there is a natural overcall of two diamonds, a bid of three diamonds is** Stayman. **If the interference is a jump to three diamonds, a** negative double **replaces** Stayman. **Responder would bid similarly with the same values and only one four card major.**

**Example 73b always plans to use a** Texas Transfer. **Whether there is no interference, or whether there is an overcall at the two or three level in any opposing suit, responder bids four diamonds which is a transfer to hearts.**

**Example 73c similarly will always use a** Texas Transfer **in all auctions. Without interference, or if there is an overcall at either the two or three level, responder will bid four hearts as a transfer to spades.**

Jumps to the three level in a minor suit are best used as game invitational. Escaping to a minor suit can be done by the use of transfers, followed by a pass. Minor suit slam auctions can be accommodated by first using **Stayman** and then bidding the minor suit.

The jump to the three level in a minor suit as an invitational call should typically show a six card suit headed by the ace-queen or the king-queen. A six card suit headed by the ace-king is too good for this invitation.

Opener is expected to bid three notrump when two things are true. Opener must hold a fit for the minor suit (high honor doubleton is fine, or at least three small cards), and must have all other suits stopped. When opener has either a poor fit for the minor suit, or has an unstopped suit, a pass is best and the minor suit contract at the three level will be played.

**Example 74:**

| a | b | c |
|---|---|---|
| ♠ 842 | ♠ AQ9 | ♠ AQ9 |
| ♥ 5 | ♥ KQ62 | ♥ K62 |
| ♦ KQ109753 | ♦ J2 | ♦ A42 |
| ♣ J6 | ♣ A1083 | ♣ A1083 |

**Example 74a is responding to an opening bid of one notrump. A jump to three diamonds shows a good diamond suit and nothing else. Opener knows to bid three notrump with a diamond fit and stoppers in all other suits, otherwise to pass.**

**Example 74b opens one notrump and hears responder jump to three diamonds. Although all outside suits are stopped opener lacks a diamond fit and must pass.**

**Example 74c opens one notrump and hears responder jump to three diamonds. With a good diamond fit and stoppers in all other suits, this opener bids three notrump.**

Major suit jumps to the three level can be played in a variety of ways. One simple method is to agree that all jumps to three of a major suit show five-five distribution in those two suits. The jump to three hearts shows values enough to invite a game (about 7 or 8 HCP), while jumps to three spades show values good enough to play game in either major suit. Opener can pass a jump to three hearts or correct to three spades with minimum values, or can carry on to four in the longer or better major suit with values that are maximum.

**Example 75:**

|      | a        |      | b        |
|------|----------|------|----------|
| ♠    | KJ1094   | ♠    | KJ1094   |
| ♥    | K10753   | ♥    | AQ1053   |
| ♦    | J6       | ♦    | J6       |
| ♣    | 4        | ♣    | 4        |

**Both Example 75 hands are responding to an opening bid of one notrump.**

**With the agreement that has just been discussed, Example 75a jumps to three hearts to show five-five in the major suits with game invitational values.**

**Example 75b jumps to three spades to show five-five in the majors with game forcing values.**

Our preference is to use the jump to three of a major suit to show a broken suit of six or seven cards, often with interest in a slam. Just because transfer bids are available there is no reason to believe that all hands with a five card or longer major suit should transfer. Particularly when responder is distributional with a 6-3-3-1 or 6-4-2-1 pattern, if that hand becomes dummy the defense has a better idea of where to look for its tricks. When responder's hand pattern is concealed, the defense remains blind for several tricks in the play.

Using this method, when responder jumps to the three level in a major suit, opener's priority is to affirm or deny possession of a high honor in that suit. Since responder's suit is known to be broken when opener does not hold a fitting honor card, it will be very dangerous to pursue a slam without a good trump fit.

Upon hearing the jump to three of a major suit, opener continues in one of three ways:

1. Without a high honor, opener bids three notrump. Responder will then correct and play game in what must be at least a 6-2 fit, but will be warned against going higher since it is known that the trump suit is ragged.
2. With a high honor in responder's known long and broken suit, a minimum opener simply raises the major suit to game.
3. Holding a high honor in responder's known long and broken suit and maximum values and controls, opener indicates all of these things by making a cue bid in a side suit to show an ace. Responder can then either sign off at game in the major or can join in the slam search by making a return cue bid or by using **Blackwood**.

**Example 76:**

| a | b | c | d |
|---|---|---|---|
| ♠ 6 | ♠ AQ | ♠ AJ4 | ♠ 843 |
| ♥ AJ9753 | ♥ 842 | ♥ K83 | ♥ KQ2 |
| ♦ A4 | ♦ KQ83 | ♦ KQ83 | ♦ KQJ3 |
| ♣ KJ104 | ♣ A962 | ♣ Q96 | ♣ AQ2 |

**Example 76a responds to an opening bid of one notrump by jumping to three hearts.**

**Example 76b has opened one notrump and hears a response of three hearts. With no heart honor, this opener rebids three notrump and passes when responder corrects to four hearts.**

**Example 76c has opened one notrump and hears a response of three hearts. With a minimum and a heart honor this opener bids four hearts.**

**Example 76d has opened one notrump and hears a response of three hearts. With good hearts and a maximum the next call is a cue bid of four clubs.**

# The Gerber convention

A response of four clubs after an opening bid of one notrump (or two notrump) is the **Gerber** convention. **Gerber** is always a jump from notrump to clubs. It asks the opening bidder to show the number of aces held.

Playing standard **Gerber,** opener bids in steps as follows: Four diamonds shows either no aces or all four aces (responder should be able to tell which), four hearts shows one ace, four spades shows two aces and four notrump shows three aces.

If responder continues by bidding five clubs, this similarly asks opener to tell how many kings are held. Opener's responses make use of the same schedule.

### Example 77:

| a | b | c | d |
|---|---|---|---|
| ♠ K4 | ♠ AQJ3 | ♠ AJ52 | ♠ A72 |
| ♥ KQ7 | ♥ J9 | ♥ J64 | ♥ A103 |
| ♦ A65 | ♦ KQJ2 | ♦ KQ84 | ♦ KQ104 |
| ♣ KQ1095 | ♣ J84 | ♣ A6 | ♣ A62 |

**Example 77a responds to an opening bid of one notrump by using the** Gerber **convention and jumps to four clubs.**

**Example 77b opens one notrump and hears responder use the** Gerber **convention by jumping to four clubs. This opener bids four hearts to show one ace. Responder 77a knows two aces are missing and signs off at four notrump.**

**Example 77c opens one notrump and hears responder use the** Gerber **convention by jumping to four clubs. This opener bids four spades to show two aces. Responder 77a knows that only one ace is missing and bids six notrump.**

**Example 77d opens one notrump and hears responder use the** Gerber **convention by jumping to four clubs. This opener bids four notrump to show three aces. When three aces are found, responder 77a may take a rosy view and bid five clubs to ask for kings. A shot at a grand slam would find the near perfect dummy because of the bonus diamond queen.**

To summarize the simple methods which are included in the new standards in response to an opening bid of one notrump:

1. Two clubs is **Stayman**, asking opener to bid a four card major suit.

A. Opener bids two diamonds to deny a four card major.

B. With both majors opener bids two hearts.

C. If responder's raise to two notrump is artificial, **Stayman** may be used to raise to two notrump. The use of two clubs as **Stayman** will not promise a four card major suit when responder's rebid is two notrump (alert).

D. If responder uses **Stayman**, then rebids three notrump, the auction promises a four card major.

E. If responder uses **Stayman**, then rebids in a minor suit, the auction shows interest in a slam in the minor. Responder does not promise a four card major.

   1. Opener denies interest in such a slam by bidding three notrump.
   2. Opener shows interest in such a slam by making a cue bid.

F. If responder uses **Stayman**, hears opener bid two hearts, and continues by bidding two spades, the auction shows four spades and game invitational values.

G. After **Stayman**, if responder bids four notrump, it shows slam invitational values in high cards and says that a major suit fit has not been found. If opener has shown four hearts and also holds four spades it is clear that there is a four-four fit in spades.

H. If responder uses **Stayman** and then jumps to four clubs that announces that a fit has been found and the bid of four clubs is **Gerber**.

2. Two diamonds is a **Jacoby Transfer** bid promising five or more hearts.

   A. Opener will usually bid two hearts as requested.

   B. Opener shows a "super acceptance" with four hearts by jumping to three hearts.

   C. Opener shows a "super acceptance" with three hearts by bidding either two spades or three clubs, showing the best side holding.

   D. When opener bids to show a "super acceptance" with three card support, responder always continues by bidding three diamonds, repeating the transfer.

3. Two hearts is a **Jacoby Transfer** bid promising five or more spades.

   A. Opener will usually bid two spades as requested.

   B. Opener shows a "super acceptance" with four spades by jumping to three spades.

C. Opener shows a "super acceptance" with three spades by bidding either three clubs or three diamonds, showing the best holding.

D. When opener bids to show a "super acceptance" with three card support, responder always continues by bidding three hearts, repeating the transfer.

4. Two spades is a transfer to minor suits.

    A. Some partnerships use two spades holding either minor

       1. When opener bids three clubs, responder will pass to show clubs.

       2. When opener bids three clubs, responder corrects to diamonds to show that suit.

    B. Some partnerships use two spades as a transfer to clubs.

       1. Opener bids three clubs with a poor hand and poor clubs.

       2. Opener bids two notrump to show a maximum with good clubs.

    C. When two spades is a club transfer, two notrump is used as a transfer to diamonds.

       1. Opener bids three diamonds to show a mediocre hand and poor diamonds.

       2. Opener bids three clubs to show a maximum with good diamonds.

    D. When two notrump is used as a transfer to diamonds, responder cannot invite a game in notrump by making that call. The use of **Stayman,** followed by a bid of two notrump, invites a notrump game (Remember that when two notrump after **Stayman** does not promise a major suit an alert is due at that time).

5. Two notrump may be a natural invitation in notrump, or can be used as a transfer to diamonds.

6. Three clubs and three diamonds are natural and invitational, typically showing six or seven card suits headed by the ace-queen or the king-queen, with no other values.

7. Three hearts and three spades are natural calls showing a broken six or seven card suit, often with values enough to invite a slam. Opener then denies a high honor in responder's suit by bidding three notrump and responder corrects to game in the major suit. Or opener affirms a high honor card in responder's suit by bidding four in that suit with no interest in a slam, or makes a cue bid to show slam interest.

8. Three notrump is natural. Responder has the values to play game in notrump.

9. Four clubs is **Gerber**. Responder is asking about the number of aces opener holds.

10. Four diamonds is a **Texas Transfer,** promising values enough to play a game and six or more cards in hearts. Responder retains control of the auction.

11. Four hearts is a **Texas Transfer,** promising values enough to play a game and six or more spades. Again, responder retains control of the auction.

12. Four spades in most partnerships has no assigned meaning.

13. Four notrump is a natural invitation to a slam in notrump. Responder will hold about 15 to 17 HCP.

14. Five of any suit has no established assigned meaning.

15. Five notrump is forcing, requiring that at least six notrump be reached, and invites opener to bid a grand slam in notrump. Responder will have 20 or 21 HCP.

16. Six of any suit is natural and to play. Responder is making an informed guess.

17. Six notrump is to play. Responder holds 18 or 19 HCP. Opener is asked to pass.

18. Seven of any denomination is to play. Seven notrump will show a balanced hand with 22 or more HCP or some hand with an extensive trick source and all aces.

This summary includes auctions that can be used by responder when the opening bid has been one notrump. It includes **Stayman** and **Jacoby** and **Texas Transfer** auctions in simple form, the **Gerber** convention and other natural and conventional auctions. Further refinements are available which will give the bidder even better tools. These refinements will be detailed in Advanced **Bridge Bidding for the Twenty First Century**.

## Opener bids two notrump

When opener starts by bidding two notrump, responder's tools are similar. Three clubs is **Stayman**, three diamonds and three hearts are **Jacoby Transfers**, three spades transfers to four clubs to escape in either minor suit, and four clubs is **Gerber.**

# Opener's notrump bid exercises

As opener, you must plan how to bid with each of these hands. Make your opening bid and/or rebid plan for each hand.

1.
♠ KJ5
♥ Q82
♦ J95
♣ AQ74

2.
♠ KJ5
♥ Q10854
♦ K6
♣ AQ3

3.
♠ AJ6
♥ K4
♦ AQJ84
♣ Q108

4.
♠ K3
♥ A74
♦ KJ10853
♣ K4

5.
♠ K5
♥ AQ
♦ KJ94
♣ AQ1073

6.
♠ A84
♥ A76
♦ A1082
♣ A63

You are responding to an opening bid of one notrump. What is your plan?

7.
♠ 8542
♥ J973
♦ Q8654
♣ —

8.
♠ KJ84
♥ 109763
♦ 85
♣ 42

9.
♠ KQ954
♥ 1073
♦ K8
♣ 962

10.
♠ KQ8
♥ A4
♦ AQ83
♣ J1076

11.
♠ Q85
♥ KJ103
♦ Q106
♣ 1094

12.
♠ 6
♥ Q8543
♦ J642
♣ Q74

13.
♠ KQ84
♥ 62
♦ K1092
♣ 864

14.
♠ AQ4
♥ K53
♦ AQ10762
♣ 4

15.
♠ 5
♥ Q95
♦ J104
♣ KJ10863

16.
♠ A6
♥ AJ975
♦ Q85
♣ 963

17.
♠ AQJ74
♥ 106
♦ KQ842
♣ 7

18.
♠ K8
♥ AJ9754
♦ 84
♣ A62

19.
♠ AQ10853
♥ 7
♦ 964
♣ Q104

20.
♠ K8
♥ K87
♦ AKQ972
♣ K6

141

With the next four hands you have responded one heart to an opening bid of one diamond. Opener rebids one notrump. What call do you make?

| 21. | 22. | 23. | 24. |
|---|---|---|---|
| ♠ 8 | ♠ 7 | ♠ KJ4 | ♠ A43 |
| ♥ K753 | ♥ AJ954 | ♥ AQ93 | ♥ AK63 |
| ♦ 96 | ♦ K62 | ♦ 104 | ♦ KJ1073 |
| ♣ QJ8642 | ♣ K952 | ♣ J973 | ♣ 2 |

With the next four hands, you have opened one diamond and rebid one notrump after a response of one heart. Responder has next bid two clubs, **New minor forcing**. What do you bid next?

| 25. | 26. | 27. | 28. |
|---|---|---|---|
| ♠ 1082 | ♠ Q83 | ♠ AQ5 | ♠ A42 |
| ♥ Q4 | ♥ 62 | ♥ 106 | ♥ KJ9 |
| ♦ KQ95 | ♦ AKJ84 | ♦ KQ954 | ♦ AQ93 |
| ♣ AQ75 | ♣ K84 | ♣ QJ3 | ♣ 1087 |

With the next four hands, you have opened one diamond and rebid one notrump after a response of one spade. Responder next bids two clubs, **New minor forcing**. What is your next call?

| 29. | 30. | 31. | 32. |
|---|---|---|---|
| ♠ AJ4 | ♠ AJ4 | ♠ A4 | ♠ A4 |
| ♥ K93 | ♥ K973 | ♥ K93 | ♥ K93 |
| ♦ A1074 | ♦ A1074 | ♦ AJ763 | ♦ AJ76 |
| ♣ J63 | ♣ J6 | ♣ 854 | ♣ Q862 |

With the next eight hands, you have responded one spade to an opening bid of one diamond. Your partner has made a jump rebid of two notrump. What is your next call?

| 33. | 34. | 35. | 36. |
|---|---|---|---|
| ♠ AQJ863 | ♠ KQ83 | ♠ AQ962 | ♠ AQ962 |
| ♥ 6 | ♥ 95 | ♥ K10874 | ♥ KJ63 |
| ♦ A85 | ♦ 842 | ♦ 85 | ♦ 86 |
| ♣ 963 | ♣ K1094 | ♣ 2 | ♣ 52 |

|  | 37. | 38. | 39. | 40. |
|---|---|---|---|---|
| ♠ | A963 | KQ864 | Q109743 | AQJ6 |
| ♥ | 4 | 5 | 62 | K83 |
| ♦ | KJ853 | 962 | A54 | Q6 |
| ♣ | A62 | A843 | 76 | Q982 |

## Answers

1. Open one club and plan to rebid one notrump. This will describe your size and shape. If partner responds in a major suit and an opponent interferes, you may need to show your fit for partner's major suit rather than rebid one notrump.

2. Open one notrump. Even though you hold a five card major suit, this hand passes all three tests for opening one notrump despite your five card major. You do have three cards in the other major suit; there is no empty doubleton; and your hand is more texturish than toppish.

3. Do not open one notrump. Your hand is too big for that call. In addition to your seventeen high card points, you also have a five card suit for which you should add one point. Count your hand as eighteen and plan to make a jump rebid of two notrump after a response at the one level.

4. Open one notrump. Although you have only fourteen high card points, your six card suit deserves two additional points and you want to be sure to protect your tenaces in your doubletons no matter what the contract.

5. Open two notrump. Again you must add a point for your long suit which gets you up to twenty. Your major suit tenaces should cause you to declare any contract, which might not happen if you open in clubs and **reverse**.

6. Open one notrump. This time you hate what you must do. You will have described a balanced hand in the range of fifteen to seventeen HCP but there is no reason for you to declare and have the lead come up to this hand. Any other opening bid will not allow you to make an accurate description.

7. Bid two clubs, the **Stayman** convention. You intend to pass any response from partner. Your otherwise useless hand will have value if one of your suits becomes the trump suit. It will be wonderful if partner bids a major suit, but if otherwise your five card diamond holding will certainly grow.

8. Again, you should use **Stayman** by bidding two clubs. If partner bids either major suit you will be happy to pass. If partner bids two diamonds to deny a four card major

suit you will sign off by bidding in your five card major suit. This auction is known as **Garbage** Stayman or **Drop Dead** Stayman.

9. Two hearts, a **Jacoby transfer** to two spades. You intend next to bid two notrump. This will show that your values are game invitational and that you have five spades.

10. Jump to four notrump. This is a quantitative invitation to a slam in notrump. If partner has a minimum that will become the contract. With more your invitation will be accepted. Holding three aces the acceptance will be a jump to slam, but with fewer aces your call of four notrump will be treated as **Blackwood**. If partner shows no aces you will sign off at five notrump, but if one ace is shown bid the notrump slam.

11. If two notrump is a natural invitation to a notrump game, bid it. Do not try to find a fit in hearts because of your flat distribution. If you must bid two clubs to invite in notrump since a notrump raise would be a transfer to diamonds, do not attempt to play hearts even if partner shows four of them. Your balanced pattern should play in notrump even if a four-four fit in hearts happens to exist.

12. Two diamonds. This is a **Jacoby transfer**, which promises that you hold five hearts. You intend to pass at your next turn. With hearts as the trump suit your hand will have more value than in notrump.

13. Two clubs, the **Stayman** convention. If partner bids two spades to show four of them, raise to three to show your invitational values with a four card fit. If partner bids two diamonds to deny a four card major suit, continue to two notrump to invite a game. If partner bids two hearts to show a four card heart suit, you should continue by bidding two spades. This shows exactly a four card spade holding (if you held five spades you would have made a transfer bid) and game invitational values. Partner will know what to do next.

14. Two clubs, the **Stayman** convention. Partner will believe that you are seeking a major suit fit. However, when you rebid three diamonds, you will show that you are interested in a slam in diamonds. Partner's next call may be three notrump to deny slam interest, or will be a cue bid to show interest in the diamond slam you have suggested.

15. Two spades—a transfer to clubs. If partner bids three clubs, as requested, you will pass. However, if partner bids two notrump to show a good hand for clubs, bid three notrump. The fit in clubs will be a source of tricks for the notrump game.

16. Two diamonds, a **Jacoby transfer** to show your five card heart suit. Your next call will be three notrump to indicate that your values are adequate for a game. Partner will pass with only two cards in hearts, but with three or more hearts will correct to four hearts.

17. Two hearts, a **Jacoby transfer**. Then bid three diamonds to show that in addition to five spades you also hold at least four diamonds. Partner will know how to continue. Partner will either affirm or deny a fit for spades while showing minimum or maximum values. Without a spade fit, the next call will affirm or deny interest in a diamond slam.

18. Two diamonds, a **Jacoby transfer** showing at least five hearts. You will next jump to four hearts. Since you have released control of the auction to partner, even though you did not have to do so, this will be recognized as an invitation to a slam in hearts.

19. Four hearts, a **Texas Transfer**. When partner bids four spades, you will pass. You have retained control over the level at which spades will be played.

20. Four clubs. This is the **Gerber** convention. If partner has three aces, you want to play seven notrump. With only two aces, you will play six notrump. There cannot be fewer than two aces in the opening bid. Your side has at least 33 HCP.

21. Three clubs. This "funny jump" shows that you have only four hearts with minimum response values, but that you also have six clubs and know that a contract of three clubs is the best place to play. You cannot bid only two clubs since that call would not show a club suit. It would be **New minor forcing**.

22. Two clubs - **New minor forcing**. You are trying to to reach game and are looking for a three card fit four your five card heart suit.

23. Raise to two notrump. Partner will know that you have game invitational values and that you do not also hold a five card heart suit. If you held five hearts, you would have used **New minor forcing** instead of raising notrump.

24. Two clubs—**New minor forcing**. You want to invite a slam in diamonds, so you must make the auction forcing in this fashion and then show your diamond fit. An immediate jump to three diamonds would only be invitational to game.

25. Two spades. This shows that you have only two hearts and also that you do not have a stopper in spades for play in notrump. It also denies five diamonds.

26. Two diamonds. This denies that you hold three hearts and shows that you do hold five diamonds. It also expresses that your call to show diamond length was superior to a call in notrump, even though you might hold a stopper in spades.

27. Three notrump. You might have opened one notrump with fourteen high card points and a five card diamond suit, but you did not like your bad holding in hearts. This jump shows maximum values and a spade stopper, but denies three hearts.

28. Three hearts. This shows maximum values for your rebid of one notrump and that you hold three card support for hearts.

29. Two spades. This shows minimum values with a three card spade fit. This is a bad thirteen because of its distribution. A good thirteen would have jumped in spades.

30. Two hearts. Yes, you do have three card support for spades, but your first obligation is to try for a four-four fit in hearts. If partner is not interested in hearts you will be happy to play in spades.

31. Two diamonds. This denies four hearts and three spades and shows five diamonds.

32. Three notrump. This denies either four hearts or three spades and shows that your values are maximum for the auction.

33. Three spades. This shows a six card suit and invites a slam in spades. Opener will not pass. This auction is forcing.

34. Raise to three notrump. This is your value call and no other contract appeals.

35. Three hearts. This promises that you have five-five in the major suits and the auction is forcing. Partner will raise hearts holding two spades and three hearts.

36. Three clubs. This is **New minor forcing**. There may be a four-four fit in hearts. If partner shows four hearts, that will be the trump suit. If partner denies four hearts and shows three spades, you will play with spades as trumps. If partner denies either four hearts or three spades, your game will be in notrump.

37. Three diamonds. Showing a fit for partner's first suit in this auction is a slam try. If partner likes the idea, you will hear a cue bid. If not, three notrump will convey a denial of your invitation.

38. Three clubs. You are trying to find a three card fit for your five card spade suit. If partner bids three hearts to show four cards there, you will simply bid three notrump, which will indicate that your checkback was because you have five spades.

39. Four spades. This jump denies extra strength and says that four spades should be the final contract.

40. Four notrump. This shows extra high card values and invites a small slam in notrump.

# CHAPTER EIGHT

## RAISING PARTNER'S SUIT

It is important to stress again the priorities of any auction. The first goal is to find a major suit fit of eight or more cards to make the trump suit. When there is no such fit, the next search is to determine if notrump is playable. Only when both of these searches fail do we settle upon playing a minor suit contract. Game contracts in major suits require ten tricks as opposed to a notrump game, which requires only nine tricks. A trump suit usually produces at least one extra trick— often more—which makes the major suit game more attractive. Minor suit games require eleven tricks—just one trick from slam. These games are rarely the most productive contract and are not to be sought unless all else fails.

When the opening bid is in a minor suit, responder first looks to bid a major suit. When there is no major, a bid in notrump is the second choice. Only when both of these options fail, does responder consider bidding the other minor or raising opener's minor.

When the opening bid is in a major suit and responder has a fit, it will be shown as soon as possible. Sometimes this can be done at responder's first turn to call. At other times, a forcing response will allow showing the nature of the raise for the major suit at responder's rebid. At either turn, expression of the major suit fit will be responder's first priority. Without other choices, responder may raise opener's minor suit.

## Raising opener's minor suit

Because an opening bid in a minor suit is often made with only three cards in the suit, when responder does not have a four card or longer major suit to bid, and does not have a balanced hand, a raise of opener's minor suit should have five card or longer support. Sometimes the raise will be made with four card support when no other action appeals.

Responder's raise of opener's minor suit must not only show an appropriate hand in fit and distribution, it must also show responder's values.

# 1. Raising with minimum response values (5+ to 9- HCP)

With minimum response values (5+ to 9- HCP) responder makes a single raise.

**Example 78:**

| a | b |
|---|---|
| ♠ 853 | ♠ 853 |
| ♥ 6 | ♥ 6 |
| ♦ Q764 | ♦ KQ96 |
| ♣ KJ965 | ♣ Q7643 |

**With Example 78a, you are responding to an opening bid of one club. Your raise to two clubs shows no major suit, an unbalanced hand, and reasonable support for clubs with minimum response values. If the opening bid is one diamond, life is not so simple. A response in clubs requires much greater values and a response of one notrump does not describe this unbalanced hand. The raise to two diamonds is not pretty, but it is the "least worst bad bid".**

**With Example 78b, you are responding to an opening bid of one club. Your raise to two clubs shows no major suit, an unbalanced hand, and reasonable support for clubs with minimum response values. If the opening bid is one diamond, a raise to two diamonds is not so unappealing, as in the previous example, because of the quality of your diamond support. In both of these examples, it is better to raise than bid diamonds when the opening bid is in clubs. There may be a decent diamond fit, but the fit for clubs is known.**

# 2. Limit raises

When responder has game invitational values (9+ to 12- HCP), a jump raise will be used. This is a change from older standards in which the jump raise was forcing, showing opening bid values. This jump raise is called a "limit" raise. It invites opener to consider a game contract, but is not forcing.

**Example 79:**

| a | b |
|---|---|
| ♠ 853 | ♠ 853 |
| ♥ 6 | ♥ 6 |
| ♦ K764 | ♦ AQJ6 |
| ♣ AQJ65 | ♣ K9875 |

With Example 79a, responder faces an opening bid of one club. A jump raise to three clubs is a perfect description. If the opening bid is one diamond, things are not so simple. A jump raise to three diamonds will not fare well unless opener holds at least four diamonds. This is likely. With three cards in both minors opener would have bid one club rather than one diamond. This jump raise is far from ideal, but is the best available description. You should always "bid where you live", which makes a raise of clubs better than a response in diamonds on both of these hands when the opening bid has been in clubs.

With Example 79b, responder is happy to make a "limit" jump raise of either minor suit.

## 3. Forcing raises

When responder holds game forcing values (12+ HCP) and no major suit to bid, there is no immediate forcing raise available. Responder can no longer make a jump raise in a minor suit to force, so often may need to temporize by bidding in the other minor suit. This appears to be awkward, but does not need to be.

If the opening bid is one diamond, responder can bid two clubs forcing the auction to game. When responder later shows and emphasizes support for diamonds, the picture will become clear. It is not so easy if the opening bid is one club. Responder will temporize in diamonds, but may later need to use **fourth suit forcing** and create a force to game before a club fit can be shown.

This complication brought about by the new standards in bidding must be faced when only simple tools are used. The second volume of this set explains **inverted minor raises**. When they are the agreement of the partnership, the awkwardness goes away. This is one of the first upgrades to be sought by those who wish to use the best of modern bidding methods. (See **Advanced Bridge Bidding for the Twenty First Century**).

### Example 80:

|  | a |  | b |
|---|---|---|---|
|  | ♠ K53 |  | ♠ K53 |
|  | ♥ 64 |  | ♥ 64 |
|  | ♦ AQ6 |  | ♦ KJ842 |
|  | ♣ KJ842 |  | ♣ AQ6 |

With Example 80a, if opener bids one diamond, this hand can make a natural game forcing response of two clubs. If the opening bid is one club, responder would like to make a forcing raise in clubs but cannot. The response must be a temporizing call of one diamond. If opener next bids one heart, this responder can place the contract by bidding three notrump. If opener rebids one notrump, a raise to three notrump is not perfect, but will probably work. If opener rebids one spade, this responder must use fourth suit forcing by bidding two hearts, then show a forcing club raise at the next turn.

With Example 80b, responder to an opening bid of one diamond bids two clubs. After this game forcing response, responder will be able to show support for diamonds at the next call and the auction will be forcing.

## 4. Splinters

Responder may have a game forcing raise with a singleton or void in a higher ranking suit. When this is the case, responder may make a **splinter** raise of the opening bid. When responder jumps to the three level in a higher ranking suit, it shows game forcing values (12+ HCP), support for the opener's minor suit (at least five cards), and shortness in the suit of the jump. This **splinter** response will allow opener to evaluate all cards immediately.

This **splinter** bid in response to the opening bid in a minor suit will show at least the values to produce a game (12+ HCP) and five card support for the opening minor suit. Responder may also use this call with six card support for the minor suit and values of a game invitation (9+ to 12-). When responder's values in high cards are only invitational the extra card in the minor suit will produce an extra trick, and will compensate adequately.

When opener holds considerable values in the suit of the **splinter,** the expressive rebid is three notrump. The values in responder's short suit will be stoppers, and the hands will not mesh well for tricks at high levels. But, when opener has no values in the suit of responder's shortness, a contract in the agreed minor suit at the five or six level will be attractive. All of the values in the two hands will be in the same suits and those fits will produce tricks.

### Example 81:

| a | b | c | d |
|---|---|---|---|
| ♠ AQ5 | ♠ AQ5 | ♠ J2 | ♠ K832 |
| ♥ 3 | ♥ 3 | ♥ AQ102 | ♥ 852 |
| ♦ KQ864 | ♦ KQ10864 | ♦ A953 | ♦ AJ953 |
| ♣ Q1093 | ♣ 1095 | ♣ K85 | ♣ A |

151

**Example 81a is responding to an opening bid of one diamond. With opening bid values, five card support, and a singleton heart, responder makes a** splinter **bid by jumping to three hearts. Although this will appear to many to be a preemptive bid, the use of this call as a** splinter **makes it far more valuable.**

**Example 81b is responding to an opening bid of one diamond. With only limit raise values, this responder should not** splinter **without a sixth card in the diamond suit. Since that sixth card is there, the** splinter **jump to three hearts is appropriate.**

**Example 81c has opened one diamond and heard a** splinter **response of three hearts. With multiple heart stoppers, this opener rebids three notrump.**

**Example 81d has opened one diamond and heard a** splinter **response of three hearts. With no wasted heart values, opener continues to describe by bidding three spades. Facing either 81a or 81b, this hand will produce a slam in diamonds because of the perfect fits.**

## Raising opener's major suit

When responder can make a descriptive raise in opener's major suit it is the first priority. Several different auctions are available to describe various types of raises.

## 1. Responder jump raises to game

The jump raise to game by responder shows five card support and not much in high card values. Ideally, responder will have some distributional feature, but even with the balanced shape of 5-3-3-2 responder may use this raise. The high cards should be in the range of about 2 to 8 HCP.

Many bidders make this their reference and are unhappy when, after the jump raise to game, the bidding side is able to take twelve tricks. Although responder has little in values, there is just enough to produce more tricks than opener can anticipate. To forestall this eventuality, responder's holdings should not include any controls that would facilitate the taking of twelve tricks. Responder should not hold any control cards—no ace or king—among the hands's meager assets. When responder holds an ace or king outside the trump suit, to distinguish between hand types, responder should first bid a **forcing notrump** then jump to game in the major suit as a rebid.

**Example 82:**

|  | a | b |
|---|---|---|
| ♠ | J9642 | J9642 |
| ♥ | 63 | 63 |
| ♦ | Q954 | K95 |
| ♣ | 103 | 1073 |

With either hand in Example 82, responder might consider raising an opening bid of one spade to four. With Example 82a, this should create no problem. With Example 82b, the presence of a control card—the diamond king—might be all that opener needs to produce twelve tricks. Instead of jumping to four spades, this responder should first use the forcing notrump and then jump to four spades as a rebid. This auction should express to opener that responder always intended to jump to four of the major suit, but did not do so at the first turn because this hand included some high card control for a slam. This might be all that opener needs to know in order to bid on and reach a makeable slam.

## 2. Responder has a fit and poor values (less than 5+ HCP)

With values that would not normally respond (0 to 5- HCP) responder should pass. However, if an opponent interferes, responder should stretch to show that support. With some values and a fit for opener's major suit, the intrusion by an opponent should cause responder to bid with a hand that otherwise would have passed.

If responder does pass and has a chance to bid on the next round, responder can show a fit for opener's major and values not quite enough to respond by belatedly raising opener's major suit.

## 3. Responder has minimum response values (5+ to 9- HCP)

Responder shows three or four card support for the opening bidder's major suit and the values of a minimum response by raising the major suit to the two level. Having raised, responder should bid further in only two circumstances:

a. If opponents enter the auction, responder should bid the agreed suit again with four cards in support of opener's major suit. With only three card support, responder should not bid again.

b. If opener makes a try for game by bidding on when the auction is uncontested, responder needs to determine whether or not the hand warrants a continuation to game (game try auctions are included in this chapter).

**Example 83:**

|  a  |  b  |  c  |
| --- | --- | --- |
| ♠ Q84 | ♠ Q84 | ♠ Q984 |
| ♥ 63 | ♥ 63 | ♥ 63 |
| ♦ 10842 | ♦ KJ82 | ♦ KJ82 |
| ♣ Q763 | ♣ 10763 | ♣ 1073 |

**With Example 83a, when opener has bid one spade, responder should plan to pass. However, if an opponent overcalls, this responder should stretch and raise to two spades. Having passed, if given another chance to bid, responder should raise spades to show a fit and some values.**

**With Example 83b, responder raises an opening bid of one spade. Having done this, responder should not bid further voluntarily.**

**With Example 83c, responder should raise an opening bid of one spade. If the auction becomes competitive, responder's fourth spade should cause a raise of spades again.**

## 4. Limit raises

With the values of a game invitation (9+ to 12- HCP), the degree of fit and the shape of the hand determine how responder will show a "limit raise". Raises in this range come in three different types. We call them the "bad" limit raise, the "good" limit raise, and the "game forcing" limit raise.

The "bad" limit raise is so described because other than its values it has no features that distinguish it. Responder's holding in opener's major suit will be exactly three cards, and there will not be a ruffing value—a singleton or void in some other suit. This raise with just three card support and a balanced hand has the fewest redeeming features that a limit raise can have.

When responder has this bad limit raise, the **forcing notrump** is used. The plan is to show the nature of this hand by making a jump rebid at the three level in opener's major suit. This set of responses was detailed in Chapter Five as we learned the **forcing notrump**.

The good limit raise grows in power because of one of two things. It either has a ruffing value (a singleton or void in some side suit) with three trumps, or it has four trumps. When responder has this good limit raise in either form, the response is a jump to the three level in the agreed major suit. Knowledge of something extra will allow opener to consider bidding a game more readily than if the raise showed only three trumps without a ruffing value as expressed by the auction which begins with a **forcing notrump**.

**Example 84:**

|  | a | b | c |
|---|---|---|---|
| ♠ | J104 | J1042 | J104 |
| ♥ | K83 | K83 | K863 |
| ♦ | AJ86 | 6 | AJ86 |
| ♣ | Q97 | AQ974 | Q7 |

**Example 84a is responding to an opening bid in either major suit. Holding a balanced limit raise, responder uses the** forcing notrump. **As a rebid, responder will jump to three of the major suit to show a limit raise with only three card support and no ruffing value.**

**Example 84b is responding to an opening bid of one heart. A jump to three hearts shows a limit raise with three card support and a ruffing value. If the opening bid had been one spade, responder's call would have instead been a** splinter.

**Example 84c is responding to an opening bid of one heart. Jump to three hearts to show a good limit raise. This time there is four card support without a ruffing value. If the opening bid had been one spade, responder would have used the** forcing notrump, **planning to show a bad limit raise by jumping to three spades as a rebid.**

## 5. Splinters

When responder holds limit raise high card strength (9+ to 12 - HCP) with four card support and a ruffing value, the auction should not stop short of game. Responder also knows that if the shortness shown fits well with opener's hand, a slam might be bid because of fits without great values. Responder shows a game forcing limit raise by making a **splinter** bid. This is a double jump in the suit of the shortness, which shows responder's values, and the location of the shortness.

**Example 85:**

|      a      |      b      |      c      |
|:-----------:|:-----------:|:-----------:|
| ♠ Q1075 | ♠ 7 | ♠ Q1075 |
| ♥ A642 | ♥ A642 | ♥ 7 |
| ♦ 7 | ♦ Q1075 | ♦ A642 |
| ♣ KJ106 | ♣ KJ106 | ♣ KJ106 |

**In response to an opening bid in either major suit, Example 85a** splinters **by jumping to four diamonds. This shows a game forcing limit raise that includes four card support for opener's major suit, and shortness in diamonds.**

**With Example 85b, when the opening bid has been one heart, responder jumps to three spades, a** splinter. **This shows four card support for hearts with a game forcing limit raise and four card trump support.**

**With Example 85c, when the opening bid has been one spade, responder** splinters **by jumping to four hearts. This shows a game forcing limit raise with four card support for spades and heart shortness.**

## 6. The Jacoby Two Notrump

With four card support for the major suit bid by the opener and the values of an opening hand, responder uses a convention known as the **Jacoby Two Notrump**. The jump response of two notrump promises values of 12+ HCP or more and four card support for the suit of the opening bid. It asks opener for a further description as it shows opening bid values and a four card fit.

Opener's rebids are:

1. A jump to four of the major with a minimum hand and no shortness.
2. Opener rebids a singleton or void at the three level.
3. Opener bids three notrump without shortness to show a sound opening bid (14+ HCP) and a five card suit.
4. Opener rebids the original major suit at the three level without shortness to show a sound opening bid (14+ HCP) and a six or seven card suit.
5. Opener jump rebids at the four level to show a second five card suit headed by two of the top three honors.

**Example 86:**

|  | a | b | c |
|---|---|---|---|
| ♠ | AQ94 | KJ1075 | KJ1075 |
| ♥ | A6 | K83 | K83 |
| ♦ | K642 | AQ83 | AJ8 |
| ♣ | J106 | 4 | 42 |

|  | d | e | f |
|---|---|---|---|
| ♠ | KJ1075 | KJ10753 | KJ1075 |
| ♥ | KQ3 | KQ3 | K8 |
| ♦ | AJ8 | A8 | AQ953 |
| ♣ | 42 | Q4 | 4 |

**Example 86a responds to an opening bid of one spade. With opening bid values and four card support for spades, responder uses the** Jacoby Two Notrump. **This jump response of two notrump describes a good hand for the auction and asks opener to rebid to show the nature of the opening bid.**

**The balance of Example 86 shows opening bidders who must rebid after a** Jacoby Two Notrump **response.**

**Opener 86b bids three clubs to show shortness in that suit.**

**Opener 86c jumps to four spades. This shows a minimum opening bid without shortness in any side suit.**

**Opener 86d bids three notrump to show no shortness, only a five card suit, and better than minimum opening bid values.**

**Opener 86e bids three spades to show no shortness, a six or seven card suit, and better than minimum opening bid values.**

**Opener 86f jumps to four diamonds. This shows a second suit of at least five cards and that the quality of that suit is excellent. Opener must have two of the top three honors to make this call. If the five card diamond suit did not meet that standard, opener would have shown shortness at the three level.**

## 7. Raises by a passed responder

When responder is a passed hand, a forcing raise is not possible. Responder still may have a hand for a simple or a limit raise. Simple raises do not change. When responder has 5+ to 9- HCP and three or four card support for opener's major suit, the previous pass changes nothing. Responder raises the major suit to the two level.

When responder as a passed hand has a limit raise (9+ to 12- HCP) and three or four card support for opener's major suit, a new viewpoint must be added. Responder takes into account the fact that opener may not have a real opening bid, and that the major suit opening bid might have been with a suit of only four cards. It behooves responder not to make a limit raise that will get the partnership too high when opener is light.

A passed hand responder should not jump to the three level to show a limit raise. It is also true that responder's previous pass makes a call of one notrump non-forcing. In order to show a limit raise, responder uses the **Drury convention**.

When responder has passed and opener has bid a major suit, the bid of two clubs as a response is not natural. It is the **Drury convention**. It shows that responder has a limit raise for opener's major suit. The form most often used is **Reverse Drury**.

Recognizing that responder's call of two clubs shows a limit raise, opener rebids to describe:

   a. When opener has a hand that would not have been opened in first or
      second seat, a simple rebid of the suit at the two level shows that
      fact. After this rebid, the auction should go no further. After the light
      opening bid, opener might have to bid and rebid a major suit of only
      four cards.

   b. When opener has full values and is happy to play game facing a
      limit raise, it is easy to jump to game in the agreed major suit.

   c. Opener's rebid of two diamonds is artificial. It announces a full open-
      ing bid and shows that opener is not sure whether a game should be
      bid. Armed with this knowledge, responder can bid a game with
      four card support and shortness in some side suit—a hand that would
      have **splintered** as an unpassed responder. If the limit raise is of any
      other type, responder can continue by making a game try in a new
      suit.

   d. If opener rebids in any other new suit, the bidding is natural, showing
      a full opening hand with interest in reaching a game or slam.

**Example 87:**

|  | a | b | c |
|---|---|---|---|
| ♠ | J93 | AJ3 | J93 |
| ♥ | KQJ5 | KQJ54 | KQJ54 |
| ♦ | A4 | A103 | AQ3 |
| ♣ | 10873 | 107 | 107 |

**In third seat, Example 87a has opened one heart. When responder bids two clubs—the** Drury convention—**this opener rebids two hearts to deny a real opening bid.**

**Example 87b has opened one heart in third seat. When responder bids two clubs—the** Drury convention—**this opener jumps to four hearts. Game should make as responder has a limit raise for the heart suit.**

**Example 87c has opened one heart in third seat. When responder bids two clubs—the** Drury convention—**opener does not know whether to reach game or not and bids two diamonds, which is artificial and announces a real opening bid.**

Use of the **Drury convention** requires several additional considerations.

a. Two clubs is artificial and shows a limit raise, so a jump raise in opener's major suit is preemptive. It shows four card or longer support and about two to seven HCP.

b. Since two clubs is conventional, when responder has a six card club suit and game invitational values (9+ to 12- HCP), as well as shortness in opener's major suit, a jump to three clubs describes this hand.

c. Although the response of one notrump to the major suit opening bid is no longer forcing, responder retains the same value range of 5+ to 12- HCP. With game invitational values of 9+ to 12- HCP, responder will not have a fit for opener's major suit, unless...

Responder may bid one spade over one heart, holding three hearts. The reason is that opener might bid one heart on a four card suit, also holding four spades. The response of one spade is geared to finding the correct fit of eight cards rather than play in hearts, where the fit might be only seven cards.

d. As a passed hand, responder might jump to two notrump. This cannot be the **Jacoby Two Notrump**. Responder does not have opening bid values. It should not be natural. With a near opening bid, responder should not want to be any higher than one notrump, if the opening has been light. The passed hand jump to two notrump in response to an opening major suit bid shows both minor suits with game invitational values. Responder must be at least five-five in the minors with 9+ to 12- HCP.

**Example 88:**

|  a  |  b  |  c  |  d  |
| --- | --- | --- | --- |
| ♠ 7 | ♠ K85 | ♠ KJ104 | ♠ 63 |
| ♥ Q974 | ♥ 4 | ♥ K83 | ♥ 9 |
| ♦ J642 | ♦ J103 | ♦ A4 | ♦ AQ954 |
| ♣ 10987 | ♣ AQ10864 | ♣ 9764 | ♣ KJ1062 |

**All Example 88 hands have passed and are responding to a third seat opening bid of one heart.**

**Example 88a makes a preemptive jump raise to three hearts.**

**Example 88b jumps to three clubs to show game invitational values, a six card club suit, and at most two hearts.**

**Example 88c might bid two clubs, the** Drury convention. **It has a limit raise for hearts. However, if opener has bid one heart on a four card suit and also has four spades, it is important to reach the correct fit. Responder bids one spade rather than use** Drury. **If opener rebids and does not raise spades, responder will next show support for hearts.**

**Example 88d jumps to two notrump. This response shows game invitational values (9+ to 12- HCP) and at least five cards in each minor suit.**

The majority of experienced tournament players use the major suit raises we have shown here. They present a simplified standard. They have substantial merit, but superior conventional agreements are available and are used by experienced players who wish to improve upon the general standard. Those who want to use the best methods are directed to **Inverted Minor Raises** and **Two Way Reverse Drury** in Volume Two.

# Game tries

After responder has made a single raise of opener's major suit, with a hand of extra values and a feeling that game is possible, opener will make another call to try for game. The game try chosen should seek to determine the degree of fit that exists. The fit being sought can be in any side suit, or even in the trump suit itself. Although responder has expressed a fit in the trump suit, the degree of that fit may be the key to finding a game contract. Or opener may need to learn of a fit in specific side suits.

With a hand that includes extra values, either in high cards or in distribution, after a single raise, opener will often make a try for game. With a suit that is only five cards, the game try will show about a good fifteen to about eighteen HCP. With six-four or five-five distribution opener might jump directly to game with minimum values in high cards.

Opener's try for game should show where help is needed. Sometimes that will be in the trump suit and sometimes that will be in another suit. Game should be reached when the correct fits exist, but not when those fits are missing. Whether or not the bidding side has twenty six HCP has no relevance. Fits take tricks, and the numbers game does not have the importance given to it by many.

**Example 89:**

| a | b |
|---|---|
| ♠ 874 | ♠ KQ4 |
| ♥ KQ109 | ♥ Q54 |
| ♦ 873 | ♦ 873 |
| ♣ 965 | ♣ Q654 |

**You respond to an opening bid of one heart by raising to two hearts with either hand in Example 89. Opener makes a game try by bidding three hearts. What do you do with each of these hands?**

**With Example 89a, most bidders will pass, falling victim to the numbers game. They have only five HCP, which is a minimum for the raise they have made. They do not understand that opener has specified that in order to make game maximum values are not needed—just good help in hearts.**

**With Example 89b, most bidders will bid on to four hearts. They hold maximum values, but they have not listened to opener's need for good hearts. With mediocre trump support, it is probably not right for this responder to**

**bid on. But, the numbers game will often cause bidders to make the wrong call.**

**Example 90:**

♠ 5
♥ J7632
♦ AKJ4
♣ AKJ

**Opener with Example 90 has bid one heart and then heard a raise to two hearts. The selected game try of three hearts sends the message that the need is for help in hearts. If Example 89a bids four hearts, game is very likely to make. Declarer will lose a spade and a heart, and if the diamond position is favorable, there will be an overtrick. If the diamond position is terrible, the club finesse will still bring the contract home. Chances for this game to make are about 85%.**

**However, if responder with 89b raises to four hearts, the likely result will be a loser in spades and three losers in hearts before the minor suit problems are addressed. Example 89b as a dummy makes game about 15%. Don't be a victim of the numbers game. When opener asks for help in the trump suit, bid game with trump help, but do not bid game even with maximum values when your trump support is poor.**

If the trump suit is not a problem, opener will need help in one or more of the side suits. A game try in a side suit should show at least three cards with some honor holding. Opener should be seeking matching honor cards in that side suit. When responder has a wonderful holding in a side suit where opener has asked for help, a direct jump to game in the agreed major suit is correct. The fits will take tricks.

Holding no help in the suit of opener's game try, that game try should be rejected. Responder should return to opener's major suit at the three level. Lack of a fit where it has been sought indicates that the facing hands will not produce tricks.

Having some help in the suit of the game try, if that help is not outstanding, a counter offer can be made. When bidding space exists, responder can show indecision by bidding in some suit between opener's game try and the agreed major suit to show that help in the suit of the game try was marginal, and to show values in the suit of the counter offer.

Example 91:

♠ AKJ85
♥ 7
♦ AQ76
♣ Q93

This opener has bid one spade and has been raised to two spades by re-sponder. Since opener has additional values and game may be possible, this opener should make a game try in a new suit where he needs help.

Many bidders will make a game try of three diamonds. They have been misled by looking to suit lengths. Their game try is based on the fact that they hold four cards in diamonds. This game try would not be descriptive. Opener needs help in both clubs and diamonds, and cannot bypass clubs to make a game try in diamonds just because there are four diamonds and only three clubs.

If responder hears a game try in diamonds and has good clubs, the club holding will not be known to be of help. With good clubs and poor dia-monds, responder will reject the game try. This will not make for a success-ful auction. Opener needs high card fits in both clubs and diamonds. The game try must be made in clubs. Opener cannot afford to bypass any suit in which help is needed when a new suit game try is made.

Example 92:

| a | b | c | d |
|---|---|---|---|
| ♠ Q73 | ♠ Q73 | ♠ Q73 | ♠ Q73 |
| ♥ KJ104 | ♥ J104 | ♥ 854 | ♥ 854 |
| ♦ 854 | ♦ 854 | ♦ KJ104 | ♦ J104 |
| ♣ J104 | ♣ KJ104 | ♣ J104 | ♣ KJ104 |

Note that all hands of Example 92 are the same. The spade holding is the same in all four hands. The holdings in the other three suits are the same, but they have been shifted so that the degree of fit changes. All of these responders have raised an opening bid of one spade to two spades and have heard a game try from partner of three clubs.

With Example 92a, responder does not have a wonderful club holding but knows that it will be helpful. This hand makes a counter offer of three hearts. Opener with Example 91) is not at all impressed that partner has heart values opposite shortness. Opener hopes that the three spade contract is not too high.

**With Example 92b, responder jumps to four spades. Wonderful support exists where opener has indicated a need, in clubs. Game will depend on what happens in diamonds. Declarer has five spade tricks and three club tricks because of the club and spade fits. If the diamond position furnishes two tricks, four spades will make.**

**With Example 92c, responder makes a counter offer of three diamonds. Opener knows that responder's club holding will provide some help and that good diamonds will fit well with opener's hand. Ten tricks will be easy, unless opener loses control to repeated heart leads. Trumps must not be drawn until a club trick is established.**

**With Example 92d, responder jumps to four spades after a game try in clubs as he did in 92b. With secondary value in diamonds also fitting with opener, the contract will make an overtrick when the diamond finesse succeeds and the contract will still be safe when the diamond finesse fails.**

We hope that you have seen from these examples that what we have preached from the early pages of this book is true. Fits take tricks. Beware of the numbers game. Do not try to determine when you do or do not have twenty-six points between the two hands in order to bid a game. Instead, determine whether the two hands fit well together or not. When they do fit well, the tricks will be there with fewer points than the numbers game wants. When there are no fits, even more than the twenty-six number will not produce enough tricks to make a game. In **Advanced Bridge Bidding for the Twenty First Century,** we introduce other game tries which are more sophisticated.

## Suit raise exercises

You are responding to an opening bid in either minor suit. What is your plan with each of these hands?

| 1. | 2. | 3. | 4. |
|---|---|---|---|
| ♠ K93 | ♠ 104 | ♠ 85 | ♠ KJ4 |
| ♥ Q108 | ♥ KJ6 | ♥ 6 | ♥ K10 |
| ♦ J64 | ♦ 85 | ♦ AKJ642 | ♦ K985 |
| ♣ 10975 | ♣ AQ10963 | ♣ KQ93 | ♣ J1062 |

| 5. | 6. | 7. | 8. |
|---|---|---|---|
| ♠ 6 | ♠ K102 | ♠ 6 | ♠ A6 |
| ♥ A95 | ♥ KJ6 | ♥ AQ4 | ♥ A85 |
| ♦ KQ854 | ♦ K1083 | ♦ Q743 | ♦ A942 |
| ♣ Q652 | ♣ QJ75 | ♣ AQ975 | ♣ J1095 |

You are responding to an opening bid in either major suit. What is your plan?

| 9. | 10. | 11. | 12. |
|---|---|---|---|
| ♠ A42 | ♠ A64 | ♠ J95 | ♠ KJ85 |
| ♥ KQ6 | ♥ KQ85 | ♥ AQ84 | ♥ AJ6 |
| ♦ Q974 | ♦ 6 | ♦ KJ973 | ♦ 9742 |
| ♣ 953 | ♣ AJ943 | ♣ 5 | ♣ Q8 |

After two or three passes it is your turn. Do you open the bidding? If so, with what call and for what reasons?

| 13. | 14. | 15. | 16. |
|---|---|---|---|
| ♠ AJ963 | ♠ J762 | ♠ AQ103 | ♠ A6 |
| ♥ 84 | ♥ AQ103 | ♥ J762 | ♥ KJ975 |
| ♦ KQ7 | ♦ 85 | ♦ 85 | ♦ QJ7 |
| ♣ 1062 | ♣ K93 | ♣ K93 | ♣ 853 |

As dealer you have passed. Partner has opened one heart in third seat. What response do you make?

| 17. | 18. | 19. | 20. |
|---|---|---|---|
| ♠ AJ87 | ♠ 95 | ♠ K7 | ♠ K74 |
| ♥ K62 | ♥ 6 | ♥ KJ62 | ♥ 6 |
| ♦ 76 | ♦ KQ974 | ♦ Q1086 | ♦ Q82 |
| ♣ K954 | ♣ AJ1062 | ♣ Q83 | ♣ KQ10853 |

## Answers

1. If the opening bid has been one diamond, respond one notrump. If the opening bid is one club, do not make the error of raising clubs. Your hand is balanced and partner might have opened with only three clubs. A response of one notrump is descriptive if you have passed, but if you have not passed, you should temporize by bidding one diamond. Do not fear that partner will raise. The opening was in clubs and partner cannot hold five or more diamonds. It would be better for

partner to declare at notrump than for you to respond one notrump and play the contract.

2. If the opening bid has been one club, you have a limit raise. Bid three clubs. If the opening bid has been one diamond, you should make the systemic response of three clubs. This shows a club suit of at least six cards and game invitational values.

3. If the opening bid has been one club respond one diamond. You intend at your rebid to jump to three clubs. This is the only jump preference that is forcing. It shows an excellent hand with both minors and a probable emphasis on diamonds. If the opening bid was one diamond, make a **splinter** response of three hearts. This shows a diamond fit of at least five cards, values enough to play at least at game, and shortness in hearts.

4. In response to either minor suit make a jump response of two notrump. This shows game invitational values and denies a four card major. You definitely want to declare so that the opening lead will come up to your hand.

5. If the opening bid is one club, respond by bidding one diamond. You hope to be able to make a rebid that shows your game invitational values. You will not be able to jump rebid three clubs because that is the one jump preference that is forcing. If the opening bid is one diamond jump to three diamonds to show a limit raise.

6. In response to an opening bid in either minor suit, jump to three notrump. This shows opening bid values (12+ to 15- HCP) and denies a four card major. This new standard has not yet been completely recognized by the rulemakers; therefore your partner will need to alert your opponents to the fact that this is not the old 16 to 18 HCP slamkiller. This hand is perfectly described and you again want to have the lead come up to your tenaces.

7. In response to one club, make a **splinter** jump response of three spades. If the opening bid is one diamond, bid two clubs. Your will show diamond support later in your game forcing auction.

8. In response to one club, bid one diamond. In response to one diamond, bid two clubs. Unless partner has some marvelous hand, your goal is to reach three notrump, but you want it to be played from partner's side rather than yours. You have no reason to have the lead come up to your hand and partner most likely holds tenace positions.

9. In response to an opening bid in either major suit, use the **forcing notrump**. Your intention is to show a bad limit raise (three card support with no ruffing value) at your rebid. If partner's rebid is at the two level in a minor suit, you will jump to opener's major at the three level. If partner either rebids the original major at the two level or makes a jump shift rebid, you will jump to game in the major to show this hand. If partner has opened with one heart and **reverses** by bidding two spades, you will bid three hearts, which is forcing. With less, you would rebid two notrump to ask partner to bid three clubs before placing the contract.

10. If the opening bid is one heart, bid a **Jacoby Two Notrump** to show an opening hand with four card trump support and ask partner to describe further. If the opening bid has been one spade, respond two clubs. Your intend to show three card spade support at your next turn. However, if partner rebids in hearts, you will make a **splinter** jump in diamonds.

11. In response to one heart, make a **splinter** jump to four clubs. If the opening bid is one spade, make a limit jump raise of three spades since you hold three card support with a side ruffing value.

12. If the opening bid is one heart, respond one spade. Your plan is to next jump to three hearts to show a bad limit raise. The auction is similar to one with which you might have started with a **forcing notrump**, but that would have denied that you hold four spades. If the opening bid is one spade, make a limit raise by jumping to three spades.

13. In either third or fourth seat, you can open one spade. The light opening bid in third is expected. In fourth, you count your Pearson points and reach fifteen. Ten high card points and five spades. Remember your guide for opening light in fourth seat. Your high card points plus your spades must equal fifteen or more.

14. In third seat, open one heart. You would like a heart lead if you defend and you leave the door open to a fit in either major suit. In fourth seat, you should pass with only fourteen Pearson points.

15. In third seat, open one club. Your hearts are poor and you can pass a response in any suit. A club lead would also be reasonable if your side defends. In fourth seat, a pass is appropriate. Note that this hand and number fourteen are the same with the major suits inverted. Opening with a four card heart suit is wrong here. You do not want hearts to be led if your side defends.

16. Open one heart in third seat. This reasonable hand is almost an opening bid in first or second seat. However, in fourth seat you need to understand the rule of fifteen and pass. You are not able either to compete in spades or defend spades.

17. Although you have a limit raise for hearts as a passed hand, you should not use **Drury**. With only three card support for hearts, you need to search for what might be a better fit in spades. Respond one spade. If you do not find a fit there, you will later show your fit for hearts.

18. Respond by jumping to two notrump. Because you are a passed hand, this jump shows heart shortness, game invitational values (9+ to 12- HCP) and at least five-five distribution in the minor suits. A perfect description.

19. Respond two clubs, the **Drury convention**. This shows your limit raise for hearts.

20. Respond three clubs. You cannot bid two clubs. That would be **Drury,** which shows a limit raise for hearts. This jump shows game invitational values (9+ to 12- HCP), no more than two hearts and at least six clubs.

# CHAPTER NINE

## HIGH LEVEL OPENING BIDS

Opening bids at the two level and higher are either preemptive or descriptive. The distinction is very important. Preemptive opening bids have severe limitations, both offensively and defensively. Their purpose is to create obstacles for the opposition. They are made with hands that have great offensive strength if the opener's long suit becomes the trump suit. Preemptive opening hands will also hold scant defensive strength. These two restrictive requirements are imperative when an opening preemptive bid is made.

Descriptive opening bids convey specific information of a constructive nature. These opening bids give information about offensive potential, but there is no limit imposed on the defensive strength held by a descriptive opening bidder. Preemptive and descriptive opening bids are totally different.

## Preemptive opening bids

Opening bids in suits at the three and four levels and five of a minor are considered to be preemptive. When a preempt is made, it is assumed that certain offensive and defensive criteria are met by the opening hand.

A preemptive opening bidder should use the rule of two, three and four to measure the level at which a preempt should be made. First determine the number of tricks available if the long suit becomes the trump suit. The rule of two, three and four is imposed so that the appropriate level of the preemptive opening can be determined and the potential penalty limited.

When the bidder's side is vulnerable and the other side is not, the rule is of two. The opening preemptive bidder must hold enough tricks to be within two of the opening.

When the vulnerability is equal, the rule is of three. The opening preemptive bidder must be able to win enough tricks to be within three of the opening.

When the bidder's side is not vulnerable and the other side is vulnerable, the rule is of four. The opening preemptive bidder must have enough tricks to be within four of the opening.

The rationale is that if the opponents double the opening preemptive bid and then defend, the contract should not be hopeless. The opening bidder expects that if the opponents double and defend, partner will be able to provide one trick towards the contract. The rule of two, three and four protects the preemptive opening bidder from a disastrous result.

When the preemptive bidder is vulnerable and is within two tricks of what has been bid, and if partner provides one trick, the result will be down only one. This is minus two hundred against a game or more for the opponents, which will be a score of at least four hundred.

Preempting at equal vulnerability is within three tricks of what has been bid. If partner provides one trick the result will be down two. This is minus three hundred when game for the opposition will provide four hundred or more, or minus five hundred when game for the opposition will produce six hundred or more.

If the preemptive bidder is not vulnerable versus vulnerable and is within four tricks of what has been bid, if partner provides one trick, the result will be down three. This is minus five hundred when at least a game for the opposition is expected, which will provide six hundred or more.

This is the factor that determines the level at which an opening preemptive bid can be made safely. If the opening bidder can count seven tricks and is vulnerable against not vulnerable opponents, the preemptive opening bid can be at the three level. With equal vulnerability, an opening preempt at the three level needs only six winners. When the vulnerability is favorable, opener can preempt at the three level with only five winners.

The defensive requirement is just as important as the offensive requirement when considering a preemptive bid. An opening preemptive bid should never include more than one defensive trick. Opener might have some residual holding which could produce a defensive trick, but should never have the expectancy of more than one defensive trick using the quick trick table (see Chapter One).

Suit length has a great deal to do with this evaluation. A six card suit headed by ace and king should be evaluated as two defensive tricks. However, a seven card suit headed by ace and king should be evaluated as only one defensive trick. The seventh card causes another hand to be short, and only one defensive trick will cash in most instances.

A preemptive bid with a hand that has more than one defensive trick creates a trap for partner. If the opponents arrive at a game and partner has only two defensive tricks and a fit for the suit of the preemptive bid, a save may be indicated. Partner may bid on as a sacrifice with the expectancy that the opponents can make the game that they have bid. This will not produce a good result when the combined defensive strength of preemptor and partner is enough to defeat the game contract bid by the opponents. The unexpected defensive trick in the opening preemptive bidder's hand will be the cause of the problem.

**Example 93:**

|  a  |  b  |  c  |
|-----|-----|-----|
| ♠ AKJ9753 | ♠ 64 | ♠ 5 |
| ♥ 62 | ♥ — | ♥ QJ10875432 |
| ♦ 7 | ♦ KQ1087532 | ♦ K6 |
| ♣ 543 | ♣ J97 | ♣ 8 |

|  d  |  e  |  f  |
|-----|-----|-----|
| ♠ 103 | ♠ A987543 | ♠ 92 |
| ♥ 7 | ♥ 53 | ♥ KQJ98543 |
| ♦ J82 | ♦ A4 | ♦ — |
| ♣ AKQJ754 | ♣ 93 | ♣ Q84 |

**Example 93a is classic for a preemptive opening bid. With seven likely offensive winners and one defensive trick, opener should bid three spades when vulnerable versus not. At any other vulnerability, the opening bid should be four spades.**

**Example 93b has seven offensive winners and no defensive tricks even though a KQ combination is rated as a trick. The length of the suit negates that defensive potential. Vulnerable versus not, opener should bid three diamonds. At equal vulnerability, four diamonds is correct, and not vulnerable versus vulnerable five diamonds suits the offensive requirements. In first or second seat, the danger exists that partner may have a good hand with a diamond fit and three notrump may be the best place to play. In third seat, the suggested action is on target. It is virtually impossible that this hand could be given the opportunity to open in fourth seat, but should that happen, look to see if everyone is playing with the same deck, then pass quickly.**

**Example 93c has seven offensive winners and half a defensive trick. The vulnerability will determine whether the opening bid should be three or four hearts.**

**Example 93d has seven offensive winners and one defensive trick. With a solid source of tricks for a possible notrump contract, this hand should preempt three clubs in third or possibly in fourth seat, but should either pass or bid one club in first or second position.**

**Example 93e has five or six tricks in its long suit plus a trick on the side. With two defensive winners, this hand should not make a preemptive opening bid. A two spade bid is acceptable.**

**Example 93f has seven offensive winners and virtually no defense. An opening bid of three or four hearts will be determined by the vulnerability.**

## Responding to preemptive opening bids

When opener has bid preemptively, responder knows what to expect. The rule of two, three and four is the criterion for most preemptive opening bids. Responder knows what values are necessary if the preemptive bid is to be advanced. When the preempt has been made vulnerable versus not, responder knows to raise with only two tricks. If the vulnerability is equal, responder needs three tricks to raise. When the opening preemptor is not vulnerable against vulnerable opponents, responder knows that the potential to take four tricks is necessary for a forward move.

Sometimes responder will have a good hand with a long suit and no fit for opener. A new suit by responder is forcing. When responder bids a new suit, opener raises when possible, bids a new suit to show a value, or repeats the suit of the preempt when that is the most descriptive call.

## Descriptive opening bids

Opening bids at the two level and of five hearts and higher are descriptive rather than preemptive. There is no restriction on defensive strength. An opening bid at the five level or higher carries a very specific message.

## Very high level opening bids

An opening bid of five hearts or more promises that the opening bidder will make that contract and has no losers outside of the trump suit. It indicates that responder can raise one level for every high honor in the trump suit. It also indicates that high cards in all other suits have no value.

**Example 94:**

| a | b | c | d |
|---|---|---|---|
| ♠ KQJ10853 | ♠ — | ♠ AKJ8 | ♠ 10875 |
| ♥ — | ♥ KJ1098543 | ♥ 72 | ♥ AQ2 |
| ♦ — | ♦ A | ♦ KQ105 | ♦ J842 |
| ♣ AKQJ74 | ♣ AKQJ | ♣ 1092 | ♣ 95 |

**Example 94a has twelve offensive winners and needs only to find partner with the spade ace in order to make seven spades. The opening bid of six spades makes that fact clear to responder.**

**Example 94b has eleven offensive winners with hearts as the trump suit. Opener bids five hearts.**

**Example 94c responds to the opening bid of five hearts. Despite opening bid values this hand should pass. It does not meet the needs expressed by the opening bid.**

**Example 94d) responds to an opening bid of five hearts. Despite minimum response values, this hand should raise to seven hearts. It contains two high honors in hearts which is all opener should need.**

## Weak two bids

In the late 1950's, the late great Howard Schenken introduced the weak two bid. By the mid sixties, virtually all serious tournament players had abandoned the old fashioned strong two bids that had previously been standard and were playing weak two bids.

Since that time, opening two bids in spades, hearts and diamonds are no longer strong and forcing. In the first three positions, they show hands with less than opening bid values (roughly 5 to 11 HCP) and a good suit, usually of six cards. Although there are those who believe that these are preemptive opening bids, they are not. They are descriptive - NOT preemptive. The need for a forcing opening bid to show strong hands is satisfied by the use of two clubs as artificial and forcing.

Preemptive opening bids are based on two things. Offensive strength is measured by tricks that can be taken from a long suit. Defensive strength should be almost completely absent. Hands with as much as two defensive tricks should not make preemptive opening bids. Because the opening weak two bid is not classified as preemptive, this distinction allows weak two bids on hands with two defensive tricks.

These opening bids usually show a six card suit of reasonable quality. The classic distributional patterns are 6-3-2-2, 6-3-3-1, and 6-4-2-1. With the last of these patterns, the bidder could hold a side four card minor suit, but never a side four card major. Six-five patterns and 6-4-3-0 patterns are not appropriate, since there is more than one true candidate to be the trump suit.

A weak two bid with a seven card suit usually happens only when the bidder is vulnerable against non-vulnerable opponents. Holding a seven card suit and not much in values, many would consider opening preemptively at the three level. However, at this particular vulnerability that opening bid would place the opener's side at risk of a large penalty. Opening with a weak two bid decreases the possibility of that penalty. Only at this particular vulnerability should a seven card suit be expected for a weak two bid.

Some adventurous souls will open with weak two bids on five card suits. In third position, this tactic has considerable merit. The bidder's partner has already passed, so there is very little risk of getting too high. The preemptive effect makes life difficult for the opposition. The opponents probably hold most of the high cards and the problem created by this weak two bid on only a five card suit will make it hard for them to determine both the level and the denomination at which they should play. A weak two bid on a five card suit in first or second seat is also acceptable if the hand is otherwise balanced and the suit is of excellent quality.

In first or second seat, weak two bids should be structured. The opening two bidder should offer information that can be trusted by a partner who has not yet passed. In third position, facing a passed partner, the weak two bidder has no such obligation. The intention should be to obstruct the opponents rather than to inform partner. In short, in third seat just about anything goes.

A weak two bid in fourth seat presents yet a different consideration. A pass will end the auction with neither a plus nor a minus score for either side. This means that a fourth seat weak two bid is made with the intention of going plus—not minus. The standards for a weak two bid in fourth seat obviously increase.

Instead of 5 to 11 HCP, a fourth seat weak two bidder should have about 10 to 13 HCP. This call should always show a good six or seven card suit, never just five. The function of this opening bid is to shut out the opponents who probably hold about half of the high card strength, although neither of them has been able to open the bidding. With both opponents silent, the other passed hand, your partner, will also hold some of the missing strength. Opener will be favored to make the two level contract.

With attention given to the position in which an opening two bid is made, a description is conveyed to the responder. This description of expected size and shape is totally different than what is expected from a bid that is preemptive rather than descriptive.

### Example 95:

| a | b | c |
|---|---|---|
| ♠ 86 | ♠ KJ97643 | ♠ 54 |
| ♥ AQJ954 | ♥ 107 | ♥ KQJ106 |
| ♦ Q9 | ♦ 82 | ♦ 942 |
| ♣ 762 | ♣ Q8 | ♣ K108 |

| d | e | f |
|---|---|---|
| ♠ A5 | ♠ KQ10953 | ♠ 103 |
| ♥ 62 | ♥ 103 | ♥ J954 |
| ♦ AJ10954 | ♦ 6 | ♦ AQ10864 |
| ♣ 843 | ♣ Q1074 | ♣ 5 |

**Example 95a is a classic weak two bid. The suit is excellent, but the worst possible (balanced) shape makes this weak two bid a minimum despite its 9 HCP.**

**Example 95b has about six offensive tricks and little defense. It might be opened three spades at favorable or equal vulnerability. However, if the vulnerability is unfavorable, a weak two bid is more reasonable.**

**Example 95c is an excellent weak two bid in third seat, despite the five card suit. It is also reasonable in first or second position.**

**Example 95d is almost good enough to open with one diamond, despite only nine high card points as it has several winners and two defensive tricks. However, a weak two bid is fine. The presence of two defensive tricks should not preclude an opening weak two bid, which is descriptive rather than pre-emptive.**

**Example 95e is a fine weak two bid. The good suit and good shape make for excellent offense. The four card minor suit is fine.**

**Example 95f should not be opened with a weak two bid except in third seat. The suit is fine and the values are right, but the four card major suit is too important and a heart fit might be missed after an opening bid of two diamonds.**

## Responding to weak two bids

When a weak two bid has been made in first or second seat and responder has not yet passed, a game or slam might be in the offing. With most poor hands, responder will pass. However, with a poor hand that includes a fit for the suit of the weak two bid, responder should make a preemptive raise. The raise can be to any higher level. The degree of fit and the lack of defensive strength in responder's hand should determine the level to which that raise should be made.

**Example 96:**

| a | b |
|---|---|
| ♠ Q83 | ♠ Q10754 |
| ♥ AJ62 | ♥ 83 |
| ♦ 95 | ♦ K962 |
| ♣ K1065 | ♣ J4 |

**If partner opens two spades, Example 96a should raise to three spades. It is likely that an opposing three level contract might make, so responder preemptively takes the three level away. It is better to block opposing action than let it happen and then raise partner.**

**If partner opens two spades, Example 96b should raise preemptively to at least the four level. Vulnerability will determine how high responder bids. Vulnerable against not a raise to the four level is probably safe enough. At any other vulnerability, this responder might even preempt to the five level.**

A responder who visualizes a game or slam will usually make a forcing call to seek information about the weak two bid. A two notrump response is forcing and asks for further description from opener. Of the several possible meanings for the call of two notrump, the simplest asks opener if the weak two bid is maximum or minimum.

When the opening bid is made with minimum values, after the response of two notrump opener rebids in the original suit. With good values for the opening two bid, opener bids to express some feature in the opening hand. Opener shows a maximum by bidding an honor card holding in some side suit. Ideally this holding will be an ace or a king, but when opener's suit is excellent there will often be no such good side suit holding. When that is true, opener does the best thing that is available. It may be necessary to invent a side suit feature just so opener can show that the weak two bid is maximum.

**Example 97:**

|   | a | b | c |
|---|---|---|---|
| ♠ | KQJ954 | KJ9765 | AKQ962 |
| ♥ | 85 | 85 | 7 |
| ♦ | J82 | Q109 | 85 |
| ♣ | K9 | J6 | J863 |

**All Example 97 hands have opened two spades. Partner has bid two notrump to find out more about the nature of the weak two bid.**

**Example 97a shows its maximum and locates a feature by bidding three clubs.**

**Example 97b rebids three spades to show a minimum for the weak two bid.**

**Example 97c has a maximum, but no real feature to bid. Opener cannot rebid spades because that would show a minimum weak two bid. The best opener can do is to bid three clubs to show a feature there.**

At other times, responder will introduce a new suit. This new suit call is forcing and expected to be natural. Opener is asked to show a fit for responder when possible, or to show a feature when maximum or rebid the original suit when minimum as before.

When the new suit is higher ranking and at the two level, opener has specific rebids to affirm or deny a fit for responder's suit.

1. Opener shows three card support headed by ace, king or queen by raising responder to the three level.
2. Opener shows ace, king or queen doubleton, or any lesser three card holding by bidding two notrump.
3. With any lesser degree of fit, opener rebids the suit of the weak two bid to show a minimum, or shows a feature with a maximum as though the response had been two notrump.

**Example 98:**

| a | b | c | d |
|---|---|---|---|
| ♠ K85 | ♠ K5 | ♠ 82 | ♠ 82 |
| ♥ 96 | ♥ 1096 | ♥ 94 | ♥ 94 |
| ♦ KQ9854 | ♦ KQ9854 | ♦ KQ9854 | ♦ AQ10985 |
| ♣ 82 | ♣ 82 | ♣ K85 | ♣ QJ3 |

**All hands of Example 98 have opened two diamonds.**

**With Example 98a, if responder bids two hearts, opener will rebid three diamonds to show minimum values without a fit for hearts. If responder bids two notrump, opener will again rebid three diamonds to show minimum values. If responder bids two spades, opener will raise to three spades to show three card support, which includes a high honor.**

**With Example 98b, if responder bids two notrump, opener will rebid three diamonds to show minimum values. If responder bids either two hearts or two spades, opener will rebid two notrump to show either a high honor doubleton or some three card holding, which does not include a high honor.**

**With Example 98c, if responder bids two notrump, opener rebids three diamonds to show minimum values. If responder bids two of either major suit, opener's rebid of three diamonds both shows minimum values and denies a fit for the major suit.**

**With Example 98d, if responder bids two notrump, opener rebids three clubs to show maximum values and a club feature. If responder bids two of either major suit, opener's rebid of three clubs both shows maximum values and a club feature, and denies a fit for responder's major suit.**

In all cases when responder has shown values by making a forcing bid, opener's rebid should be the best available description. When the response and rebid are not at the two level using the schedule shown above, opener will make the best descriptive call that can be found. Priority is always given to showing good or bad values, and affirming or denying a fit for a major suit shown by responder.

# The opening bid of two clubs

When opener has a wonderful hand and wants to be sure that responder will bid, an opening bid of two clubs is used. This opening bid is artificial and forcing. It says nothing about the club suit. It simply says that opener's hand is so good that a simple opening bid might be passed. Fearing that a game (or slam) might be missed if a simple non-forcing opening bid is made, opener bids two clubs to be sure that responder's first call is not a pass.

This call is the replacement for old fashioned strong two bids in each of the suits. Opener may hold a very strong balanced hand, or may have a suit oriented hand which will win nine or more tricks without help from responder. This two club bid not only replaces natural forcing opening bids, but also allows opener to show opening bids of 22 or more HCP with balanced hands.

## Responder's priorities

When opener bids two clubs, responder must express something about values. Responder will usually bid two diamonds—an artificial waiting response—to allow opener to show the nature of the strong opening hand. Responder will rarely make any other call. Only with a hand that needs to convey a special message will responder disrupt the auction by bidding otherwise.

With less than an ace, a king or two queens, responder holds negative values. If opener rebids in notrump, responder is not required to bid again and may pass. But, when opener's rebid is in a suit, the auction is forcing and responder must rebid to show or deny values.

If responder holds a very good long suit, a response in that suit is often the best description. A response of two in a major suit shows a five card or longer suit headed by two of the top three honors as well as some additional values.

A positive response in a minor suit should show even more. Since more space is being used, the hand shown should be even more impressive. Responder should hold a very good six card suit to bid three in either minor. When responder does not have such a good suit to show, the artificial waiting response of two diamonds should be used. This will allow opener to continue to show the nature of the strong two club opening bid.

**Example 99:**

| a | b | c | d |
|---|---|---|---|
| ♠ AQ1085 | ♠ AQ1085 | ♠ 85 | ♠ 85 |
| ♥ 954 | ♥ 954 | ♥ K54 | ♥ Q53 |
| ♦ 85 | ♦ 85 | ♦ AQ1085 | ♦ AQ10985 |
| ♣ 753 | ♣ K53 | ♣ 954 | ♣ 54 |

**All hands of Example 99 are responding to an opening bid of two clubs.**

**Example 99a has the required suit for a two spade response, but nothing extra. It is better for this responder to mark time by making the waiting response of two diamonds.**

**Example 99b has the same spade suit as before. The extra value of the club king should cause this responder to bid two spades.**

**Example 99c has the same suit and values as 99b. However, a response of three diamonds would use a great deal of bidding space and responder's suit is only five cards. The waiting bid of two diamonds is better.**

**Example 99d has a sixth card in the diamond suit as well as an outside value. This hand describes well by responding three diamonds.**

## Opener's rebids

With a balanced hand of 22 HCP or more, opener starts with two clubs. A rebid of two notrump shows 22 to 24 HCP. With 25 to 27 HCP, opener rebids three notrump. With 28 to 30 HCP, opener rebids four notrump. With greater values, opener bids more. Since I have never had a hand that big, I won't worry about just how much more.

Opener's rebid in a suit promises at least five cards in that suit and a hand that will produce about nine tricks without help from responder. It is forcing and suggests that an opening one bid would not have been appropriate.

## Responder's rebids

Responder's rebid is expected to announce values or lack of values. When responder does not have values, the cheapest call that can be made at the three level conveys that message. This call will usually be three clubs. If opener's rebid is in a minor suit, responder's artificial negative call will be in the next higher ranking suit (specifically three diamonds if opener bids three clubs, or three hearts if opener rebids three diamonds). This artificial negative rebid announces no aces or kings and denies as much as two queens. It also tends to deny a fit for the suit of opener's rebid.

When opener rebids in notrump, responder is no longer forced. Opener's rebid has pinpointed the values of the opening hand. Responder may continue using **Stayman**, or a **Jacoby Transfer**, or a **Texas Transfer,** or by use of the **Gerber convention**. Or responder can simply determine that notrump should be played at some level and can bid to that level to invite opener to bid more. As expressed in Chapter Seven, responder can add the points shown by the opener's rebid to this hand's points and determine the level at which to bid.

**Example 100:**

|  | a |  | b |  | c |  | d |
|---|---|---|---|---|---|---|---|
| ♠ | 852 | ♠ | 852 | ♠ | J853 | ♠ | 1062 |
| ♥ | J10862 | ♥ | J1062 | ♥ | 10743 | ♥ | J8 |
| ♦ | 5 | ♦ | 9862 | ♦ | 98654 | ♦ | 8543 |
| ♣ | 9874 | ♣ | 86 | ♣ | — | ♣ | K973 |

|  | e |  | f |  | g |
|---|---|---|---|---|---|
| ♠ | QJ4 | ♠ | 852 | ♠ | KQ2 |
| ♥ | K10 | ♥ | K109743 | ♥ | 964 |
| ♦ | 10742 | ♦ | 5 | ♦ | K3 |
| ♣ | KJ96 | ♣ | 1086 | ♣ | KQJ93 |

**All Example 100 hands have responded with a waiting bid of two diamonds, after an opening bid of two clubs. The opening bidder has rebid two notrump to show 22 to 24 HCP and a balanced hand.**

**Example 100a will probably be a useless hand unless hearts becomes the trump suit. Responder should use a** Jacoby Transfer **by bidding three diamonds and pass when opener bids hearts.**

**Example 100b has no reason to bid further. Pass will end the auction and declarer will play two notrump.**

**Example 100c should play in a suit rather than in notrump. Responder should use** Stayman **by bidding three clubs. Regardless of opener's next call responder will pass.**

**Example 100d should simply raise to three notrump.**

**Example 100e can visualize a slam, if opener has maximum values. Responder jumps to four notrump to invite that slam.**

**Example 100f wants to play game in hearts. A jump to four diamonds is a** Texas Transfer, **after which responder will pass.**

**Example 100g knows the combined values of the two hands are at least 36 HCP. Responder jumps to four clubs, the** Gerber **convention. If opener shows all four aces, responder bids seven notrump. If an ace is missing, responder stops at six notrump.**

When opener has rebid in a suit, responder has certain priorities. If responder is broke, the expression of negative values is primary. With no fit, responder rebids as cheaply as possible at the three level as an artificial negative. Opener's rebid in a suit is forcing; responder will not pass.

With negative values and a fit for opener's major suit, responder will jump to game in that suit. This jump to game promises three cards in opener's major suit, denies an ace or a king, and also denies a singleton or a void in any side suit. It is assumed that the fit will be enough to produce a game in opener's major suit even though responder does not have high card values.

When responder holds any control for a possible slam, a simple raise to the three level will show positive values and a fit. When responder holds a fit and has not jumped to game, the auction indicates a control for a possible slam contract.

When opener has rebid in a suit and responder has positive values, but no fit, priority falls to showing a five card or longer suit. Responder's bid of any new suit shows positive values as well as at least five cards in the bid suit.

With positive values, no fit for opener's suit, and no five card suit to show, responder rebids in notrump. This is responder's last priority after opener has rebid in a suit.

If a two club opener rebids to show a suit, then repeats that suit, the auction is no longer forcing and responder may pass. However, if the two club opener shows a suit and then rebids in yet another suit, the auction remains forcing and responder should not pass.

### Example 101:

| a | b | c |
|---|---|---|
| ♠ Q85 | ♠ Q85 | ♠ Q85 |
| ♥ 96 | ♥ 6 | ♥ 6 |
| ♦ 87432 | ♦ 87432 | ♦ 87432 |
| ♣ 1062 | ♣ 10862 | ♣ Q1062 |

|     | d        |     | e        |
|-----|----------|-----|----------|
| ♠   | 96       | ♠   | 96       |
| ♥   | Q84      | ♥   | Q84      |
| ♦   | KJ862    | ♦   | KJ82     |
| ♣   | J63      | ♣   | J763     |

All hands of Example 101 have bid two diamonds as a waiting bid, after an opening bid of two clubs. Opener next bids two spades, which promises a suit at least five cards long.

Example 101a jumps to four spades. This shows a negative response in values, but promises a spade fit of at least three cards. It also denies that responder holds a shortness control (singleton or void), which might be useful at a slam contract.

Example 101b bids three clubs, an artificial negative. When responder later shows support for spades, opener will know that there is probably a shortness control as well as a fit for spades in responder's hand.

Example 101c raises to three spades. This promises a positive response as well as a fit for spades.

Example 101d bids three diamonds. This denies a fit for spades and promises five or more diamonds as well as the values of a positive response.

Example 101e bids two notrump. This shows positive values, denies a fit for spades and shows that responder does not have a five card or longer suit.

## Summary

1. Opener's bids at the three or four levels and at five of a minor are preemptive. It must be stressed that preemptive opening bids show offensive strength and deny defensive strength. A preemptive opening bid denies more than one defensive trick.

2. Opener's descriptive opening bids are at the two level or of five hearts or higher.
   A. Opening bids of five hearts or higher are very descriptive and promise that in order for more tricks to be made, responder must furnish high honors in the trump suit.
   B. Opening weak two bids vary by position.

1. In first and second seat, they show 5 to 11 and are highly structured.
2. In third seat, they show 5 to 11 HCP and are at whim.
3. In fourth seat, they are good hands with good suits and about 10 to 13 HCP.

3. It should be stressed that opener should not seek to bid two clubs. Human nature causes people to want to show power, and bidding two clubs often gives a rush of adrenalin to one who makes that call. This feeling of power often obscures the true needs of the auction. Opener should bid two clubs only when it is necessary. When responder holds only one useful card, that should be enough to provide the tricks necessary for game facing a two club opening bid. Do not stretch to open two clubs.

## High level opening bid exercises

With each of the following hands, consider your opening bid. Would you pre-empt? Would you pass? Would you open with a bid at the one level? How would you bid in first or second position? In third position? In fourth position?

1.
- ♠ AQ109753
- ♥ 9
- ♦ A86
- ♣ 84

2.
- ♠ 6
- ♥ 83
- ♦ KJ987543
- ♣ J4

3.
- ♠ 9
- ♥ AJ10962
- ♦ 632
- ♣ A43

4.
- ♠ KQ8542
- ♥ 6
- ♦ J9754
- ♣ 3

5.
- ♠ Q852
- ♥ AQ9753
- ♦ 8
- ♣ 54

6.
- ♠ 6
- ♥ KJ10973
- ♦ Q4
- ♣ 10982

7.
- ♠ AQJ942
- ♥ 5
- ♦ A102
- ♣ 963

8.
- ♠ 5
- ♥ —
- ♦ QJ10
- ♣ QJ10876532

9.
- ♠ QJ10987543
- ♥ —
- ♦ AK
- ♣ AK

| 10. | 11. | 12. |
|-----|-----|-----|
| ♠ 7 | ♠ 10 | ♠ — |
| ♥ AKJ10854 | ♥ A102 | ♥ KQ2 |
| ♦ K32 | ♦ AJ976543 | ♦ J84 |
| ♣ 65 | ♣ 4 | ♣ A1087654 |

| 13. | 14. | 15. |
|-----|-----|-----|
| ♠ AQJ104 | ♠ KQ108764 | ♠ KJ4 |
| ♥ 62 | ♥ 3 | ♥ 4 |
| ♦ QJ8 | ♦ J105 | ♦ AQJ1083 |
| ♣ 1094 | ♣ 82 | ♣ J62 |

| 16. |
|-----|
| ♠ 2 |
| ♥ QJ10975 |
| ♦ 76 |
| ♣ AJ43 |

You are responding to an opening bid of two hearts. What action do you take?

| 17. | 18. | 19. | 20. |
|-----|-----|-----|-----|
| ♠ AJ6 | ♠ J64 | ♠ 64 | ♠ K842 |
| ♥ Q85 | ♥ Q85 | ♥ Q85 | ♥ 6 |
| ♦ A8 | ♦ K8 | ♦ AJ62 | ♦ A963 |
| ♣ K9842 | ♣ K9842 | ♣ AK104 | ♣ A1094 |

You have opened two hearts and partner has responded two spades. What is your rebid?

| 21. | 22. | 23. | 24. |
|-----|-----|-----|-----|
| ♠ J84 | ♠ J8 | ♠ 8 | ♠ K64 |
| ♥ AQ9864 | ♥ AQ9864 | ♥ AQ9864 | ♥ KJ10964 |
| ♦ 63 | ♦ K85 | ♦ 97 | ♦ Q42 |
| ♣ Q8 | ♣ 62 | ♣ J843 | ♣ 5 |

What is your opening bid on each of these hands?

| 25. | 26. | 27. | 28. |
|-----|-----|-----|-----|
| ♠ 6 | ♠ AQ8 | ♠ — | ♠ AQJ9 |
| ♥ AKQ976 | ♥ KQ103 | ♥ KQJ8643 | ♥ AQ |
| ♦ AKQ852 | ♦ Q6 | ♦ KQJ9 | ♦ AK1032 |
| ♣ — | ♣ AKQ4 | ♣ A6 | ♣ 83 |

You are responding to an opening bid of two clubs. What call do you make?

| 29. | 30. | 31. | 32. |
|---|---|---|---|
| ♠ K93 | ♠ AJ5 | ♠ KQJ94 | ♠ KQ8 |
| ♥ 6 | ♥ 6 | ♥ 6 | ♥ Q1042 |
| ♦ 942 | ♦ A7542 | ♦ 853 | ♦ A6 |
| ♣ AKJ864 | ♣ K1094 | ♣ 10872 | ♣ J963 |

You have responded two diamonds (waiting) to partner's opening bid of two clubs. Partner has rebid two spades. What is your next call?

| 33. | 34. | 35. | 36. |
|---|---|---|---|
| ♠ 84 | ♠ 84 | ♠ J874 | ♠ J82 |
| ♥ Q8632 | ♥ A842 | ♥ A65 | ♥ 85 |
| ♦ J654 | ♦ J103 | ♦ 2 | ♦ Q972 |
| ♣ 92 | ♣ Q653 | ♣ K10973 | ♣ A654 |

You have responded two diamonds (waiting) to partner's opening bid of two clubs. Partner has rebid two notrump. What is your next call?

| 37. | 38. | 39. | 40. |
|---|---|---|---|
| ♠ QJ87432 | ♠ 8 | ♠ KJ82 | ♠ K85 |
| ♥ 6 | ♥ 10642 | ♥ 53 | ♥ J6 |
| ♦ Q84 | ♦ J6542 | ♦ 10874 | ♦ QJ74 |
| ♣ 92 | ♣ 973 | ♣ J64 | ♣ K1086 |

## Answers

1. Open one spade. This hand has too much defense for a preemptive opening bid. It has both the offensive and defensive strength for an opening one bid.

2. You have seven probable tricks on offense and none on defense. Open three diamonds if vulnerable against not, but open four diamonds at any other vulnerability.

3. Open two hearts in any position, even fourth. You like your suit and want to keep your opponents from bidding spades.

4. Pass. Your spade suit is fine for a weak two bid but your shape is wrong. If partner has no spades, you could easily miss as much as a game in diamonds. You can enter the auction later.

5. Pass. Again your suit is fine for a weak two bid, but you should not risk missing a fit in spades.

6. Two hearts in first, second or third seat. If you are acting after three passes—very unlikely—do not open Pandora's box. Pass and hope an opponent (not partner) has missed an ace.

7. Open one spade in any of the first three positions. Open two spades in fourth.

8. You have eight offensive tricks with clubs as trumps and no defense at all. Open four clubs if vulnerable versus not, but five clubs otherwise.

9. Open five spades. All you need for more tricks is for partner to hold one or both missing spade honors. Partner will know to raise with those cards.

10. Open one heart in first or second seat. Do not preempt with this much defense. If partner has passed, an opening bid of four hearts is acceptable.

11. Open one diamond or pass. Again, you hold too much defense for a preemptive opening bid.

12. Open one club or pass. Your suit is poor and you have too much defense to preempt.

13. Open two spades in any position except fourth. This is a very good five card suit.

14. Open three spades unless vulnerable versus not, in which case two spades is fine.

15. Open one diamond in the first three seats. Open two diamonds in fourth.

16. Open two hearts in the first three seats. Pass in fourth.

17. Two notrump. If partner has a good hand, you want to be in a heart game.

18. Three hearts. Make it difficult for the opponents to enter the auction.

19. Four hearts. This hand is far better than number 17 even though both have 14 HCP.

20. Pass. Your high cards will be of help even though you have no fit.

21. Two notrump. This shows a minor fit for spades. You promise high honor doubleton or three cards without a high honor.

22. Three diamonds. This denies a spade fit and shows a maximum weak two bid with a diamond feature.

23. Three hearts. This denies a spade fit and shows a minimum weak two bid.

24. Three spades. This shows three spades including a high honor.

25. One heart. DO NOT open two clubs. If you make that error, the opponent next to bid may overcall and be raised preemptively to the five or six level. Then you will have to guess which suit to introduce. If you guess wrong, you may go down at the five level when a slam in the other suit is cold. Do not be concerned about playing one heart. Too many high cards are outstanding. Your rebid will be six diamonds.

26. Two clubs. Although you should try not to open two clubs, when your hand is balanced and 22 HCP or more, you have no alternative. You will rebid two notrump.

27. One heart. Yes, you do have at least nine winners, but two clubs would be a joke. With only sixteen HCP, you need not fear that you will play one heart.

28. One diamond. Yes, you do have 20 HCP, but that does not make your hand a two club opening bid. You may have only five tricks!! If partner responds one heart, you can jump shift in spades. If partner responds one notrump, you can **reverse** to two spades.

29. Respond three clubs. This shows a good hand with a good club suit. If you mark time with a two diamond response, partner will never have a clue that your suit is so good.

30. Two diamonds (waiting). You can show your opening bid values later. Let partner tell you about the strong two bid.

31. This hand is borderline. It may be best to show your good spade suit. Your only extra value is the spade jack, but that is a powerful card. Remember that if you make a positive response in spades, you make it difficult for partner to describe the strong opening hand. If you make the waiting bid of two diamonds, you can show your spade suit later.

32. Two diamonds. Again you want to hear about partner's strong two bid. There is no rush to show your values.

33. Three clubs—an artificial negative. Given the chance, you will show your heart suit later. For now, you must deny values.

34. Two notrump. This shows the values of a positive response as it denies both a spade fit and a five card suit.

35. Four diamonds. This is a **splinter** that shows positive response values, four card support for spades, and a singleton or void in diamonds.

36. Three spades. This shows at least three card support as well as positive response values.

37. Four hearts. This is a **Texas Transfer,** asking partner to bid four spades. You will then pass.

38. Pass. You would like to explore for a suit fit but are not able to do so.

39. Three clubs—the **Stayman convention**. If partner holds four spades, you want to play game in that suit. Otherwise you will correct to three notrump.

40. Jump to four notrump. If partner holds maximum values, your high cards will usually produce a slam in notrump.

# CHAPTER TEN

## INTRUDING WHEN THEY HAVE OPENED THE BIDDING

The fact that your opponents have opened the bidding does not mean you are required to remain silent. There are several reasons and ways that your side might enter the auction begun by the opponents. Sometimes your entry into the auction will be constructive—sometimes obstructive. Sometimes you will suggest a trump suit for your side—at other times, you will ask partner to select a trump suit. At times, you will just show a good balanced hand and let partner determine where to go. At times, you desperately want a certain lead.

When you enter the auction bidding a suit or bidding notrump, you will have either made an overcall or a balancing bid. It is important that you understand the difference between these two auctions. An overcall is after a bid by your right hand opponent (RHO). You make a balancing bid after two passes when another pass would end the auction.

## Overcalls

Bidding after your right hand opponent has opened or responded is an overcall. Your overcall can be in a suit or in notrump. It can be a simple call or it can be a jump. There are several reasons to make an overcall:

1. The hand may belong to your side in a partscore, a game or a slam.
2. The overcall can be for the purpose of lead direction.
3. If the overcall finds partner with a huge fit, your side may be able to take a profitable sacrifice at a high level.
4. The overcall may simply throw the opposition off balance, causing them to play at the wrong level or in the wrong suit.

There are various kinds of overcalls.

# Simple overcalls in notrump

An overcall made in notrump without jumping shows a hand that might have opened one notrump—balanced and roughly in the range of 15 to 17 HCP. The overcall must include honor cards in the suit (or suits) bid by the opponents, which gain in value because of placement. The overcall not only shows a balanced hand in the suggested range, it also guarantees at least one stopper in the suit bid by RHO.

Overcalling one notrump should be the best expression of your hand. Some hands that you would have opened one notrump should not overcall one notrump. When they open in your short suit, it is probable that a takeout double would be better. Your overcall of one notrump should show at least three cards in the suit bid in front of you. You should have at least one stopper in that suit—more is preferred.

If you play notrump when your holding in RHO's suit is short or tenuous, it may not be possible to break communications between the defending hands—a tactic that is often necessary for the contract to succeed. In such cases, you need to consider some other bid.

**Example 102:**

|  | a | b | c |
|---|---|---|---|
| ♠ | AJ8 | Q1074 | AJ8 |
| ♥ | K1094 | K6 | K104 |
| ♦ | A6 | KJ1094 | Q62 |
| ♣ | KJ83 | AQ | AQ75 |

**All of the hands in Example 102 should open one notrump. If RHO has opened the bidding, some will be appropriate for an overcall of one notrump.**

**Example 102a should overcall one notrump if RHO bids one spade, heart or club. In each case, the hand has a potential double stopper in the suit of the opening bid as well as a balanced hand in the correct range. If the opening bid is one diamond, there is only one stopper that must be played early. A better description would be a takeout double. This hand has support for all of the unbid suits and is flawed for an overcall in notrump.**

**Example 102b is semibalanced but has good doubletons, which would cause opener to bid one notrump. If RHO bids either one spade or one diamond, the overcall of one notrump describes well. If the opening bid is one club, a takeout double would not be good because of the poor support for hearts. The double stopper in clubs makes the overcall of one notrump the best choice,**

though far from ideal. If RHO bids hearts, an overcall in notrump is very dangerous. Although a takeout double is not ideal, it is probably better than the notrump overcall.

Example 102c is a good overcall of one notrump if RHO bids in spades, hearts or clubs. Each suit has a flexible stopper, maybe two. But, if RHO bids diamonds, the overcall is shaky. With a diamond lead, this hand may be forced to spend its stopper at trick one, leaving that suit wide open if declarer later loses the lead. Still, no other bid describes very well either. Give the edge to a takeout double rather than a notrump overcall.

## Advancing an overcall in notrump

An overcall in notrump is a complete description. The modern advancer (the advancer is the partner of an intruder who has overcalled, doubled, or made a cue bid) can use the same system as the responder to an opening bid of one notrump. The old standard for advancer was to make natural suit bids and use a cue bid in opener's suit as **Stayman**.

**Jacoby Transfers** in modern methods have caused a change in standard. The transfer bid might be in the suit of the original opening bid (which cannot be both a **transfer** and **Stayman**)   The modern standard for advancing the overcall of one notrump is to use **Stayman** and **Jacoby**. Instead of using a cue bid as **Stayman**, responder uses two clubs, leaving the **transfer** response for the advancer.

## Jump overcalls in notrump

Jump overcalls in notrump are not needed to show strong balanced hands. Holding a very good balanced hand, first make a takeout double, then bid notrump to show a hand too good for an original overcall of one notrump. If your hand is monstrous, you can first double, then cue bid in order to find out what your partner has before settling into notrump at some level.

An interesting concept applies to doubles and to bids in notrump. They either mean what they say, or the exact opposite of what they say. Double means that an opposing contract will fail and the doubler wants to increase the penalties. But, when double is the first call of a competitive bidder, its meaning is exactly opposite. Instead of wanting to penalize the opposing bid, double expresses the desire to compete and asks partner to select from among the unbid suits. The takeout double is a standard bidding method.

Voluntary bids in notrump normally show balanced hands in a specific range. However, when a bid in notrump is used in a very unusual way, its meaning is exactly the opposite of standard. Instead of showing a strong balanced hand, the bidder shows a very unbalanced hand, which is usually quite weak. This is called the "unusual notrump". It has become a standard bidding application and should be understood by all serious bidders.

A jump overcall in notrump at the two, four, five or six level is the "unusual notrump". It shows a hand with at least five-five distribution in the two lowest ranking unbid suits. The values of the hand will never be intermediate. The "unusual notrump" overcaller will either be preempting in two suits, or making a slam try in those two suits.

One of the basic precepts of preemption is this: When a bidder has preempted, the entire offensive value of the hand has been expressed. A bidder who has preempted should never volunteer another call. This means that the preemptive bid should be made at the highest possible level when the rule of two, three, and four is applied. A bidder who uses the "unusual notrump" to preempt should bid at the highest possible level, and then never bid again.

If an "unusual notrump" bidder makes another bid, it shows values at the opposite end of the scale. Instead of a preempt in two suits it is a slam try in two suits. Intermediate hands that are too good for preempts, but not good enough to suggest slam, should be shown by overcalling in one of the suits. The overcaller has values enough to later bid the other suit in most auctions.

**Example 103:**

| a | b | c | d |
|---|---|---|---|
| ♠ 7 | ♠ — | ♠ 86 | ♠ A6 |
| ♥ 84 | ♥ — | ♥ 5 | ♥ — |
| ♦ KJ1094 | ♦ KQJ974 | ♦ AKJ93 | ♦ AKJ95 |
| ♣ QJ987 | ♣ QJ108543 | ♣ KQJ84 | ♣ KQ10974 |

**The hand of Example 103a is a classic two-suited preemptive bid of two notrump if the opening bid has been in a major suit. It has two reasonable minor suits (the two lowest ranking suits) with good offense if a fit can be found, but very little defense.**

**Example 103b presents the ultimate two suited preempt. It has ten winners if either clubs or diamonds are trumps, and has no defensive tricks. This hand**

should preempt at some high level. A competitive bid of four, five, or even six notrump can easily be justified based on the auction.

Example 103c should overcall in diamonds after an opposing major suit bid. The shape is correct but the values are wrong for the use of the "unusual notrump". This overcaller hopes to be able to show clubs at the next turn to bid.

Example 103d needs very little to make a slam in one of the minor suits. If partner has a fit for either suit and any fitting high card, twelve tricks should be easy. This bidder uses the "unusual notrump" and then raises when partner selects one of the suits. This indicates that the bidder is trying for a slam. If the bid had been preemptive there would be no further call.

A jump overcall of three notrump shows the desire to play that contract. The hand that makes such a bid will have a source of tricks, and stoppers in other suits, most particularly a stopper in the suit that has been bid by RHO.

### Example 104:

&spades; K3
&hearts; A6
&diams; AKQJ843
&clubs; J5

Example 104a is a classic for a jump overcall of three notrump when RHO has bid in a major suit. After a one spade opening bid this call is a favorite.

## Overcalls in suits

Simple overcalls in suits usually show at least five cards and a suit of reasonable quality. When the overcaller's hand has values, the overcall shows length and seeks a fit. Although the suit is expected to be of good quality, sometimes the overcaller will have no choice but to suggest a suit that is mediocre because of a hand that is otherwise very reasonable. It is impossible to find a fit if no one bids the suit.

At times you will hold a good suit and little else. Although you have no strong desire to declare, you do want partner to lead your suit. If you do not give partner help by making an overcall, the defense may give up a cheap trick on the opening lead. This is reason enough to overcall a good suit even when you have a poor hand.

Ideally, the overcall will show a hand with values and good suit. On a practical basis, the overcall will sometimes show a good hand with a bad suit, or a bad hand with a good suit. Either reason is valid.

**Example 105:**

| a | b | c |
|---|---|---|
| ♠ AQ1084 | ♠ J9874 | ♠ KQJ93 |
| ♥ K5 | ♥ A5 | ♥ 85 |
| ♦ QJ72 | ♦ KJ3 | ♦ 1096 |
| ♣ 84 | ♣ AJ8 | ♣ 764 |

**Example 105a would open the bidding if given the first chance to bid. If RHO opens in clubs, diamonds, or hearts, this hand is a good overcall of one spade. Both suit and hand are good.**

**Example 105b has a poor suit with opening bid values. After RHO opens the bidding overcall in spades despite the bad suit. This hand is a one spade opening bid. If spades are not bid and partner has a fit, it will go undiscovered.**

**Example 105c has a good suit and little else. After RHO opens the bidding, overcall one spade to provide partner with help should there be a problem on opening lead.**

## Overcalls on four card suits

In his 1979 book, *The Complete book on Overcalls in Contract Bridge*, Mike Lawrence was the first to suggest that a four card suit overcall might be the best call available in some auctions. Until that book, overcalls on four card suits were considered unacceptable. Lawrence gave three basic rules for such an overcall.

    1. Four card overcalls should be made only at the one level.
    2. The four card suit should be of very good quality.
    3. The overcaller should have length in the suit bid by RHO.

With a good four card suit and length in opener's suit, the intruder will be short in one or both of the remaining suits. This gives the hand the wrong shape for a takeout double. Because the suit must be good, the overcall will provide lead direction on defense. The third rule is the safety factor.

Holding length in RHO's suit, the overcaller expects to find shortness in the two remaining hands. This increases the likelihood of a fit for your suit in the hand of your partner. If the overcalled suit becomes the trump suit, there is also a strong advantage in the play. Declarer will be able to ruff losers in the long side suit in dummy with no fear of being overruffed.

**Example 106:**

| a | b | c |
|---|---|---|
| ♠ 63 | ♠ K3 | ♠ K6 |
| ♥ AKJ8 | ♥ A853 | ♥ AJ105 |
| ♦ AQ742 | ♦ AQ742 | ♦ Q2 |
| ♣ 94 | ♣ J9 | ♣ KQ986 |

**Example 106a is perfect for an overcall of one heart when RHO has bid one diamond. All three criteria are met. If the opening bid is one club some action must be taken and the overcaller has to guess which suit to bid (solution for this problem in *Advanced Bridge Bidding for the Twenty First Century*).**

**Example 106b should not overcall one heart after RHO bids one diamond, because the heart suit is not good enough. An overcall of one notrump would be a better idea. Even a pass could be right.**

**Example 106c was a problem in the Master Solver's Club of the *Bridge World* magazine. If RHO bids one club it meets the criteria for an overcall of one heart. However, in the problem RHO had bid one diamond. Despite no diamond length, sixteen expert panelists out of 28 voted for an overcall in hearts.**

## Overcalls at the two level

Overcalls at the two level require good suits. A contract that requires eight tricks, rather than just seven, offers more opportunity to an opponent who holds a trump stack and senses a large penalty. The danger factor at the two level is far greater than at the one level. If your overcall must be at the two level, it will be far better to have a bad hand with a good suit than to have a good hand with a bad suit.

**Example 107:**

| a | b | c |
|---|---|---|
| ♠ KQ5 | ♠ 974 | ♠ J63 |
| ♥ AJ8 | ♥ K6 | ♥ 4 |
| ♦ J6 | ♦ 862 | ♦ 1062 |
| ♣ K8753 | ♣ AQJ94 | ♣ AQJ974 |

**Example 107a has 14 HCP. An overcall of two clubs after RHO bids one diamond is a death trap. If LHO holds the hand of Example 107b, it will be easy to determine that a large penalty is in the offing. Your 14 HCP may produce only three tricks. You may take no tricks at all in your trump suit. LHO can pass and convert a reopening double for penalties. If you feel the urge to enter the auction because of your 14 HCP, make a takeout double.**

**Example 107c is far better for a two club overcall despite only 8 HCP. This good suit should produce five tricks and there is virtually no danger of running into a trump stack.**

## Advancing partner's overcall

When partner has overcalled in a suit, the advancer needs to know how to continue. With many nondescript hands a pass is in order. This is advancer's checklist.

1. Raise the overcall as you would have raised if partner had opened the bidding in a major suit. This requires about 5+ to 9 HCP and three card support. The importance of this raise must be stressed. Partner will often have a good enough hand so that what is needed to bid a game or to compete further is knowledge of a fit. Withholding that information runs partner out of gas quickly. DO NOT FAIL TO RAISE PARTNER'S OVERCALL WHEN YOU ARE ABLE TO DO SO.

2. A change of suit is corrective. A new suit by responder is forcing, but responder's rule does not apply to an advancer. A change of suits by advancer is a search for a better place to play and is not forcing.

   If the overcall was in a major suit and the advancer removes to a minor suit, it denies a fit for the major. Advancer will hold at most a doubleton in support of the major and be bidding a suit at least five cards long.

If the overcall was in a minor suit and advancer removes to a major suit, there is no denial of a fit. Major suit contracts are more to be sought than those in minors, and advancer might be trying to improve the contract despite a fit for the overcall.

A change from one major suit to the other or from one minor suit to the other does not deny a fit. It simply suggests that advancer believes that a contract in the corrected suit would be superior.

3. A jump in a new suit shows the values of an opening bid (or more) and a good six card suit. It is descriptive and forward going, but it is not forcing.

4. A jump raise of the overcall is strictly preemptive. It promises a four card fit and very few (if any) values.

5. A jump cue bid is a power raise for the overcall. It promises a four card or longer fit and at least a good 10 HCP.

6. Advancer shows all other good hands and starts forcing auctions by making a simple cue bid. The cue bid elicits information from the overcaller. With minimum hands the overcaller will repeat the suit as cheaply as possible. With better hands the overcaller will make the call that best expresses the nature of the hand, but will not repeat the suit of the overcall cheaply.

Advancer's usual hand for the cue bid will include three card support for the overcall, and values enough to suggest game. The advancer will also use the cue bid to build a forcing auction. A cue bid followed by a new suit makes the auction forcing. This correlates with items 2 and 3 above. Advancer can correct as shown in item 2, move forward as in item 3, or force by cue bidding and then introducing a new suit.

**Example 108:**

| a | b | c |
|---|---|---|
| ♠ 85 | ♠ 8652 | ♠ 7 |
| ♥ Q973 | ♥ Q84 | ♥ 854 |
| ♦ A1062 | ♦ J83 | ♦ KQ9753 |
| ♣ K93 | ♣ K93 | ♣ A105 |

|       d       |       e       |       f        |
|:-------------:|:-------------:|:--------------:|
| ♠ AQ975       | ♠ J32         | ♠ AK10953      |
| ♥ 82          | ♥ KQJ974      | ♥ Q2           |
| ♦ K73         | ♦ Q2          | ♦ 7            |
| ♣ 984         | ♣ 83          | ♣ KQ75         |

|       g       |       h       |       i        |
|:-------------:|:-------------:|:--------------:|
| ♠ 8753        | ♠ Q1094       | ♠ KQ5          |
| ♥ J9          | ♥ KQ8         | ♥ A432         |
| ♦ 7           | ♦ 64          | ♦ 103          |
| ♣ Q98754      | ♣ AJ102       | ♣ K742         |

|       j       |       k       |
|:-------------:|:-------------:|
| ♠ J963        | ♠ AKQ5        |
| ♥ KQ1095      | ♥ 74          |
| ♦ 82          | ♦ 3           |
| ♣ 64          | ♣ KQJ1073     |

**All Example 108 hands are advancers whose partner has overcalled.**

**With Example 108a, the auction has been one diamond on your left and an overcall of one spade by partner. One notrump shows scattered minimum response values without a spade fit.**

**With Example 108b, after LHO has opened and partner has overcalled at the one level in any suit, raise the overcall. You would have raised if partner had made a major suit opening bid.**

**With Example 108c, partner has overcalled one spade after an opening bid of one club. Your correction to two diamonds denies a fit for spades and shows at least five cards in your suit.**

**With Example 108d, partner has overcalled one diamond. Despite a fit for diamonds, you visualize a better result at a spade contract. Correction to spades shows at least five cards and does not deny a diamond fit.**

**With Example 108e, partner has overcalled one spade after an opening bid of one club. Despite your fit for spades you correct to your excellent heart suit.**

With Example 108f, partner has overcalled one heart after an opening bid of one club. Assuming RHO, passes show your opening bid values and good suit by jumping to two spades.

With Example 108g, partner has overcalled one spade after an opening bid of one diamond. If responder passes or makes a negative double, **make a preemptive raise of the overcall by jumping to three spades.**

With Example 108h, partner has overcalled one spade after an opening bid of one diamond. **Make a jump cue bid of three diamonds to show a "power raise" for spades with four card support.**

With Example 108i, partner has again overcalled one spade after an opening bid of one diamond. **Make a simple cue bid of two diamonds with your good raise for the overcall without four card support. If partner's next call shows a bad overcall, you will subside, but if partner shows a good overcall, bid four spades.**

Examples 108j and 108k are the hands of a partnership. After an opening bid of one diamond, 108j overcalled one heart for lead directional purposes. Advancer began with a cue bid of two diamonds and the overcaller rebid two hearts to show a bad hand. Advancer's next call was three clubs, which was forcing. The overcaller then simply bid three hearts (some call was required) after which advancer bid three spades. This was music to the ears of the overcaller who raised to four spades. An excellent auction during which both overcaller and advancer understood what each meant and bid to the excellent game.

## Jump overcalls in suits

Jump overcalls in suits are preemptive. They show hands with suits of at least six cards and not much defensive strength. These replace strong jump overcalls, which do not happen often. The frequency of a hand with just a good suit after an opposing opening bid far exceeds that of a hand with great strength as well as a long suit. Strong jump overcalls did not happen often, but preemptive jump overcalls happen with great frequency.

When partner makes a preemptive jump overcall it is probable that if your side declares, partner's suit should be the trump suit. The long trump suit will probably be worth four or five tricks. When that suit is not the trump suit partner's hand will usually have little value.

The hand that makes a preemptive jump overcall will usually have a six or seven card suit with reasonable texture and little else. Knowing this, the advancer will have a good idea of how the auction should continue.

With no fit for the suit of the overcall, the advancer will usually pass. Whatever high cards advancer holds will be useful if partner is allowed to declare. It is when the advancer has a fit that action should be taken.

With minimum values, advancer should raise the overcall to an appropriate level. When advancer does not have much in high cards, the greater the fit, the higher the level at which the raise should be made. A fit of three cards should inspire a single raise. A fit of four cards should inspire a jump raise to the four or five level. The purpose is to make the opponents guess whether to double and defend or bid on, maybe to a contract that cannot be fulfilled. We expect that if our side declares the contract will be doubled, and we will surrender less than the amount of the game (or slam) that the opponents can make.

Holding a good hand without a fit, the advancer can pass, hoping the high cards will allow the contract to make. With a good hand and a fit, the advancer should probe to get more information about the nature of the jump overcall. If the jump overcall has been at the three level, this is difficult. If the jump overcall is to a higher ranking suit at the two level, advancer can use two notrump as a probe for information.

In such auctions when the jump overcaller has minimum values for the auction and the advancer probes by bidding two notrump, a simple rebid of the suit conveys that information. When the jump overcaller has a good hand for the auction, a rebid in a new suit will show some feature. Refer to auctions that are opened with a weak two bid.

**Example 109:**

|   | a | b | c |
|---|---|---|---|
| ♠ | KJ10973 | 8 | Q84 |
| ♥ | 62 | A94 | 9853 |
| ♦ | 4 | KJ753 | KJ53 |
| ♣ | J872 | K1054 | K10 |

|   | d | e |
|---|---|---|
| ♠ | Q854 | Q85 |
| ♥ | 953 | 953 |
| ♦ | KJ53 | A53 |
| ♣ | K10 | AK109 |

**Example 109a is classic for a jump to two spades after an opening bid at the one level.**

**Example 109b facing this jump overcall should pass (no fit). Hopefully, the high cards will help fulfill the contract.**

**Example 109c holds a fit and little defense. Raise the jump overcall to the three level.**

**Example 109d holds a better fit and should raise preemptively to the four or five level, depending on vulnerability.**

**Example 109e has a fit and good values. This advancer should use two notrump to probe for information about the jump overcall.**

## Balancing

Balancing bids are made after two passes. They occur when responder passes the opening bid and in other auctions where opener's side stops at a low level.

### Balancing in notrump

A balancing bid of one notrump when responder has passed usually shows less than an opening bid or an overcall in notrump. It still shows a balanced hand, but with about 10 to 14 HCP. When the opening bid has been in a minor suit, the balancer does not necessarily have a stopper in the suit of the opening bid.

Holding a standard notrump of 15 to 17 HCP, balancer will usually double. A rebid in notrump will show these better values.

When the opening bid has been in a major suit, a stopper is expected. There is also a space problem. If the balancer has 15 or 16 HCP, it still may best to bid one notrump. A double might cause a response at the two level, requiring a rebid of two notrump.

A jump to two notrump in balancing position is not the "unusual notrump". It shows a balanced hand in the range of 18+ HCP.

It is possible to advance either the balancing notrump or the balancing jump in notrump with the systems shown in Chapter seven. It is standard to do so facing the balancing jump in notrump, but not many bidders use **Stayman** and **Jacoby** facing the simple balancing notrump. Most probably, they should.

Example 110:

|  | a | b | c |
|---|---|---|---|
| ♠ | K84 | K84 | AK4 |
| ♥ | Q1073 | Q1073 | KQ73 |
| ♦ | AJ3 | AJ3 | AJ3 |
| ♣ | J42 | KQ6 | K94 |

With all hands of Example 110, the auction has been opened by LHO and there have been two passes.

Example 110a balances with a bid of one notrump. This shows a balanced hand in the range of 10 to 14 HCP. If the opening bid was in a major suit, a stopper is expected, but not if the bid was in a minor suit.

Example 110b balances with a double when the opening bid has been in a minor suit. This hand would have opened by bidding one notrump, but it is too big for a balance of one notrump after a minor opening. You show these values in balancing position by first making a takeout double, then bidding in notrump. If the opening bid was in a major suit, it would be better to balance by bidding one notrump. A double might cause partner to bid at the two level, and you would then need to bid two notrump.

The denomination of the opening bid and the position determine how you will describe. If you were making an overcall, you would always bid one notrump, but in balancing position meanings are different.

Example 110c jumps to two notrump. This describes a hand that is better than an opening bid of one notrump. It is a balanced hand with a good 18 HCP to about 20. It is not the "unusual notrump".

## Jumps in the balancing position

After an opening bid and two passes, if balancer jumps in a suit, it is not a preemptive bid. Jump overcalls are preemptive, but balancing jumps are not. A jump in the balancing position shows an opening hand or more with a good six card suit. The high card range for this call is about 12 to 16 HCP.

Please understand:

THERE ARE NO WEAK JUMPS IN THE BALANCING SEAT. ALL JUMPS SHOW GOOD HANDS.

Most suit bids in the balancing position will show five or more. But, it may be necessary to bid a four card suit when nothing else will suffice. Doubles in the balancing position will be variable. At times, the balancing double will be simply to protect, and can be on less than substantial values. After the opening bid, partner might have been strapped despite reasonable values. A double by the balancer takes that fact into account.

A call by the balancer is made with the understanding that the balancer is bidding all of the values held by that side. The balancer knows that responder is weak and that opener has not made a forcing opening bid. Therefore the balancer's partner may well have values that could not be expressed.

**Example 111:**

|  a  |  b  |  c  |
|-----|-----|-----|
| ♠ KJ974 | ♠ AQJ8 | ♠ A64 |
| ♥ 62 | ♥ 63 | ♥ 3 |
| ♦ A93 | ♦ 843 | ♦ AQ53 |
| ♣ K52 | ♣ KJ95 | ♣ K8652 |

**After an opening bid of one heart and two passes, Example 111a is a classic for a balancing bid of one spade.**

**After an opening bid of one diamond and two passes, Example 111b cannot double for takeout with no support for hearts. The best call is one spade, despite only four cards.**

**After an opening bid of one heart and two passes, Example 111c doubles. The spade support is not wonderful, but if partner bids spades, this hand should not disappoint. However, the expected action is a penalty pass by partner and this hand has adequate defense.**

## Balancing when the opponents have stopped at a low level

When responder has bid and the auction stops at the two level, if the opponents have found a fit, it is usually right to balance. If neither member of our side has overcalled, the most likely balancing action will be a takeout double. Sometimes the balancer could not overcall at the two level, and now can bid a suit.

If the opponents have found a fit of eight or more cards, our side will almost always also have such a fit. With the values in the deck divided fairly evenly, sometimes both their contract and ours will make. At other times, we will go down one, which will not be a problem, or our balance may cause the opponents to compete further and be one trick too high.

Much will depend not only upon the fits that are found, but also the placement of key cards. The placement of missing key cards in one opposing hand or the other may be favorable to one side or the other. At times, the placement will favor neither side.

When the opponents have not found a fit, you will know not to balance when you have length in their suit. If you are short in the opponents' suit, your partner probably has a stack. In either case, if the opponents do not have a fit, your side probably also has no good fit.

**Example 112:**

|  | a | b | c |
|---|---|---|---|
| ♠ | 83 | 83 | 83 |
| ♥ | KQ74 | AQ1043 | KJ10 |
| ♦ | KJ62 | KJ6 | Q972 |
| ♣ | 1074 | 1042 | AJ83 |

|  | d | e | f |
|---|---|---|---|
| ♠ | 8542 | A97 | QJ8 |
| ♥ | 6 | Q62 | 62 |
| ♦ | KQ103 | KJ543 | KJ97 |
| ♣ | AQ76 | 107 | KJ104 |

**Example 112a is in balance position after the auction: 1♠ - pass - 1NT - pass, 2♥ - pass - 2♠ - pass, pass - ?. You should not balance. The auction indicates that the opponents have found a five-two fit and your partner has a four card stack, and you have a stack in opener's second suit.**

**Example 112b is in balance position after the auction: 1♣ - pass - 1♠ - pass, 2♠ - pass - pass - ?. Your suit was not good enough for an overcall, but the opponents have found a fit and stopped. You expect to find enough of a heart fit and enough in values to have a play for three hearts. Although you have only 10 HCP, your side has about half of the deck. Balance by bidding your suit.**

**Example 112c is in balance position after the auction: 1♠ - pass - 2♠ - pass, pass - ?. The opponents have found a fit so your side should also have one. Balance with a takeout double.**

**Example 112d is in balance position in the auction: 1♠ - pass - 2♠ - pass, pass - ?. You know that your partner is very short in spades and should have a fit for one of your minor suits. Your balance of two notrump asks partner to pick a minor. This is NOT a balancing 10-14 HCP notrump—it is a form of the "unusual notrump".**

**Example 112e is in balance position in the auction: 1♥ - pass - 1♠ - pass, 2♣ - pass - 2♥ - pass, pass - ?. Do not balance. The opponents have not found a true fit, but hearts will break well for them. Your suit was too ragged for an overcall, and it is also too ragged for a balance now.**

**Example 112f is in balance position in the auction: 1♥ - pass - 2♥ - pass, pass - ?. It is clear to balance with double. They have found a fit and your side also has one, as well as about half of the points in the deck.**

In summary, overcalls and balancing bids are of two extremely different natures. Many bidders do not know the difference and run into trouble because they are not speaking a standard language. Do not mistake a balance for an overcall. Each is based on completely different parameters.

## Takeout doubles

A common intrusion into an auction begun by the opponents is a double as a takeout call. Although the call of **double** literally means that the opponents will not make their contract and the doubler wants to reap increased penalties, when double is the first call made as an entry into the auction, the meaning is quite different.

As an initial entry into the auction, double is not for penalties, but its completely opposite meaning is that the intruder wants partner to select a trump suit. The doubler will have reasonable values and support for the unbid suits. As an aside, when the takeout double was introduced, the Portland Club (London's most conservative) would not allow its use!

The double for takeout today is the most commonly used of all bidding conventions. It is so common that its meaning is universally known. The classic takeout double has at least two defensive tricks, roughly the values of an opening bid, and support for all of the unbid suits. The more perfect the distribution, the lower the HCP requirements, but the defensive requirement is a must.

Example 113:

|   | a | b | c |
|---|---|---|---|
| ♠ | KJ8 | KJ84 | KJ84 |
| ♥ | AQ3 | AQ3 | AQ73 |
| ♦ | 62 | 62 | 6 |
| ♣ | K10952 | K1092 | K1092 |

All Example 113 hands are next after an opening bid of one diamond.

Example 113a has a five card club suit, but the quality is not good enough for an overcall at the two level. Also, the hand has excellent three card support for each of the major suits. An overcall in clubs would not only be dangerous—it also might cause a playable fit in a major suit to be missed. You don't have to be happy about it, but a takeout double is your best entry into the auction.

Example 113b is an excellent takeout double, even with only three hearts.

Example 113c will satisfy even the most rigid purists. Four card support for all of the unbid suits makes this example classic. All three of these hands are best described with a takeout double.

## Responding to takeout doubles

When partner has made a takeout double, you are sometimes under duress. You cannot pass unless you hold length and values in opener's suit. Pass would convert the takeout double into a penalty double. If that is your choice, you must hold not only length in the opening bidder's suit, but you must also have good texture. It must be clear that your trumps are better than those of the opening bidder. After such a penalty pass, a trump lead by the doubler is mandatory (even if he is void).

With length in opener's suit but a poor holding, you cannot convert for penalties, and you must bid something. Sometimes you will not be happy to bid, but have no option.

Example 114:

|   | a | b |
|---|---|---|
| ♠ | QJ10975 | 1074 |
| ♥ | 62 | 86432 |
| ♦ | A42 | Q6 |
| ♣ | 75 | J83 |

**With Example 114a, LHO has opened one spade and partner has doubled for takeout. You have better spades than the opener and can pass for penalties. Although the bidder has five spades, after the ace and king are history, the rest will probably not win tricks. You have four spade winners. Partner will lead a trump to hasten your removal of declarer's trumps.**

**With Example 114b, LHO has opened one heart and partner has doubled for takeout. Although you have five hearts, you have no tricks in the heart suit. A penalty pass is not a good idea. You hate to bid, but a call of one spade is your best.**

A takeout double shows support for the unbid suits. When you bid one of those suits, you should think of your call as a raise of a suit shown by the double. So should partner. You do not need great values to raise one of partner's suits. Needing to call when RHO passes, a simple bid will not show much, either in length or in values. With less than the values to invite a game, your response to partner's double will be such a simple call. With values in opener's suit, you can bid notrump at an appropriate level.

An advance of a takeout double when there is no further action by the opponents should reflect values as follows:

1. A simple bid shows 0 to 9- HCP.
2. A jump response shows 9+ to 12- HCP and invites a game.
3. A jump to game indicates that you know what game to bid.
4. A cue bid shows at least the values to invite a game, but suggests that you need guidance. You are asking partner to pick the trump suit.
5. A double jump below the level of game (when that is possible) is preemptive. It shows length in the suit of the jump, but denies values.
6. If the advancer bids in competition after partner's takeout double, this bid shows some values but does not promise more than a simple raise for one of the doubler's suits. The advancer is raising a suit that the doubler has shown. The doubler should not believe that the advancer is showing game invitational values.
7. When advancer has length in more than one suit, it is always right to show a major suit rather than to bid a minor. Responding to the takeout double in a minor suit denies as many as four cards in a major. Even with six cards in a minor suit, bid a four card major suit when you have one. If a game is to be bid, it will be in a major suit, so ignore long minor suits in favor of major suits whenever you have a choice.

**Example 115:**

|  | **a** | **b** | **c** |
|---|---|---|---|
| ♠ | KQ875 | KJ85 | KJ10875 |
| ♥ | A62 | A62 | 83 |
| ♦ | 854 | 854 | 864 |
| ♣ | Q3 | Q63 | J2 |

|  | **d** | **e** | **f** |
|---|---|---|---|
| ♠ | KQ93 | KJ83 | KQ84 |
| ♥ | AJ82 | 82 | 62 |
| ♦ | 864 | 7 | 854 |
| ♣ | J2 | Q109843 | J963 |

In all hands of Example 115, LHO has opened one diamond and partner has made a takeout double.

With Example 115a, you have the values for a game and know what game to bid. Jump to four spades.

With Example 115b, invite a game by jumping to two spades.

With Example 115c, make a preemptive jump to three spades.

With Example 115d, cue bid to ask partner to pick the suit.

With Example 115e, do not make the error of bidding clubs. Respond in spades.

With Example 115f, bid one spade. If responder bids one notrump or raises to two diamonds, bid two spades. Remember that you are raising a suit that partner has shown. Your call shows the values of a raise, not of a free bid.

## Rebidding after a takeout double

After making a takeout double, be careful not to get excited when partner bids a suit that you have suggested. Remember that partner's call is a simple raise of a suit that your takeout double has suggested. If your original call has shown all of your values, you have no license to bid further, even though you are pleased with what you have heard from partner. Perhaps the most common bidding error is a restatement of the same values that a takeout bidder has already shown.

When the advancer has made a simple call showing less than game invitational values and the takeout doubler volunteers another call, it suggests that if the advancer has maximum values for a non-invitation, game should be bid. The advancer has shown 0 to 9- HCP. If the takeout doubler bids again, it shows at least a good 17 HCP. Human nature often causes a pleased takeout doubler to forget that partner was forced to bid. A raise with much less when game is not a prospect will often cause the auction to get out of hand.

A simple raise should take into account that advancer might have a hand such as Example 114b. Remember that the advancer's call when the opponents are silent can easily be made under duress rather than by choice. Advancer may hold only three cards in the suit bid and no values at all.

Jump raises of the advancer's response require substantial values. The takeout doubler must be prepared for a call from advancer that has shown virtually no values. Even when the advancer has shown values, the doubler should be cautious. When the fit is minimal, game is not assured even when the takeout double is good and the advancer invites.

**Example 116:**

| a | b | c |
|---|---|---|
| ♠ KJ95 | ♠ KQ95 | ♠ KQJ5 |
| ♥ AJ86 | ♥ AK86 | ♥ AK3 |
| ♦ 105 | ♦ 6 | ♦ 6 |
| ♣ KJ3 | ♣ AQJ3 | ♣ AKJ94 |

| d | e |
|---|---|
| ♠ 10842 | ♠ A842 |
| ♥ 952 | ♥ 1073 |
| ♦ 9743 | ♦ 9743 |
| ♣ 75 | ♣ AQ |

**Example 116a has made a takeout double of a one diamond opening bid. Advancer bids one of either major. The takeout doubler has no further call. Even if opener rebids two diamonds, a raise to two spades would be an overstatement of doubler's values.**

**Example 116b has made a takeout double of one diamond and advancer has bid in a major suit. Since advancer may have no values at all, this excellent hand should not do more than make a jump raise to the three level.**

**Example 116c has made a takeout double of one diamond and advancer has bid one spade. This doubler should** splinter **to four diamonds, believing that a contract of four spades is safe.**

**Example 116d has bid one spade in response to a takeout double of one diamond. If any of the three doublers shown above bids again, the contract may be at too high a level. Facing Example 116a, a contract of two spades will fail. Facing Example 116b, a contract of three spades might fail. Facing Example 116c, a contract of four spades will probably make, but is not sure fire.**

**Example 116e would make a jump response to show invitational values. Facing Example 116a, game is a reasonable prospect but not a sure thing.**

## Is it really for takeout?

There are hands that are simply too good for an overcall either in a suit or in notrump. When your hand fits this description start by making a takeout double. Partner will believe that your hand is typical for a takeout double. Presumably you have an opening bid or more with support for all of the unbid suits. At your rebid, you will correct that impression.

After a takeout double and a response, it will be unexpected for the doubler to bid another suit. Instead of a double for takeout, the auction shows a hand with fine values, whose bidder feared that an overcall might be passed and a game missed.

**Example 117:**

|  | a |  | b |
|---|---|---|---|
| ♠ | A6 | ♠ | KQ84 |
| ♥ | AKJ975 | ♥ | KJ3 |
| ♦ | AQ6 | ♦ | AQ6 |
| ♣ | 83 | ♣ | A83 |

**After an opening bid of one club or one diamond, Example 117a fears that an overcall of one heart will not suffice. A game might easily be missed. Double for takeout, and after the advancer bids, correct to hearts. The message of the auction is of a very good hand with a very good suit.**

**After an opening bid in any suit, Example 117b knows that an overcall of one notrump will not show the correct values. Double for takeout and then correct to notrump. The auction shows a hand with values too great for a notrump overcall.**

## The numbers game—again

There are bidders who do not understand the takeout double. They do not understand that it is a tool to find fits, or to show a superlative hand. They use the double to show an opening bid without regard for distribution. Their doubles show that they have thirteen HCP. When they overcall, they deny as much as thirteen HCP. These bidders have no concept of what takeout doubles are all about, but they are in the bridge arena, so be prepared.

Playing in sanctioned ACBL clubs and tournaments, everyone is required to have listed agreements on a convention card, which must be displayed for the convenience of the opponents. The modern convention card requires an indication of doubles that are not really for takeout, but are made to show values regardless of distribution. The card also indicates that this non-standard approach must be accompanied by an alert. This is simply a caution. Be prepared for this abortive approach. When not informed, you may be entitled to redress if you can demonstrate injury.

## Cue bids

The modern use of a cue bid as an entry into the auction makes far more sense than the old fashioned Goren requirement. The old standard was so absurd that it rarely happened. It used a cue bid to show about 20 HCP with shortness (usually a void) in the suit that had been bid by the opposing side.

Today's cue bid shows a hand with two suits and moderate values. The most common usage is the **Michaels** cue bid.

The cue bid shows two suits of at least five cards and less than opening bid values. The range is usually 6 to 11 HCP. A cue bid of a minor suit opening bid shows both majors. A cue bid of a major suit opening bid shows the other major and one of the minor suits.

When the opening bid is in a major suit and the advancer has no fit for the other major suit, a bid of two notrump asks the intruder to name the minor.

With a fit in a major suit and reasonable values, advancer can jump to invite a game. Or, advancer may have values enough to bid a game expecting it to make. With a huge fit for a known suit and no defense, advancer can make a preemptive jump to a high level.

**Example 118:**

|  | a | b | c |
|---|---|---|---|
| ♠ | KJ975 | KQ954 | KQ954 |
| ♥ | Q10843 | AJ863 | 7 |
| ♦ | 6 | 6 | 92 |
| ♣ | 72 | 72 | KJ853 |

|  | d | e | f |
|---|---|---|---|
| ♠ | Q862 | Q862 | 74 |
| ♥ | K2 | K2 | 853 |
| ♦ | 853 | 853 | AQ63 |
| ♣ | AK84 | A854 | Q1094 |

**Example 118a is a typical minimum hand for a** Michaels **cue bid after a minor suit opening bid.**

**Example 118b is a typical maximum.**

**Example 118c would make a** Michaels **cue bid after an opening bid in hearts, but would have to overcall in spades after an opening bid in diamonds.**

**Example 118d faces an auction in which the opening bid is one diamond and partner has made a** Michaels **cue bid. This hand should jump to game in spades because of the fits for both major suits and club controls.**

**Example 118e in the same auction should invite a game by jumping to three spades.**

**When the opening bid has been one heart and partner has made a** Michaels **cue bid, Example 118f should bid two notrump to ask for the intruder's minor suit.**

## Intruder's exercises

With each of the following hands, it is your turn after an opening bid of one diamond on your right. What call do you make and why?

|  | 1. | 2. | 3. | 4. |
|---|---|---|---|---|
| ♠ | KJ85 | 4 | 7 | Q10985 |
| ♥ | A976 | KJ10974 | AKJ6 | AJ642 |
| ♦ | 5 | 853 | AQ843 | 7 |
| ♣ | KQ87 | Q62 | 854 | 54 |

5.
♠ KJ7
♥ QJ83
♦ A6
♣ KQ54

6.
♠ 85
♥ QJ974
♦ 5
♣ KJ1085

7.
♠ AKJ1092
♥ AQ5
♦ 83
♣ A7

8.
♠ AJ6
♥ QJ92
♦ AJ73
♣ K4

With each of the following hands, the auction has begun with one club on your left and two passes. What call do you make and why?

9.
♠ Q94
♥ K106
♦ K82
♣ KJ104

10.
♠ A1083
♥ KQ65
♦ QJ102
♣ 5

11.
♠ K8
♥ A4
♦ J1054
♣ QJ1093

12.
♠ QJ83
♥ A6
♦ KJ7
♣ KQ54

13.
♠ K3
♥ KQJ963
♦ A52
♣ 82

14.
♠ K8
♥ AJ104
♦ AQ7
♣ AQ93

15.
♠ KQ952
♥ AJ874
♦ 7
♣ 83

16.
♠ AQ1085
♥ KQ3
♦ J94
♣ 96

With each of the following hands, the auction has begun with one diamond on your left. Your partner has made a takeout double and the next opponent has passed. What call do you make and why?

17.
♠ KQ105
♥ A62
♦ 43
♣ J1087

18.
♠ K87
♥ 106
♦ QJ104
♣ Q432

19.
♠ Q5
♥ 862
♦ KQ10985
♣ J3

20.
♠ AJ6
♥ KJ1084
♦ 4
♣ A1098

21.
♠ Q862
♥ 5
♦ 83
♣ KJ9432

22.
♠ 862
♥ J105
♦ 9742
♣ J87

23.
♠ KJ9854
♥ 1073
♦ 852
♣ 7

24.
♠ KQ84
♥ AJ93
♦ 754
♣ 64

With each of the following hands, there has been an opening bid of one heart on your left and partner has overcalled one notrump. RHO passes. What call do you make and why?

| 25. | 26. | 27. | 28. |
|---|---|---|---|
| ♠ J83 | ♠ KQ83 | ♠ KQ873 | ♠ 854 |
| ♥ 1076 | ♥ 52 | ♥ 52 | ♥ 72 |
| ♦ K854 | ♦ K1096 | ♦ 10864 | ♦ J6 |
| ♣ KJ6 | ♣ 1098 | ♣ J3 | ♣ AK10854 |

With each of the following hands, you have made a takeout double after an opening bid of one diamond and partner has responded one spade. What is your next call and why?

| 29. | 30. | 31. | 32. |
|---|---|---|---|
| ♠ AQ82 | ♠ AQ82 | ♠ QJ104 | ♠ Q107 |
| ♥ AK3 | ♥ A83 | ♥ AK7 | ♥ KJ102 |
| ♦ 84 | ♦ 84 | ♦ — | ♦ 84 |
| ♣ A1074 | ♣ A1074 | ♣ AK9853 | ♣ AQ94 |

With each of the following hands, you have made a takeout double after an opening bid of one diamond and partner has responded one spade. Opener has rebid two diamonds. What is your next call and why?

| 33. | 34. | 35. | 36. |
|---|---|---|---|
| ♠ KQ87 | ♠ AQ97 | ♠ AQ97 | ♠ AQ97 |
| ♥ AJ2 | ♥ AJ2 | ♥ A92 | ♥ AQ2 |
| ♦ 75 | ♦ 75 | ♦ 5 | ♦ — |
| ♣ Q1072 | ♣ K1093 | ♣ AKJ104 | ♣ AKJ1042 |

With each of the following hands, there has been an opening bid of one diamond on your left and partner has made a cue bid to show both major suits with five to eleven HCP. What call do you make and why?

| 37. | 38. | 39. | 40. |
|---|---|---|---|
| ♠ KQ95 | ♠ 102 | ♠ K106 | ♠ K93 |
| ♥ QJ2 | ♥ K9 | ♥ KJ3 | ♥ KJ874 |
| ♦ 6 | ♦ J1073 | ♦ 1075 | ♦ 7 |
| ♣ K10874 | ♣ 98652 | ♣ A986 | ♣ A654 |

## Answers

1. Double. This is a classic takeout double of a one diamond opening bid.

2. Two hearts. Another classic. If ever you should make a preemptive jump overcall, this is the hand.

3. One heart. At the one level with a chunky suit and length in the suit that has been bid in front of you, this meets all requirements for a four card suit overcall.

4. Two diamonds. Playing Michaels you have a perfect description with this cue bid.

5. Double. Do not overcall one notrump. If the opening bid had been in any other suit an overcall of one notrump would have been your best description. However, when the opening bid is one diamond show your support for all of the other suits rather than suggest a contract in notrump.

6. Two notrump. This is the "unusual notrump" which shows a preempt in the two lower of the unbid suits. You show at least five-five distribution with reasonable suit quality and very little defense.

7. Double. Your hand is too good for an overcall of one spade. Bid spades at your next turn and partner will then know that you have a very good hand with a very good suit.

8. One notrump. You would have opened one notrump. You have length in diamonds and a double stopper.

9. One notrump. In balancing seat this is 10 to 14 HCP with a balanced hand.

10. Double. A classic either in direct seat or when balancing.

11. Pass. No good place to play except in clubs. Since they bid the suit first let us defend.

12. Double. Too good to bid one notrump in balance seat although you would have overcalled one notrump if a one club bid had been made on your right.

13. Two hearts. A jump in a suit in the balance seat shows an opening bid and a good six card suit.

14. Two notrump. This jump in the balance seat shows a very good balanced hand - more than an opening notrump.

15. Two clubs. This is still Michaels even though it is made in balancing position.

16. One spade. This is an opening bid, an overcall, or a balance of one spade.

17. Two spades. Facing a takeout double, invite game with more than minimum values.

18. One notrump. You show minimum response values (5+ to 9- HCP) with some length and values in diamonds.

19. Pass. You have at least four trump tricks in diamonds. This is the trump quality that you need in order to convert a takeout double for penalties. If partner doesn't lead a trump, he is void.

20. Four hearts. You have the values to be in a game and should have at least eight hearts between your two hands.

21. One spade. Do not make the error of bidding clubs. In responding to a take-out double, make major suits a priority.

22. One heart. Don't you hate this auction? Do the best you can. It's not a perfect world.

23. Three spades. Your double jump is preemptive. You show a long suit and sparse values.

24. Two diamonds. Let partner pick the suit. Why do it yourself and guess wrong? If partner is four-three in the majors you could easily pick the wrong one. Partner will select and also show a specific value range. If partner bids at the two level you will pass. If partner jumps to show extras you will raise to game.

25. Pass. You have enough to help one notrump make, but not enough to bid higher.

26. Two clubs. Enough in values to try for a game. Use **Stayman** to try for the eight card spade fit on the way.

27. Two hearts. Make your **Jacoby Transfer** as though partner had opened in notrump. Pass and let partner play the spade partial.

28. Three notrump. Your source of tricks in clubs should be plenty for partner. Even with only two small clubs when partner ducks the first round the suit should run.

29. Two spades. Partner does not have as much as a good nine HCP. With maximum values for the non-jump partner will know to bid on toward a game. You have advertised at least a good 17 HCP.

30. Pass. Yes, you like your hand and the auction, but your partner has simply raised the spades you announced with your takeout double. And that bid might have been forced holding no values at all.

31. Four spades. This is what you need to be in a game. If partner has real values an understanding of how good your hand has to be should be apparent and a move toward a slam should be made when partner's values are at all reasonable.

32. Pass. This hand should not excite you. It is a dead minimum.

33. Pass. Do not bid two spades. You have already described your hand. Do not show the extra values that you do not have.

34. Two spades. You would not have made this call if there had not been a rebid by opener. This does not invite game, but shows good values for your takeout double and willingness to compete for that reason.

35. Three spades. In or out of competition this hand is good enough to invite a game. Remember that partner might have no values and only three spades.

36. Three diamonds. If partner shows any signs of life you will consider a slam. If partner signs off by bidding only three spades you will carry on to four.

37. Three spades. With fits in both major suits you figure to have tricks even when partner has a minimum hand. With a good hand partner will put you in game.

38. Two hearts. No fit and a bad hand. Do the best you can.

39. Three diamonds. You want partner to pick the suit and show maximum or minimum values. Respect whatever decision is made.

40. Four hearts. With a ten card fit, great distribution, and a spade honor you want to be in game even when partner's values are minimum.

# CHAPTER ELEVEN

## WHEN THEY INTRUDE

## Defending against overcalls

When the opponents overcall, they often take away precious bidding space. On those occasions, you may need to change your approach to the auction. At other times the overcall will not interfere with the action that you had planned to take.

## Bidding at the one level

When the overcall allows you to bid at the one level, your response of one notrump is natural, limited, and non-forcing. The range is 5+ to 9- HCP and guarantees at least one stopper in the suit of the overcall. When partner opens one heart and RHO overcalls one spade, your bid of one notrump is no longer forcing. It is descriptive.

When you are able to bid a suit at the one level, your call is the same as if the overcall had not happened. When you have not previously passed, your new suit bid promises four or more cards and unlimited values. When the overcall has been one heart and you bid one spade, this usually promises a five card suit—with only four you would use a **negative double** (discussed later in this chapter) instead of bidding.

A call at the one level must not be classified as a "free bid". A free bid is a call made in a suit at the two level or higher after there has been an overcall. A call of two notrump is natural and invitational after the overcall. Free bids are discussed later in this chapter.

### Example 119:

| a | b | c |
|---|---|---|
| ♠ K74 | ♠ KJ6 | ♠ KJ1074 |
| ♥ QJ83 | ♥ 84 | ♥ 62 |
| ♦ 8642 | ♦ Q1072 | ♦ Q83 |
| ♣ 105 | ♣ J984 | ♣ 1074 |

| d | e |
|---|---|
| ♠ KJ83 | ♠ KJ104 |
| ♥ A7 | ♥ 62 |
| ♦ 842 | ♦ Q83 |
| ♣ 9643 | ♣ 10742 |

With Example 119a, your partner has opened one club and there has been an overcall of one heart. Bid one notrump to show a minimum response with stoppers in hearts.

With Example 119b, your partner has opened one heart and there has been an overcall of one spade. Bid one notrump to show a minimum response without a heart fit and with stoppers in spades.

With Example 119c, your partner has opened one club and there has been an overcall of one heart. Your response of one spade is forcing and shows five or more spades. If the overcall had been one diamond, you would have shown four or more spades. When the overcall is one heart, with only four spades you would have made a negative double rather than bid one spade.

With Example 119d, your partner has opened one club and there has been an overcall of one diamond. Your bid of one spade shows at least four cards and is forcing.

With Example 119e, your partner has opened one diamond and there has been an overcall of one heart. Rather than bid one spade, which would show a five card suit, you make a negative double.

## Raising partner

A raise of partner's opening bid should be made whenever possible—particularly if that bid was in a major suit. Although a single raise normally shows 5+ to 9- HCP, you should stretch to show your fit in competition. Partner may be unable to compete with a good hand unless you let it be known that you have a fit and some values. Knowledge of the fit is extremely important. With good shape and a working four HCP, do not remain silent just because you have less than a normal raise.

To show a limit raise or more for partner's suit, make a cue bid. The overcall has given you a new weapon that was not there before. A jump raise of partner's suit can now be preemptive rather than invitational (limit).

**Example 120:**

|   | a | b | c |
|---|---|---|---|
|   | **a** | **b** | **c** |
| ♠ | A85 | Q93 | 8 |
| ♥ | 84 | 1075 | Q974 |
| ♦ | Q32 | 83 | J763 |
| ♣ | KQ1074 | Q10982 | 10942 |

|   | d | e |
|---|---|---|
|   | **d** | **e** |
| ♠ | 85 | 8 |
| ♥ | K63 | K63 |
| ♦ | QJ95 | QJ953 |
| ♣ | 9863 | 9864 |

With Example 120a, partner has opened one club and there has been an overcall of one heart. Bid two hearts to show a good raise for clubs.

With Example 120b, partner has opened one spade and there has been an overcall of two diamonds. Although you would have passed if there had been no overcall, in competition you should stretch to raise. Bid two spades.

With Example 120c, partner has opened one heart and there has been an overcall of one spade. Make a preemptive jump raise of three hearts. You do not expect that partner will make three hearts, but you must create an obstacle for the opponents and make them guess what to do. Maybe they will encounter enough trouble because of your preempt to get to the wrong place. You expect a minus score, so don't worry about being too high.

With Example 120d, partner has opened one diamond and there has been an overcall of one spade. Make a simple raise to two diamonds.

With Example 120e, partner has opened one diamond and there has been an overcall of one spade. Make a preemptive raise by jumping to three diamonds.

## Free bids

Bids at the one level or raises of partner after an overcall are not classified as free bids. Bidding a new suit at the two level or higher after the overcall qualifies as a free bid. The free bid requires certain minimums. You are expected to have at least five cards in your suit. At the two level, a free bid shows at least game invitational values (9+ HCP or more). At the three level or higher, a free bid shows opening bid values and is forcing to game.

A free bid at the two level guarantees another call at your next turn. When you plan and make your free bid, you must also plan your next probable action. Sometimes your planned continuation will need to be changed when the auction takes an unexpected turn. Do what seems to be most descriptive at that time.

**Example 121:**

|  | **a** | **b** | **c** |
|---|---|---|---|
| ♠ | 85 | 108 | 7 |
| ♥ | A92 | A95 | KQJ105 |
| ♦ | AQJ92 | Q73 | K72 |
| ♣ | 1073 | AK1095 | A964 |

**With Example 121a, partner has opened one club and there has been an overcall of one spade. Your hand is good enough for a free bid of two diamonds. You have a suit of at least five cards and game invitational values. If the overcall had been two spades, your choice would not be so easy. A free bid of three diamonds would be forcing to game. Since your suit is excellent and you would have opened the bidding, you should probably bid freely even in that auction, but it is not clear.**

**With Example 121b, partner has opened one diamond and there has been an overcall in spades. Your free bid of clubs is fine whether it must be at the two or three level.**

**With Example 121c, partner has opened one diamond. After an overcall of two or three spades, you have a clear free bid in hearts.**

## Action doubles

When responder has bid and there has been an overcall, opener will often have no reason to bid. Opener will not have a fit for responder, a suit that should be rebid, or a two suited hand that calls for a rebid in the second suit.

After opener passes and if advancer also passes, responder may have a problem. When responder's values are at least enough to invite a game (9+ HCP or more), it will be clear that pass is not a logical alternative. The opening bidder's side will have most of the high card strength. Responder may not have a clear-cut call, but will know that pass cannot be right.

Responder should double to express that the hand belongs to the opening side, but that responder has no idea of the correct action. Opener should understand that this double is not for penalties, but is made to keep the auction alive. Responder asks opener to make an intelligent decision.

This double is an intelligent bridge action. Experienced players understand that the double is not for penalties. However, inexperienced players may have no such understanding. An alert is technically required for this double for that reason.

**Example 122:**

| a | b | c |
|---|---|---|
| ♠ AJ75 | ♠ AJ75 | ♠ AJ75 |
| ♥ 964 | ♥ 1096 | ♥ K83 |
| ♦ 853 | ♦ KJ83 | ♦ 1062 |
| ♣ J72 | ♣ J7 | ♣ K95 |

**With Example 122a, partner has opened one club and you have responded one spade. After an overcall of two diamonds, there have been two passes. With no extra values, your choice should be pass.**

**With Example 122b, partner has opened one club and you have responded one spade. After an overcall of two diamonds, there have been two passes. Your choice is between double and two notrump. Double will not be for penalties, and partner is unlikely to leave it in. Two notrump is the likely choice.**

**With Example 122c, partner has opened one club and you have responded one spade. After an overcall of two diamonds, there have been two passes. Your values indicate that the hand belongs to your side, but there is no clear action indicated by your hand. This is the hand for an action double.**

## Negative doubles

The **negative double** has become a standard bidding tool. When you double after an overcall, your double is not for penalty—it is a specific takeout call. It says that you would like to have made a free bid but could not because you lacked either the strength or the suit length, which would have been promised by the free bid. It also promises length in unbid major suits.

Doubling an overcall in hearts promises four or more spades. When the overcall has been made in spades, it promises four or more hearts. After a one diamond overcall, the **negative double** shows exactly four-four in the major suits. With four in one major and five or more in the other, bid your longer suit. Unfortunately, the overcall of two clubs after an opening bid of one diamond makes life complicated.

Holding four cards in one major and three in the other, the **negative double** is probably your best description, even though it is not ideal. If you hold six or more spades but lack the values to make a free bid, you can use the **negative double**. At your rebid, you can correct from hearts to spades without increasing the level at which partner has bid. Remember, partner believes you have both majors and may bid a lot in hearts.

When both majors have been bid, the **negative double** shows both minor suits. Again, with long diamonds you can use this call and correct from clubs to diamonds without increasing the level.

**Example 123:**

| a | b | c |
|---|---|---|
| ♠ K4 | ♠ 84 | ♠ QJ873 |
| ♥ AQJ6 | ♥ KQ975 | ♥ AJ102 |
| ♦ KJ82 | ♦ QJ72 | ♦ 8 |
| ♣ 954 | ♣ 106 | ♣ 642 |

| d | e | f |
|---|---|---|
| ♠ AQ4 | ♠ AQ64 | ♠ KQ93 |
| ♥ J1074 | ♥ J1073 | ♥ 854 |
| ♦ 62 | ♦ 62 | ♦ 10862 |
| ♣ 8754 | ♣ 854 | ♣ Q4 |

| g | h | i |
|---|---|---|
| ♠ KJ86 | ♠ KQ10874 | ♠ 62 |
| ♥ AJ9 | ♥ Q3 | ♥ 4 |
| ♦ 64 | ♦ J82 | ♦ AJ954 |
| ♣ 10742 | ♣ 65 | ♣ Q10862 |

| j | k |
|---|---|
| ♠ 62 | ♠ Q10983 |
| ♥ 43 | ♥ K7 |
| ♦ AJ9754 | ♦ A62 |
| ♣ Q106 | ♣ 854 |

With Example 123a, partner has opened one club and there has been an overcall of one spade. Although you hold fourteen HCP, you cannot make a free bid for lack of a five card suit. You do have four hearts, which allows you to make a negative double.

With Example 123b, partner has opened one club and there has been an overcall of one spade. This time you have a five card suit, but cannot make a free bid since you are short in values. Make a negative double to show that you have at least four hearts. You may get a later chance to bid hearts to show at least five, in which case partner will know that you did not have values enough for a free bid.

With Example 123c, partner has opened one club and there has been an overcall of one diamond. Do not make a negative double. Bid one spade. A negative double would show exactly four cards in each major suit. When you are five-four in the majors in this auction, you must bid your five card suit.

With Example 123d, partner has opened one club and there has been an overcall of one diamond. Do not make the error of making a negative double. That would promise four cards in both major suits. Respond one heart.

With Example 123e, partner has opened one club and there has been an overcall of one diamond. Your negative double promises four cards in each major suit. If the opening bid had been one diamond and the overcall two clubs, you would be happy to make a negative double since you have four cards in each major.

With Example 123f, partner has opened one club and there has been an overcall of one heart. A bid of one spade would promise a five card suit, so you make a negative double to show a response with exactly four spades.

With Example 123g, partner has opened one diamond and there has been an overcall of two clubs. Your most descriptive call is a negative double, even though you have only four-three in the majors.

With Example 123h, partner has opened one diamond and there has been an overcall of two clubs. You cannot make a free bid despite your good suit, but you can make a negative double to encourage partner to compete. If partner bids hearts (which is likely), you will correct to spades without increasing the level at which the contract will be played.

**With Example 123i, partner has opened one heart and there has been an overcall of one spade. You can describe perfectly by making a** negative double, **which shows both minor suits.**

**With Example 123j, partner has opened one heart and there has been an overcall of one spade. When you make a** negative double, **partner will believe that you have both minors. When he bids clubs (likely), you can correct to diamonds without increasing the level.**

**With Example 123k, partner has opened one diamond and there has been an overcall of one heart. Your response of one spade is forcing and shows a five card or longer suit.**

Opener's rebids when responder has made a negative double should be understood. When opener bids a new suit and the auction appears to be a **reverse**, it is not. Opener is merely bidding another suit in which he holds length. What might appear to be a jump shift is also different. Opener is required to show the extent of the values held at this rebid, and will jump with good hands, but this is not a game forcing jump shift rebid.

Holding length and strength in the suit of the overcall, responder will often wish to penalize the overcaller. Since you have adopted the **negative double**, an immediate penalty double is not possible. You must pass the overcall without pause and hope that partner will reopen with a double if the advancer passes.

After an overcall and two passes, the opening bidder must consider that the responder wanted to double for penalties but could not. Ask yourself this question: "If partner could have doubled for penalties and had done so, would I have left that double in or would I have bid on?" Looking at any hand that would have left a penalty double in, opener should reopen with double so that partner can pass and convert it to penalties.

With a hand that is completely offensive, opener would not have allowed a penalty double to stay in, and with such a hand will not reopen with double. Opener's rebid shows the completely offensive nature of the hand.

**Example 124:**

| a | b | c |
|---|---|---|
| ♠ K96 | ♠ 8 | ♠ K92 |
| ♥ 5 | ♥ AKQ10975 | ♥ QJ74 |
| ♦ Q962 | ♦ AQJ3 | ♦ Q6 |
| ♣ AKJ83 | ♣ 6 | ♣ AJ85 |

226

With Example 124a, you have opened one club and there has been an overcall of one heart. After two passes, it is your turn again. Your shortness in hearts and the absence of a heart raise by advancer indicates that partner probably wanted to double the overcall for penalties. You would have honored a penalty double if partner had made one, so you should double to enable partner to convert to penalty.

Example 124b has opened one heart and there has been an overcall of one spade. After two passes, you must make a decision. With a hand that is all offense, you would not have sat for a penalty double if partner could have made one. Bid what your hand indicates. Jump to four hearts.

Example 124c has opened one club and there has been an overcall of one heart. After two passes, you again have a decision. Your heart holding indicates that partner probably did not want to double for penalties. It is likely that the overcaller has a very good hand since neither your partner nor the advancer took action. Further action would probably not be good for your side. Pass.

## Defending against overcalls in notrump

Following an overcall of one notrump, showing a good balanced hand, double by responder is not a **negative double**. It is a true penalty double. A double of the notrump overcall assumes that opener and responder have the values to beat the overcall at least two tricks. When responder's values are game invitational or more (9+ HCP), this will usually be the best choice.

Should responder have an excellent offensive hand and want to pursue a game despite the overcall of one notrump, the only forcing call available is a cue bid of two notrump. This cannot reasonably show the desire to play a contract of two notrump. Taking eight tricks for a score of 120 cannot be as good as the penalty for taking eight tricks on defense, which would be 300 or 500. When responder makes this cue bid, opener must bid on to describe further.

### Example 125:

|  | a | b | c |
|---|---|---|---|
| ♠ | 7 | KJ7 | KJ9753 |
| ♥ | KQ9754 | A1084 | A108642 |
| ♦ | J63 | Q1093 | — |
| ♣ | 842 | 106 | 7 |

**With Example 125a, partner has opened one club and RHO has overcalled one notrump. Your bid of two hearts is competitive and not forcing.**

**With Example 125b, partner has opened one club and RHO has overcalled one notrump. Double for penalties.**

**With Example 125c, partner has opened one club and RHO has overcalled one notrump. Your distribution indicates that game in one of the major suits is likely. Cue bid two notrump. Then, when you bid spades your bid will be forcing. You will also have a chance to bid hearts.**

## Defending against the unusual notrump

Most often, the **unusual notrump** will be a jump to the two level after the opening bid. Since the intruder has shown two specific suits, responder has available two cue bids in those suits. In most auctions, the opener will have bid a major suit and the **unusual notrump** overcall would show both minors. The standard defensive bidding structure is known as **unusual versus unusual**.

The two minor suit cue bids are used to show at least game invitational values (9+ HCP), and focus on one of the two major suits—either the suit of the opening bid or the other major. After an opening bid in spades, a cue bid of three diamonds shows a limit raise (or more) for spades. A cue bid of three clubs shows at least five hearts with game invitational values (9+ HCP) or more. After an opening bid in hearts, a cue bid of three clubs shows a limit raise (or more) for hearts. A cue bid of three diamonds shows at least five spades with game invitational values (9+ HCP) or more. A CUE BID OF THEIR HIGHER SUIT SUPPORTS OR SHOWS OUR HIGHER SUIT—A CUE BID OF THEIR LOWER SUIT SUPPORTS OR SHOWS OUR LOWER SUIT.

When responder has less than game invitational values with either a fit for opener's major or a good holding in the unbid major, that is expressed and values are denied by a direct call at the three level. A raise of opener's major suit shows a single raise (5+ to 9- HCP) with three card or longer support. A call in the other major shows a good six card suit as it denies game invitational values (9+ HCP) or more.

Double of the **unusual notrump** call by responder indicates the desire to defend against at least one of the suits. It encourages opener to double if the advancer selects a suit and opener has defensive values at that contract.

Example 126:

|  a | b | c |
|---|---|---|
| ♠ Q83 | ♠ KJ93 | ♠ A9 |
| ♥ KJ94 | ♥ AJ65 | ♥ AQJ85 |
| ♦ 842 | ♦ 6 | ♦ 932 |
| ♣ 653 | ♣ 8542 | ♣ 1074 |

|  d | e |
|---|---|
| ♠ 84 | ♠ 96 |
| ♥ KQJ973 | ♥ 10874 |
| ♦ 63 | ♦ AQJ8 |
| ♣ 854 | ♣ K5 |

With Example 126a, partner has opened in a major suit and RHO has overcalled two notrump. Bid three of partner's major. You show a single raise under pressure.

With Example 126b, partner has opened in a major suit and RHO has overcalled two notrump. Make a cue bid to show a good raise for partner. If partner has bid spades, cue bid three diamonds. If partner has bid hearts, cue bid three clubs.

With Example 126c, partner has opened one spade and RHO has overcalled two notrump. Cue bid three clubs to show a good hand with a heart suit.

With Example 126d, partner has opened one spade and RHO has overcalled two notrump. Bid three hearts to show a good suit with less than game invitational values.

With Example 126e, partner has opened one spade and RHO has overcalled two notrump. Double to show good defense against at least one of the suits shown by the overcall.

## Defending against takeout doubles

When the intrusion is a takeout double, a response of one notrump shows a minimum response hand (5+ to 9- HCP) that is reasonably balanced. It denies a fit if the opening bid has been in a major suit and is definitely non-forcing.

As with overcalls, showing a fit for the opening bid has strong priority, particularly when it is in a major suit. Responder should stretch to show a fit with minimal values.

When responder has a limit raise or more for opener's suit, after the takeout double, a jump response of two notrump shows that fact. A jump raise becomes preemptive.

**Example 127:**

|  | a | b | c |
|---|---|---|---|
| ♠ | A6 | KJ6 | 7 |
| ♥ | K93 | 74 | QJ85 |
| ♦ | 10754 | Q1082 | J962 |
| ♣ | 8653 | J963 | 8765 |

|  | d | e |
|---|---|---|
| ♠ | A4 | 108 |
| ♥ | KQ7 | Q109 |
| ♦ | 10762 | Q862 |
| ♣ | J854 | 10953 |

**With Example 127a, partner has opened one heart and RHO has made a takeout double. Raise to two hearts as you would have without the interference.**

**With Example 127b, partner has opened one heart and RHO has made a takeout double. Bid one notrump to show no fit and scattered minimum response values.**

**With Example 127c, partner has opened one heart and RHO has made a takeout double. Jump to three hearts preemptively.**

**With Example 127d, partner has opened one heart and RHO has made a takeout double. Jump to two notrump to show a limit raise.**

**With Example 127e, partner has opened one heart and RHO has made a takeout double. You would have passed without interference, but you should stretch and raise to two hearts after the double (or if there had been an overcall).**

New suit responses at the one level are natural and forcing. In essence, they ignore the takeout double. However, a new suit at the two level after the takeout double is non-forcing. It is a correction by responder who will have very limited values, no fit for opener's suit, and at least five cards in the suit of the response.

**Example 128:**

| a | b | c |
|---|---|---|
| ♠ 7 | ♠ Q9874 | ♠ 8542 |
| ♥ Q84 | ♥ K4 | ♥ Q963 |
| ♦ KQ1095 | ♦ AJ963 | ♦ K3 |
| ♣ 9863 | ♣ 5 | ♣ J94 |

**With Example 128a, partner has opened one spade and RHO has made a takeout double. Your response of two diamonds shows a suit of at least five cards, shortness in spades, and is non-forcing.**

**With Example 128b, partner has opened one club and RHO has made a takeout double. Do not make the error of redoubling just because you have ten points. If you do and LHO preempts in hearts, you may never get to mention both of your suits. Your response of one spade is natural and forcing.**

**With Example 128c, partner has opened one club and RHO has made a takeout double. Ignore the double and make your natural (forcing) response of one heart.**

## Redoubles

At one time, the standard was that when responder held game invitational values (9+ HCP or more), redouble was the only permitted call. Responder's failure to redouble denied having those values.

The jump to two notrump to show those values and a fit for opener was the first deviation that was accepted. It is clear that, when a fit exists, it is a good idea to keep the opponents out of the auction.

In *Judgment at Bridge*, which was published in 1976, Mike Lawrence first postulated that with certain good hands it was a better idea to bid a suit naturally at the one level, rather than woodenly redouble to show strength. Particularly when responder has two suits, redouble might be followed by a preemptive call from the advancer and responder would have not yet expressed either of the two suits. Facing the danger of preemptive action makes the showing of a suit a better idea than simply redoubling to show strength.

Essentially, the redouble is used for one of two reasons today.

1. Responder is unable to bid naturally in a suit because that call would be non-forcing. A new suit at the two level might be passed since that call denies values. Responder first redoubles to show values, and the suit is introduced on the next round of bidding.
2. Responder is short in opener's suit and has length and strength in all of the unbid suits. The redouble warns opener not to get in the way since responder expects to reap a juicy penalty wherever the opponents settle.

When responder has redoubled and later doubles an opposing contract, the double is clearly for penalties.

**Example 129:**

| a | b |
|---|---|
| ♠ 84 | ♠ 6 |
| ♥ A6 | ♥ KJ94 |
| ♦ AQ1085 | ♦ A1085 |
| ♣ J963 | ♣ QJ93 |

**With Example 129a, partner has opened one spade and RHO has made a takeout double. Since a response of two diamonds would not be forcing, you should start with redouble. At your next turn, you will show your diamond suit and partner will know that you have at least game invitational values in addition to your suit.**

**With Example 129b, partner has opened one spade and RHO has made a takeout double. You are ready to punish any opposing contract. Your redouble warns partner to let you have your say at your next turn.**

## Defending against Michaels cue bids

As with the **unusual notrump**, a cue bid shows two suits. Usually, both suits are known. When the opening bid is in a minor suit, it shows both majors. Responder has two specific cue bids to be used for the best purposes.

It makes little sense to use major suit cue bids to seek minor suit fits. When the enemy has the majors but our side has strength, our first goal will be a contract in notrump. For such a contract to succeed, we will need stoppers in the major suits that are held by the opposition.

When the opponents have cue bid in opener's minor suit to show both majors, responder has these available auctions:

1. A raise of opener's minor suit is competitive. It shows a good fit (five cards or more) and denies good values.
2. A response in the unbid minor suit is natural and non-forcing. It shows at least five cards of reasonable texture.
3. A bid in notrump shows stoppers in both major suits. With game invitational values (9+ to 12- HCP), responder bids two notrump. With greater values, responder bids three notrump.
4. A cue bid of a major suit promises a stopper in that suit with at least game invitational values, and denies a stopper in the other major.

When the opening bid has been in a major suit and the minor suit is not known, only one cue bid is available. Responder will bid notrump with a stopper in that known suit at the level of the values held. With game invitational values or more, responder will cue bid to ask opener for a stopper in the known suit.

In competitive auctions in which our side is trying to get to a notrump contract, these rules govern the auction:

1. When one suit has been shown, a bid in notrump promises a stopper in that suit. With values but no stopper, a cue bid asks for a stopper.
2. When two suits have been bid or shown, a bid in notrump promises stoppers in both of those suits. A cue bid shows a stopper— it does not ask for one.

**Example 130:**

| a | b | c |
|---|---|---|
| ♠ KJ5 | ♠ KJ5 | ♠ 975 |
| ♥ AQ4 | ♥ AQ4 | ♥ AQ4 |
| ♦ 97632 | ♦ K9762 | ♦ KQ763 |
| ♣ J5 | ♣ J5 | ♣ J5 |

| d | e | f |
|---|---|---|
| ♠ AQ4 | ♠ AJ6 | ♠ 974 |
| ♥ 975 | ♥ 74 | ♥ 8 |
| ♦ KQ763 | ♦ K1073 | ♦ AKJ954 |
| ♣ A5 | ♣ QJ84 | ♣ K76 |

With Example 130a, partner has opened one club and RHO has cue bid to show both majors. Bid two notrump to show game invitational values and stoppers in both majors.

With Example 130b, partner has opened one club and RHO has cue bid to show both majors. Bid three notrump to show game going values and stoppers in both majors.

With Example 130c, partner has opened one club and RHO has cue bid to show both majors. Bid two hearts to show at least game invitational values and a stopper in hearts, which also denies a spade stopper.

With Example 130d, partner has opened one club and RHO has cue bid to show both majors. Bid two spades to show at least game invitational values with a stopper in spades, and to deny a heart stopper.

With Example 130e, partner has opened one heart and RHO has cue bid to show spades and an unknown minor. Your bid of two notrump promises game invitational values, and that you have a spade stopper. You also happen to have a stopper in the intruder's other suit, no matter which minor it might be.

With Example 130f, partner has opened one heart and RHO has cue bid to show spades and an unknown minor. Bid two spades—the known suit of the opponents—to ask for a stopper.

## Exercises on combating intrusion

With each of these hands, partner has opened one club and there has been an overcall of one heart. What action do you take and why?

| | 1. | 2. | 3. | 4. |
|---|---|---|---|---|
| ♠ | AJ753 | KJ3 | A2 | KJ103 |
| ♥ | 64 | Q1053 | 64 | 84 |
| ♦ | Q1082 | J964 | AKJ953 | AQ92 |
| ♣ | 94 | 85 | 874 | 1073 |

| | 5. | 6. | 7. | 8. |
|---|---|---|---|---|
| ♠ | KJ3 | 842 | K74 | Q6 |
| ♥ | Q1053 | AQ974 | 8 | 85 |
| ♦ | KJ96 | K103 | A632 | KQ8753 |
| ♣ | J4 | 85 | KQ974 | 1073 |

With each of these hands, partner has opened one diamond and RHO has made a jump overcall of two spades. What action do you take and why?

| 9. | 10. | 11. | 12. |
|---|---|---|---|
| ♠ 84 | ♠ 74 | ♠ 84 | ♠ KJ5 |
| ♥ AQ1085 | ♥ Q102 | ♥ AQ10853 | ♥ Q82 |
| ♦ K7 | ♦ 83 | ♦ 74 | ♦ J9 |
| ♣ K1094 | ♣ AQ10853 | ♣ Q102 | ♣ KJ1084 |

| 13. | 14. | 15. | 16. |
|---|---|---|---|
| ♠ KQ1085 | ♠ 84 | ♠ 9 | ♠ AQ9 |
| ♥ 65 | ♥ AQ105 | ♥ A85 | ♥ 85 |
| ♦ A82 | ♦ A62 | ♦ Q63 | ♦ Q83 |
| ♣ 1083 | ♣ KJ84 | ♣ AQ10974 | ♣ AQ1074 |

With each of these hands, partner has opened one club and RHO has overcalled one notrump. What action do you take and why?

| 17. | 18. | 19. | 20. |
|---|---|---|---|
| ♠ K7 | ♠ 843 | ♠ 843 | ♠ KQ9542 |
| ♥ KJ84 | ♥ KQ10863 | ♥ KJ862 | ♥ AJ10632 |
| ♦ QJ1095 | ♦ J84 | ♦ J84 | ♦ 7 |
| ♣ 102 | ♣ 2 | ♣ 102 | ♣ — |

With each of these hands, partner has opened one club and RHO has made a takeout double. What action do you take and why?

| 21. | 22. | 23. | 24. |
|---|---|---|---|
| ♠ K7 | ♠ KJ9 | ♠ KJ103 | ♠ 874 |
| ♥ QJ84 | ♥ QJ6 | ♥ QJ104 | ♥ 3 |
| ♦ 10973 | ♦ 10952 | ♦ KQ92 | ♦ Q95 |
| ♣ 862 | ♣ 854 | ♣ 6 | ♣ KJ9864 |

| 25. | 26. |
|---|---|
| ♠ 1093 | ♠ 7 |
| ♥ A82 | ♥ KJ862 |
| ♦ J8 | ♦ AQ753 |
| ♣ AQ1084 | ♣ J6 |

With each of these hands, partner has opened one spade and RHO has made a take-out double. What action do you take and why?

| 27. | 28. | 29. | 30. |
|---|---|---|---|
| ♠ Q84 | ♠ 8 | ♠ 82 | ♠ 6 |
| ♥ 63 | ♥ J92 | ♥ Q952 | ♥ K3 |
| ♦ 10942 | ♦ 1074 | ♦ KJ4 | ♦ 10874 |
| ♣ Q1083 | ♣ QJ9743 | ♣ J1073 | ♣ AQJ963 |

| 31. | 32. |
|---|---|
| ♠ KJ3 | ♠ QJ83 |
| ♥ 95 | ♥ 6 |
| ♦ AQ62 | ♦ J976 |
| ♣ J953 | ♣ 10543 |

With each of these hands, partner has opened one diamond and RHO has cue bid to show both majors. What action do you take and why?

| 33. | 34. | 35. | 36. |
|---|---|---|---|
| ♠ 104 | ♠ AJ4 | ♠ 854 | ♠ AQ3 |
| ♥ KQ8 | ♥ K102 | ♥ 63 | ♥ KQ4 |
| ♦ 975 | ♦ 1098 | ♦ Q6 | ♦ 85 |
| ♣ AJ863 | ♣ Q963 | ♣ KQ10974 | ♣ K10942 |

With each of these hands, partner has opened one heart and RHO has cue bid to show spades and an undefined minor. What action do you take and why?

| 37. | 38. | 39. | 40. |
|---|---|---|---|
| ♠ 82 | ♠ AJ10 | ♠ AJ7 | ♠ AJ95 |
| ♥ 74 | ♥ 7 | ♥ 74 | ♥ 63 |
| ♦ Q84 | ♦ K104 | ♦ K104 | ♦ KQ7 |
| ♣ AKQJ96 | ♣ KQJ954 | ♣ QJ974 | ♣ J642 |

# Answers

1. One spade. You show that you have response values and a five card suit.

2. One notrump. Minimum response values and a heart stopper.

3. Two diamonds. Your free bid shows at least game invitational values and at least a five card suit.

4. Double. You show at least the values of a response and promise exactly four spades.

5. Two notrump. You show game invitational values and at least one stopper in hearts.

6. Pass in tempo. You cannot make a penalty double, so you wait for partner to reopen with double. You will pass and convert that double to penalties.

7. Two hearts. You show at least a limit raise for clubs.

8. Pass. You do not have the values for a free bid and cannot make a **negative double** without hearts. If partner reopens with a double, you will be able to show your diamond suit.

9. Three hearts. You have the values and suit length to make a game forcing free bid at the three level.

10. Pass. See problem eight. You do not have the values for a free bid despite your fine suit, and do not have enough hearts to make a **negative double**.

11. Double. You have the suit length for a free bid in hearts but do not have the values to bid at the three level. Given the chance, you will bid three hearts at your next turn.

12. Two notrump. You show spade stoppers and game invitational values.

13. Pass. You cannot make a penalty double but, if partner reopens with a double, you will pass and convert it to penalties.

14. Double. You have plenty of values but no suit long enough for a free bid. You show at least game invitational values and four or more hearts.

15. Three clubs. You have the values and suit length for a game forcing free bid.

16. Three notrump. Spade stoppers and enough values for game.

17. Double. This is for penalties. Lead the diamond queen.

18. Two hearts. After the notrump overcall, your suit bid is not forcing. You just want to play a heart partial.

19. Pass. It would be pushy to bid two hearts, even though that would be non-forcing.

20. Two notrump. This is your only forcing call since a new suit would not force. You will bid three forcing spades next, and then show hearts.

21. One heart. Natural and forcing. Ignore the double. Bid hearts, not diamonds.

22. One notrump. Minimum scattered response values.

23. Redouble. You are ready to double any contract.

24. Three clubs. Strictly preemptive.

25. Two notrump. You show a limit raise.

26. One heart. Natural and forcing. Do not redouble just because you have ten points. You must start to show your suits.

27. Two spades. Stretch to raise in competition.

28. Two clubs. Natural and non-forcing—also showing spade shortness.

29. One notrump. Show your minimum response values and scattered cards.

30. Redouble. If you bid clubs now, you show a weak hand. Bidding clubs at your next turn will show this hand.

31. Two notrump. You show a limit raise or better.

32. Three spades. Strictly preemptive and very standard.

33. Two hearts. Heart stopper and no spade stopper with at least game invitational values.

34. Two notrump. Stoppers in both majors and game invitational values.

35. Three clubs. Natural and non-forcing.

36. Three notrump. Both majors stopped and values enough for game.

37. Two spades. Three clubs would not be forcing, but a cue bid of the known suit is. Partner will not know whether you have a heart raise or need a stopper in spades, but will make a descriptive bid.

38. Three notrump. Double spade stopper and a stopper in the presumed other suit, as well as a source of tricks.

39. Two notrump. Similar to the previous example but not as good.

40. Double. You show a good hand that wants a shot at the opposing contract.

# CHAPTER TWELVE

## SLAM BIDDING

By this time, an important concept should be understood. THE BEST SLAM TRY AUCTIONS TAKE PLACE BELOW THE LEVEL OF GAME. Good hands preserve bidding space in which information can be exchanged. When one partner suggests a slam at the three level, the other can either accept or reject the idea.

When fits have been discovered that will produce the needed tricks, controls can be sought. When both fits and controls are present, slams can often be bid and fulfilled on about half of the high card strength in the deck.

Here are a few of the auctions we have observed in which slam tries can be made.

### 1. Fits can be found by auctions that appear to be game tries.

What appears to be a game try can be a slam try in disguise. After the single raise of a major suit, opener can make what appears to be a try for game. If responder accepts the try, good fits will be known and opener can then make a further move toward slam. If the game try is rejected, opener knows that the hands do not fit well, and will settle for game.

### Example 131:

| a | b | c |
|---|---|---|
| ♠ AKJ863 | ♠ Q92 | ♠ Q92 |
| ♥ 5 | ♥ KJ84 | ♥ 1093 |
| ♦ A9 | ♦ Q76 | ♦ KJ84 |
| ♣ AK54 | ♣ 1093 | ♣ Q76 |

Opener with Example 131a bids one spade and is raised to two. Four spades appears to be virtually iron-clad and many will jump to that game. A sensitive bidder may feel that slam is possible if responder has the right values. A game try of three clubs may smoke out the fitting values that could produce twelve tricks.

Responder with Example 131b has no help in clubs and rejects the game try by bidding three spades. Knowing that the hands do not fit well, opener 131a signs off at four spades. These hands fit so poorly that even four spades is no cinch.

Responder with Example 131c has a club card, which should be of help. At worst, this hand would accept the club game try and bid four spades. At best, this responder will make a counter-offer by bidding three diamonds. Knowing that responder has useful values in clubs and diamonds, opener can jump to six spades. He does not need to seek controls since he holds controls in all suits. Although it is not iron-clad, this slam is an exceptionally good bet. Note that both 131b and 131c are the same hand with suits interchanged. The tricks that are generated come from the fits that exist, not from a number of high card points.

> **2. When a fit has been found and** fast arrival **has not been used, slam has been suggested.**

If either partner could have used **fast arrival**, but instead has shown good values and a fit while keeping the auction at a low level, that partner has shown interest in a slam. The other partner can reject the slam suggestion by bidding game in the agreed suit, or can show interest in the suggested slam by showing some value in another suit.

> **Example 132:**

|  | a | b |
|---|---|---|
| ♠ | AQ1083 | KJ6 |
| ♥ | AJ4 | 852 |
| ♦ | 954 | A7 |
| ♣ | Q6 | AKJ103 |

Example 132a opens one spade and gets a response of two clubs. With no other descriptive rebid, opener bids two spades. When responder next bids three spades, opener knows that a slam has been invited, since responder did not jump to four spades, which would have been fast arrival. Having shown minimum values of 12+ to 15- HCP, opener now evaluates and likes his good trumps, his fitting club honor, and his control in hearts. He shows his heart control with a cue bid of four hearts.

Example 132b hears an opening one spade bid and responds two clubs. After opener rebids two spades, this responder shows his extra values by raising to three spades. Since a jump to four spades would be fast arrival, **this simple raise shows the spade fit and interest in a slam. (If opener had rebid either two hearts or two diamonds, this hand would have shown its spade fit and extra values by jumping to three spades.) After responder's rebid of three spades, opener's cue bid of four hearts spurs responder to seek a slam.** Blackwood **will find two aces with opener, which confirms enough controls to cause slam to be bid. Twelve tricks are easy on the combined holding of 29 HCP.**

### 3. Fourth suit forcing auctions may suggest slam.

Slam tries below the game level can be made in auctions where **fourth suit forcing** has been used. Responder first makes the auction forcing to game, but does not rush to bid game. When opener notes a slam invitation, he can accept it by making a cue bid or reject it by just bidding game in the agreed suit.

### Example 133:

| a | b |
|---|---|
| ♠ QJ74 | ♠ AK95 |
| ♥ 106 | ♥ AQJ93 |
| ♦ A54 | ♦ 72 |
| ♣ AQ83 | ♣ K4 |

**Example 133a opens one club and after a response of one heart rebids one spade. Responder next bids two diamonds,** fourth suit forcing. **Opener's next call is two notrump, which denies three hearts, shows minimum values of 12 or a bad 13 HCP, and confirms a diamond stopper. When responder next bids three spades, opener recognizes that a four card fit has been shown and that the auction invites a slam. Responder might have used** fast arrival **by jumping to four spades instead of using** fourth suit forcing, **which would have shown the spade fit and values enough for game but no interest in a slam. The actual auction shows responder's slam interest. Since opener has limited his values, he shows his control with a cue bid in clubs. Responder shows more than opening bid values, since he did not bid four spades over one spade instead of using** fourth suit forcing.

**Example 133b bids one heart after an opening bid of one club. When partner rebids one spade, responder does not jump to game in spades (fast arrival), but uses** fourth suit forcing **by bidding two diamonds. After opener's rebid of two notrump, responder shows his four card spade fit and slam interest by bidding three spades. Opener's cue bid of four clubs brings a heart cue bid from responder. Opener tries one more time with five diamonds and responder jumps**

to six spades. Another excellent slam is reached on a combined holding of only 29 HCP.

**4. Responder may suggest slam after using** New Minor Forcing.

Another auction which may provide for a low level slam try is one in which **New Minor Forcing** is used. Even though opener may rebid one notrump to show a balanced minimum opening bid, responder may know that slam is possible. **New Minor Forcing** is used to issue that slam invitation.

**Example 134:**

| a | b |
|---|---|
| ♠ A95 | ♠ 7 |
| ♥ 93 | ♥ AK85 |
| ♦ A864 | ♦ 96 |
| ♣ A1096 | ♣ KQJ754 |

**Example 134a has a choice of opening bids. Planning a rebid of one notrump, the opening bid of either minor suit is acceptable. Some expert opinions insist that one diamond is mandatory—other expert opinions are just as strongly in favor of an opening bid of one club. This opening bidder chose to bid one club, which was a distinct help to the responder. After a response of one heart, opener rebid one notrump to show 12 to 14 HCP and a balanced hand. Having a hand with no tenaces this opener was not eager to become declarer at notrump, but needed to describe the size and shape of the opening hand. Responder continued by bidding two diamonds**—new minor forcing. **Opener next bid two notrump to show a hand with minimum values (12 or a bad 13 HCP), exactly two hearts and a stopper in spades. Responder's next call was a natural slam try of three clubs. Having shown limited values, opener was happy to agree to the try for slam by cue bidding three diamonds.**

**Example 134b responded to an opening bid of one club by bidding one heart. After opener rebid one notrump, this responder used** new minor forcing **by bidding two diamonds to build a forcing auction and try for a club slam. Opener's rebid of two notrump was encouraging since it showed exactly two hearts, and responder knew that in a club contract, there would be no heart losers. Responder then bid three clubs to show his club fit and interest in slam. When opener next bid three diamonds to show slam interest and a diamond control, this responder knew that a slam in clubs should be bid. The contract of six clubs was cold and the combined holding of the two hands was only 25 HCP.**

### 5. Responder may make slam tries after using Stayman.

Many slam tries below the game level occur after an opening notrump bid. Responder can start with **Stayman** and introduce a minor suit slam try at his rebid. Opener can show interest by making a cue bid, or deny interest by bidding three notrump.

### Example 135:

| a | b | c |
|---|---|---|
| ♠ KQ83 | ♠ A8 | ♠ 92 |
| ♥ AQ98 | ♥ AQ96 | ♥ K5 |
| ♦ QJ3 | ♦ A93 | ♦ K107 |
| ♣ J5 | ♣ Q854 | ♣ AK10763 |

**Example 135a opens one notrump and when responder uses** Stayman **by bidding two clubs bids two hearts. When responder next bids three clubs to show a hand interested in a club slam, opener rejects the invitation by bidding three notrump. This opener is minimum without a club fit and few controls.**

**Example 135b opens one notrump and, when responder uses** Stayman **by bidding two clubs, bids two hearts. When responder next bids three clubs to show a hand interested in a club slam, opener shares that interest because of maximum values, a club fit, and excellent controls. Opener might start by cue bidding to show a control, but could just jump to six clubs because the hand has controls everywhere.**

**Example 135c responds to an opening bid of one notrump with** Stayman **by bidding two clubs. After opener's rebid, responder bids three clubs to show a club suit with interest in a slam. The continuation of the auction will depend on opener's reaction to this slam invitation.**

### 6. When responder to an opening notrump has shown a two-suited hand with game forcing values by using a Jacoby Transfer, that auction may also have slam overtones.

After an opening bid of one notrump and a **Jacoby Transfer**, which shows that responder holds a five card or longer major suit, when responder then bids a minor suit at the three level, the auction is forcing to game and responder is at least five-four in the suits he has shown. Responder may just be painting his pattern on the way to reaching a game, but may also have a hand which is interested in slam.

Opener can have several hand types.

1. A true fit for responder's major without slam interest. Opener jumps to game in responder's major suit, using **fast arrival**.
2. A true fit for responder's major with slam interest. Opener shows his fit and good values by bidding responder's major at the three level. This leaves room for responder to make further slam tries, or to sign off at game.
3. A doubleton in responder's major and no slam interest. Opener just bids three notrump.
4. A doubleton in responder's major and interest in slam in responder's second suit. Opener cue bids a control to show this hand type.

**Example 136:**

| a | b | c |
|---|---|---|
| ♠ KQ985 | ♠ J73 | ♠ A103 |
| ♥ 63 | ♥ KQ72 | ♥ AK72 |
| ♦ 4 | ♦ AQ85 | ♦ K985 |
| ♣ AQ1054 | ♣ K9 | ♣ K9 |

| d | e |
|---|---|
| ♠ J3 | ♠ J3 |
| ♥ KQ72 | ♥ AK72 |
| ♦ AQ5 | ♦ AQ5 |
| ♣ K932 | ♣ K932 |

**Example 136a responds to an opening bid of one notrump by bidding two hearts, a** Jacoby Transfer **to show at least five spades. After opener bids two spades, responder continues by bidding three clubs, which is natural and game forcing.**

**Example 136b has a spade fit but no slam interest. This opener jumps to four spades, using** fast arrival **to deny slam interest.**

**Example 136c might well have shown a super acceptance for spades in reply to the** Jacoby Transfer. **If not, after responder's rebid, this opener bids three spades to show a true fit for spades and interest in a slam.**

**Example 136d has a fit for responder's second suit but, with minimum values, has no slam interest. This opener signs off at three notrump.**

**Example 136e shows interest in a slam in responder's second suit by making a cue bid of three diamonds.**

The auctions and examples we have shown are a few of the situations in which a slam try can be shown below the level of game. Others should be recognized when they occur. When it is known what game should be played, and in a forcing auction either partner takes a detour, that detour should be understood as a probe for slam. Partner can then deny slam interest by bidding the indicated game, or can show agreement with the slam idea by bidding to show side values or controls.

Other slam auctions will not be so cooperative. Sometimes, one partner knows of fits and tricks sources and simply sets out to find out about controls. Two standard conventions are used to ask partner to show the number of aces held.

# Blackwood

After suit agreement, a bid of four notrump asks partner to show the number of aces held. Responses are according to this schedule.

> Five clubs shows zero or four aces.
> Five diamonds shows one ace.
> Five hearts shows two aces.
> Five spades shows three aces.

Based on the number of aces that are held, the **Blackwood** bidder can sign off in the agreed suit at the five level, bid a slam in the agreed suit, or continue to seek a possible grand slam.

When the four notrump bidder continues by bidding five notrump, the auction says:

> 1. Partner, we have all of the aces.
> 2. I am interested in a grand slam.
> 3. If you hold some asset beyond what you have already communicated, please bid a grand slam now.
> 4. If you do not have that extra asset, continue by telling me how many kings you hold. Use the same schedule at the six level as was used to show aces at the five level.

When the **Blackwood** bidder determines that slam should not be bid, a contract of five notrump may appear to be the best available. The **Blackwood** bidder cannot bid five notrump to play there since that would be a grand slam try. When it is possible, the

**Blackwood** bidder continues by bidding the highest-ranking suit at the five level that cannot be a possible trump suit. This asks partner to sign off by bidding five notrump.

Many tournament players use **Roman Keycard Blackwood**—a variation in which the trump king is treated as a fifth ace, and also transmits information about the trump queen. If this idea intrigues you, see *Advanced Bridge Bidding for the Twenty First Century.*

## Gerber

The other convention that asks partner to show the number of aces held is the **Gerber** convention. **Blackwood** is used after suit agreement. **Gerber** is used in auctions where notrump has been bid.

After a natural opening bid or rebid of one or two notrump, a jump to four clubs is **Gerber**. It asks partner to show the number of aces held using this schedule:

> Four diamonds shows zero or four aces.
> Four hearts shows one ace.
> Four spades shows two aces.
> Four notrump shows three aces.

If the asker continues by bidding five clubs, this says:

> 1. Partner, we have all of the aces.
> 2. I am interested in a grand slam.
> 3. If you have any undisclosed asset, please bid the grand slam now.
> 4. If you cannot bid the grand, show me the number of kings you hold using the same response schedule at the five level.

When three notrump has been bid, a removal to four clubs is NOT the **Gerber** convention. It is either a slam try in a previously bid club suit, or a club cue bid in support of a previously bid suit. In either case, the removal of three notrump is always a forcing slam try. It is never because of fear that three notrump will not make.

When three notrump has been reached and the bidder's partner needs to know about aces by number, **Gerber** is a jump to five clubs. The same schedule of responses applies after the **Gerber** call of five clubs.

As was expressed in Chapter Seven, raises of notrump are always quantitative. A raise of notrump to the four level is never **Blackwood**. In notrump auctions, **Blackwood** never applies. Ace-asking in notrump auctions makes use of the **Gerber** convention instead.

## Cue bidding to show controls

As useful as these two conventions can be, there will be hands in which their use will not provide the necessary information regarding controls. Two specific hand types exist in which knowledge of the number of aces partner holds will not serve adequately.

When the slam seeker has a void, **Blackwood** will not provide the needed information. Unless all of the aces are accounted for, the slam seeker will not know whether partner has shown a useful ace, or whether that ace is in the void suit.

Similarly, when the slam seeker has two losers in an unbid suit, when **Blackwood** indicates that there is one missing ace, the opposition may be able to capture the first two tricks in the danger suit. **Blackwood** will not provide the information necessary for slam to be bid reasonably.

**Example 137:**

| a | b | c |
|---|---|---|
| ♠ AKJ953 | ♠ Q1062 | ♠ Q1062 |
| ♥ — | ♥ AQ5 | ♥ Q753 |
| ♦ 96 | ♦ Q753 | ♦ AQ5 |
| ♣ AKQ82 | ♣ 76 | ♣ 76 |

**Example 137a opens one spade and receives a limit raise of three spades from partner.** Blackwood **would do no good. Opener has both a void and two fast losers in an unbid suit. A cue bid of four clubs should elicit a return cue bid from responder when responder holds a red suit control.**

**Example 137b cue bids the heart ace. Knowing that there is no control in diamonds, opener settles for game in spades.**

**Example 137c cue bids the diamond ace. Opener can safely bid slam in spades once he knows that partner holds a diamond control.**

# Jumps to five of a major suit

When opener jumps to the five level in an agreed major suit, he indicates a specific need. Three informative auctions are possible.

1. When no side suit has been singled out, the jump to five in the agreed major suit asks for good trump quality.
2. When an opponent has bid a side suit, the jump to five of the agreed major asks for second round control in that suit. Holding second round control, partner bids six in the agreed major suit. With first round control of the enemy's suit, partner cue bids that suit. With no control, partner passes and the contract is at the five level.
3. In an uncontested auction in which only one suit remains unbid, the jump to five of the agreed major asks for second round control of that unbid suit. Again, with second round control, partner bids six of the agreed suit, with first round control, partner cue bids that suit, and with no control, partner passes and the contract is at the five level.

**Look again to Example 137a. After an opening bid of one spade and an overcall of two diamonds, responder bids three diamonds to show a limit raise (or more) for spades. Opener jumps to five spades to ask for a diamond control.**

**Example 137b has no diamond control and passes.**

**Example 137c bids six diamonds to show first round control in that suit.**

### Example 138:

| a | b | c |
|---|---|---|
| ♠ J109754 | ♠ Q863 | ♠ AQ83 |
| ♥ A5 | ♥ Q42 | ♥ Q42 |
| ♦ AKQ102 | ♦ J7 | ♦ J7 |
| ♣ — | ♣ KQ106 | ♣ Q1065 |

**Example 138a opens one spade. After a limit raise of three spades from responder, opener jumps to five spades, asking responder to bid six with good trumps.**

**Example 138b has poor trump quality and passes.**

**Example 138c has good trump quality and raises to six spades.**

**Example 139:**

|  | a | b | c |
|---|---|---|---|
| ♠ | A6 | KQ83 | K873 |
| ♥ | AQJ93 | K84 | K84 |
| ♦ | 94 | J72 | A73 |
| ♣ | AK83 | Q95 | Q65 |

**Example 139a opens one heart and rebids two clubs after a one spade response. Responder next jumps to three hearts to show three card support and game invitational values. Opener visualizes a heart slam if responder has a diamond control. Opener jumps to five hearts, which asks opener to bid on with a control in diamonds, or pass without that control.**

**Example 139b passes and the contract is five hearts, which is easy.**

**Example 139c bids six diamonds to show first round control, and opener bids six hearts.**

## The grand slam force

An unexpected jump to five notrump is known as the **grand slam force**. It asks partner to bid seven in the agreed suit if he holds two of the top three honors in the agreed suit. With any lesser holding, partner signs off at six in the agreed suit. Variations that refine this convention are found in *Advanced Bridge bidding for the Twenty First Century*.

**Example 140:**

|  | a | b |
|---|---|---|
| ♠ | KJ97532 | AKQJ4 |
| ♥ | — | AK6 |
| ♦ | A | — |
| ♣ | AKQ104 | K10875 |

**Example 140a opens one spade and is raised to two. Opener jumps to five notrump. If responder holds the ace and queen of spades, the grand slam will be bid. Even when responder holds only three small spades, six spades is not an unreasonable contract.**

**Example 140b opens one spade and receives a response of two clubs. Opener's jump to five notrump sets clubs as the trump suit, and asks responder to bid seven with the ace and queen of clubs. Six clubs should be a reasonable contract in any case.**

## Summary

The ability to make slams depends on several things.

I. Fits produce tricks. Finding fits and suggesting slam can happen in several auctions.
    A. Game tries find fits and may be slam tries in disguise.
    B. Auctions when **fast arrival** has not been used suggest slams.
    C. Use of **fourth suit forcing** may build slam try auctions.
    D. Use of **New Minor Forcing** may build slam try auctions.
    E. Responder may make slam tries after using **Stayman**,
    F. Opener may show or deny slam interest after a **Jacoby Transfer** and a suit rebid by responder.
    G. All auctions in which game is forced, the trump suit (or notrump) is known, and a detour is taken suggest slam. Partner can deny by bidding the indicated game, or agree with a further expression of value in a new suit.
II. When fits are known, controls can be sought.
    A. The **Blackwood** convention is used after suit agreement.
    B. The **Gerber** convention is used in notrump auctions.
        1. **Gerber** is always a jump from notrump to clubs.
        2. Three notrump removed to four clubs is not **Gerber.**
            a. It can be a slam try in a previously bid club suit.
            b. It can be a cue bid in support of a previously bid suit.
            c. The removal of three notrump to four of a minor suit is always a slam try.
    C. Cue bids can be used in certain auctions.
        1. Cue bids can show slam interest in lieu of signing off at an agreed game.
        2. Cue bids can show agreement to suggested slams.
        3. Cue bids can be used when **Blackwood** would not provide useful information.
            a. The cue bidder holds a void.
            b. The cue bidder holds two fast losers in an unbid suit.
III. Special auctions are available.
    A. Jumps to five of a major suit can have one of three meanings.
        1. In uncontested auctions they ask for good trumps.

        a. Partner will pass with bad trumps.

        b. Partner will bid six with good trumps.

    2. When an opponent has overcalled this jump asks for control of that suit.

        a. Partner will pass with no control.

        b. Partner will bid six with second round control.

        c. Partner will cue bid with first round control.

    3. When only one suit is unbid this jump asks for control of that suit.

        a. Partner will pass with no control.

        b. Partner will bid six with second round control.

        c. Partner will cue bid with first round control.

B. The grand slam force is an unexpected jump to five notrump.

    1. Bid seven when you have two of the top three honors.

    2. Bid six with a lesser honor holding.

# FINAL EXERCISES

The final exercises are organized as follows:

1-20      Opening Bids
21-28     Responses
29-36     Opener's Rebids
37-48     Responder's Rebids
49-60     Responder's Rebids after a Forcing Notrump
61-68     Responder's Rebids after Opener Reverses
69-84     Responses to One Notrump
85-92     Responder's Rebids after Opener Jumps to Two Notrump
93-100    Responder's Rebids after Opener Rebids One Notrump
101-108   Intrusions After the Opponents Open the Bidding
109-120   Responder's Bids after an Overcall
121-136   Responder's Bids after a Takeout Double
137-140   Responder's Bids after a Michaels Cue Bid
141-144   Responder's Bids after an Unusual Notrump
145-152   Advancing Overcalls
153-160   Advancing Takeout Doubles
161-164   Game Tries
165-168   Responses to Game Tries
169-172   Opener Plans Possible Rebids for Difficult Hands

With each of the following hands, you are the opening bidder. Determine what call you would make in first or second seat, in third seat if different, and in fourth seat if different. If the vulnerability makes a difference, make that fact known.

| 1. | 2. | 3. | 4. |
|---|---|---|---|
| ♠ Q107 | ♠ AKJ854 | ♠ 9 | ♠ AQJ3 |
| ♥ K4 | ♥ 6 | ♥ AKQJ1074 | ♥ 104 |
| ♦ K109874 | ♦ A107 | ♦ 1084 | ♦ AKJ |
| ♣ AQ | ♣ 1094 | ♣ J6 | ♣ KQ104 |

| 5. | 6. | 7. | 8. |
|---|---|---|---|
| ♠ K94 | ♠ AK87 | ♠ J | ♠ 7 |
| ♥ Q87 | ♥ AJ62 | ♥ Q4 | ♥ AKJ84 |
| ♦ KQJ842 | ♦ J84 | ♦ AQ109854 | ♦ AQ1095 |
| ♣ 8 | ♣ 93 | ♣ 942 | ♣ A6 |

9.
- ♠ K10876
- ♥ J2
- ♦ 5
- ♣ AKJ54

10.
- ♠ KQ97
- ♥ AQ4
- ♦ 84
- ♣ KQ103

11.
- ♠ AKJ9762
- ♥ 8
- ♦ 4
- ♣ AJ104

12.
- ♠ Q1082
- ♥ KQJ5
- ♦ K83
- ♣ 104

13.
- ♠ J75
- ♥ K942
- ♦ AK5
- ♣ Q93

14.
- ♠ QJ1087653
- ♥ —
- ♦ A
- ♣ AKQJ

15.
- ♠ 8
- ♥ A1097543
- ♦ A95
- ♣ 82

16.
- ♠ 84
- ♥ 72
- ♦ AKQJ1072
- ♣ 96

17.
- ♠ KQ952
- ♥ 7
- ♦ A93
- ♣ Q1087

18.
- ♠ AKJ10
- ♥ J9743
- ♦ A4
- ♣ 62

19.
- ♠ KQ105
- ♥ Q1082
- ♦ 76
- ♣ A93

20.
- ♠ QJ4
- ♥ KQ1083
- ♦ K9
- ♣ KQ7

With the hands that follow, you are responding to an opening bid of one heart. Determine the response you would make. If position or vulnerability makes a difference, include that information.

21.
- ♠ 85
- ♥ KJ6
- ♦ A973
- ♣ K1065

22.
- ♠ A52
- ♥ 9
- ♦ K74
- ♣ AQJ854

23.
- ♠ A95
- ♥ AJ83
- ♦ 62
- ♣ AK72

24.
- ♠ KQ9
- ♥ 7
- ♦ 107643
- ♣ J852

25.
- ♠ 7
- ♥ QJ73
- ♦ AJ82
- ♣ K1054

26.
- ♠ K85
- ♥ J6
- ♦ Q842
- ♣ Q1093

27.
- ♠ K73
- ♥ A1084
- ♦ 62
- ♣ KJ42

28.
- ♠ 752
- ♥ 6
- ♦ 984
- ♣ KQJ1065

With these hands, you are rebidding after opening one club and receiving a response of one heart. What rebid you make?

| 29. | 30. | 31. | 32. |
|---|---|---|---|
| ♠ 9763 | ♠ A65 | ♠ AJ4 | ♠ Q1087 |
| ♥ A65 | ♥ 9763 | ♥ KQ75 | ♥ KJ6 |
| ♦ A8 | ♦ A8 | ♦ 5 | ♦ AQ |
| ♣ KQ72 | ♣ KQ72 | ♣ AKJ98 | ♣ AQ103 |

| 33. | 34. | 35. | 36. |
|---|---|---|---|
| ♠ AKJ4 | ♠ 7 | ♠ Q108 | ♠ 4 |
| ♥ Q2 | ♥ Q2 | ♥ 5 | ♥ KJ96 |
| ♦ 7 | ♦ AKJ4 | ♦ Q975 | ♦ AQ4 |
| ♣ AKQ973 | ♣ AKQ973 | ♣ AKJ103 | ♣ AQJ82 |

With these hands, you have responded one heart to an opening bid of one diamond. After partner rebids one spade, it is your turn. What is your rebid?

| 37. | 38. | 39. | 40. |
|---|---|---|---|
| ♠ 83 | ♠ 9 | ♠ 65 | ♠ 92 |
| ♥ KJ842 | ♥ AJ82 | ♥ AQ1093 | ♥ KQ76 |
| ♦ 10 | ♦ Q10973 | ♦ Q84 | ♦ Q104 |
| ♣ QJ765 | ♣ K65 | ♣ K109 | ♣ KJ84 |

| 41. | 42. | 43. | 44. |
|---|---|---|---|
| ♠ K1053 | ♠ 104 | ♠ K1053 | ♠ Q84 |
| ♥ AK82 | ♥ AQJ973 | ♥ AKQ2 | ♥ K1072 |
| ♦ 106 | ♦ 92 | ♦ 92 | ♦ 82 |
| ♣ K84 | ♣ K84 | ♣ AJ3 | ♣ J843 |

| 45. | 46. | 47. | 48. |
|---|---|---|---|
| ♠ J76 | ♠ KQ87 | ♠ Q8 | ♠ 8 |
| ♥ KQJ4 | ♥ AK93 | ♥ AJ93 | ♥ AKQ9753 |
| ♦ A102 | ♦ Q762 | ♦ J10762 | ♦ 765 |
| ♣ 863 | ♣ 5 | ♣ 84 | ♣ K2 |

With these hands, you have made a **Forcing Notrump** response to an opening bid of one heart. Opener has rebid two clubs. What is your next call?

| 49. | 50. | 51. | 52. |
|---|---|---|---|
| ♠ K84 | ♠ A84 | ♠ KQ5 | ♠ K9 |
| ♥ J6 | ♥ 6 | ♥ 97 | ♥ AJ6 |
| ♦ Q987 | ♦ Q987 | ♦ AQ107 | ♦ K1087 |
| ♣ Q1062 | ♣ KJ1053 | ♣ 10754 | ♣ 9865 |

| 53. | 54. | 55. | 56. |
|---|---|---|---|
| ♠ Q84 | ♠ K84 | ♠ 1085 | ♠ K7 |
| ♥ 6 | ♥ 6 | ♥ 93 | ♥ 5 |
| ♦ Q987 | ♦ AQJ953 | ♦ AJ10 | ♦ QJ10743 |
| ♣ KJ1053 | ♣ J54 | ♣ KQ964 | ♣ 8652 |

With hands 57, 58 and 59, partner has opened one spade and you have bid a forcing notrump. Partner rebids two diamonds. What call do you make? With hand 60, partner's rebid has been either two spades or three diamonds. What call do you make in each case?

| 57. | 58. | 59. | 60. |
|---|---|---|---|
| ♠ J5 | ♠ 8 | ♠ Q6 | ♠ KJ5 |
| ♥ KJ84 | ♥ J93 | ♥ KQ1072 | ♥ 86 |
| ♦ 972 | ♦ 542 | ♦ 1042 | ♦ A962 |
| ♣ AQ93 | ♣ KQJ973 | ♣ J65 | ♣ QJ65 |

With the hands that follow, you have responded one spade to an opening bid of one club. Partner's rebid has been a **reverse** of two hearts. How do you continue?

| 61. | 62. | 63. | 64. |
|---|---|---|---|
| ♠ KQ982 | ♠ K973 | ♠ K9753 | ♠ AQJ953 |
| ♥ 86 | ♥ J6 | ♥ QJ83 | ♥ K2 |
| ♦ Q643 | ♦ 9763 | ♦ 543 | ♦ 10762 |
| ♣ 102 | ♣ Q75 | ♣ 9 | ♣ 5 |

| 65. | 66. | 67. | 68. |
|---|---|---|---|
| ♠ KQ83 | ♠ QJ965 | ♠ QJ83 | ♠ AJ653 |
| ♥ J82 | ♥ KQ104 | ♥ J92 | ♥ 3 |
| ♦ AQJ | ♦ 10 | ♦ AQ5 | ♦ Q92 |
| ♣ 943 | ♣ Q82 | ♣ 876 | ♣ KJ93 |

With the following hands, you are responding to an opening bid of one notrump. How do you plan the auction?

| 69. | 70. | 71. | 72. |
|---|---|---|---|
| ♠ 8743 | ♠ KJ8 | ♠ 8 | ♠ A8 |
| ♥ J962 | ♥ AQ4 | ♥ A93 | ♥ K5 |
| ♦ Q10754 | ♦ QJ103 | ♦ K62 | ♦ KQJ9753 |
| ♣ — | ♣ A82 | ♣ KQ10954 | ♣ K2 |

| 73. | 74. | 75. | 76. |
|---|---|---|---|
| ♠ AJ102 | ♠ K93 | ♠ KJ763 | ♠ AQ1097 |
| ♥ K873 | ♥ QJ105 | ♥ 982 | ♥ KJ85 |
| ♦ 6 | ♦ J92 | ♦ K5 | ♦ 92 |
| ♣ 10754 | ♣ A106 | ♣ J104 | ♣ 84 |

| 77. | 78. | 79. |
|---|---|---|
| ♠ 73 | ♠ AQ5 | ♠ AQJ10972 |
| ♥ AJ1098 | ♥ KQ | ♥ 8 |
| ♦ KQ853 | ♦ AJ104 | ♦ KQ4 |
| ♣ 5 | ♣ K1076 | ♣ K6 |

| 80. | 81. | 82. |
|---|---|---|
| ♠ 84 | ♠ 85 | ♠ QJ9753 |
| ♥ 3 | ♥ KQ93 | ♥ 9 |
| ♦ AQ109753 | ♦ AJ72 | ♦ KJ5 |
| ♣ 965 | ♣ J104 | ♣ 742 |

| 83. | 84. |
|---|---|
| ♠ 74 | ♠ 872 |
| ♥ KQ109752 | ♥ Q9642 |
| ♦ K86 | ♦ 3 |
| ♣ 3 | ♣ J853 |

With the following hands, you have responded one spade to an opening bid of one club. Partner's rebid has been a jump to two notrump. How do you continue?

| 85. | 86. | 87. |
|---|---|---|
| ♠ KQ84 | ♠ KQJ852 | ♠ AJ1064 |
| ♥ J62 | ♥ J62 | ♥ J62 |
| ♦ Q1073 | ♦ Q107 | ♦ Q107 |
| ♣ 95 | ♣ 5 | ♣ 95 |

88.
- ♠ AJ1064
- ♥ KJ1032
- ♦ 82
- ♣ 6

89.
- ♠ QJ105
- ♥ 1097
- ♦ Q1073
- ♣ 86

90.
- ♠ QJ105
- ♥ AK7
- ♦ QJ85
- ♣ J10

91.
- ♠ KQ109875
- ♥ K7
- ♦ KQ4
- ♣ 2

92.
- ♠ AKJ976
- ♥ 5
- ♦ AJ10
- ♣ 1092

With the following hands, you have responded one heart to an opening bid of one diamond. Partner has rebid one notrump. How do you continue?

93.
- ♠ 854
- ♥ AJ1073
- ♦ J4
- ♣ AQ6

94.
- ♠ KJ105
- ♥ QJ76
- ♦ 82
- ♣ AJ6

95.
- ♠ J32
- ♥ QJ876
- ♦ 54
- ♣ K82

96.
- ♠ J8
- ♥ AK42
- ♦ KQ10973
- ♣ 5

97.
- ♠ J7
- ♥ K952
- ♦ 8
- ♣ QJ10843

98.
- ♠ 9
- ♥ KQ8643
- ♦ 842
- ♣ AJ5

99.
- ♠ KQ8
- ♥ K872
- ♦ 104
- ♣ QJ64

100.
- ♠ K102
- ♥ AQJ10742
- ♦ 85
- ♣ 4

With the following hands, it is your turn to bid after an opposing opening bid of one club. What action do you take and why?

101.
- ♠ QJ102
- ♥ K4
- ♦ A108
- ♣ AJ93

102.
- ♠ K62
- ♥ KQJ92
- ♦ 10974
- ♣ 5

103.
- ♠ AQ4
- ♥ KJ109
- ♦ K854
- ♣ 52

104.
- ♠ Q10972
- ♥ AQ864
- ♦ 85
- ♣ 3

105.
- ♠ A4
- ♥ AKJ1082
- ♦ KQ32
- ♣ 6

106.
- ♠ QJ102
- ♥ AK8
- ♦ QJ65
- ♣ K2

107.
- ♠ 2
- ♥ AKJ5
- ♦ 853
- ♣ KJ1074

108.
- ♠ 9
- ♥ KJ972
- ♦ QJ1087
- ♣ J2

With the following hands, you have observed an opening bid of one club by your partner and an overcall of one spade. What action do you take and why?

| 109. | 110. | 111. | 112. |
|---|---|---|---|
| ♠ KJ8 | ♠ 84 | ♠ 84 | ♠ 84 |
| ♥ Q65 | ♥ A62 | ♥ KQ109 | ♥ A62 |
| ♦ J8432 | ♦ AK1094 | ♦ K1073 | ♦ 987 |
| ♣ 95 | ♣ 1063 | ♣ J42 | ♣ AQ1043 |

With the following hands, you have observed an opening bid of one heart by your partner and an overcall of two clubs. What action do you take and why?

| 113. | 114. | 115. | 116. |
|---|---|---|---|
| ♠ J64 | ♠ AJ8 | ♠ A105 | ♠ AQJ102 |
| ♥ Q1084 | ♥ 54 | ♥ KQ93 | ♥ J3 |
| ♦ J9653 | ♦ J1062 | ♦ Q862 | ♦ K105 |
| ♣ 7 | ♣ KQ86 | ♣ 54 | ♣ 863 |

| 117. | 118. | 119. | 120. |
|---|---|---|---|
| ♠ 853 | ♠ A1082 | ♠ K9762 | ♠ Q5 |
| ♥ KJ10 | ♥ Q6 | ♥ KJ103 | ♥ K8753 |
| ♦ 98742 | ♦ J976 | ♦ 6 | ♦ 109642 |
| ♣ 63 | ♣ K84 | ♣ A54 | ♣ 8 |

With the following hands, you have observed an opening bid of one diamond by partner and a takeout double. What action do you take and why?

| 121. | 122. | 123. | 124. |
|---|---|---|---|
| ♠ AQ875 | ♠ Q83 | ♠ K96 | ♠ QJ10875 |
| ♥ 83 | ♥ Q76 | ♥ K52 | ♥ 8 |
| ♦ 2 | ♦ K109 | ♦ KQ765 | ♦ Q63 |
| ♣ KJ986 | ♣ J642 | ♣ 82 | ♣ 982 |

| 125. | 126. | 127. | 128. |
|---|---|---|---|
| ♠ QJ93 | ♠ KJ93 | ♠ 7 | ♠ J96 |
| ♥ KQ107 | ♥ Q4 | ♥ 853 | ♥ 84 |
| ♦ 6 | ♦ 8632 | ♦ K98753 | ♦ KQ107 |
| ♣ K1098 | ♣ Q65 | ♣ J102 | ♣ 10762 |

With the following hands, you have observed an opening bid of one heart by your partner and a takeout double. What action do you take and why?

| 129. | 130. | 131. | 132. |
|---|---|---|---|
| ♠ A6 | ♠ 82 | ♠ KJ9 | ♠ 1062 |
| ♥ KQ3 | ♥ KJ9 | ♥ 82 | ♥ 7 |
| ♦ 108652 | ♦ 108652 | ♦ J1073 | ♦ J95 |
| ♣ Q94 | ♣ 1094 | ♣ Q984 | ♣ KQ10952 |

| 133. | 134. | 135. | 136. |
|---|---|---|---|
| ♠ Q62 | ♠ A62 | ♠ AJ3 | ♠ AJ1075 |
| ♥ Q853 | ♥ KQ84 | ♥ 62 | ♥ 64 |
| ♦ 6 | ♦ Q10976 | ♦ KQJ942 | ♦ Q82 |
| ♣ 97542 | ♣ 7 | ♣ 98 | ♣ 943 |

With the following hands, you have observed an opening bid of one club from your partner and a Michaels Cue Bid of two clubs by your right-hand opponent. What action do you take and why?

| 137. | 138. | 139. | 140. |
|---|---|---|---|
| ♠ 105 | ♠ AQ4 | ♠ 86 | ♠ 862 |
| ♥ KJ3 | ♥ KJ3 | ♥ 5 | ♥ 5 |
| ♦ AJ82 | ♦ QJ942 | ♦ KQ10854 | ♦ KJ53 |
| ♣ Q1094 | ♣ 82 | ♣ J1053 | ♣ KQ1085 |

With the following hands, you have observed an opening bid of one spade by your partner and an **unusual notrump** overcall at the two level. What action do you take and why?

| 141. | 142. | 143. | 144. |
|---|---|---|---|
| ♠ Q85 | ♠ 84 | ♠ AQ82 | ♠ 62 |
| ♥ K963 | ♥ K972 | ♥ A732 | ♥ KQJ987 |
| ♦ 954 | ♦ AKJ7 | ♦ 42 | ♦ J6 |
| ♣ K82 | ♣ 853 | ♣ 1098 | ♣ 854 |

With the following hands, you have observed an opening bid of one diamond on your left. Partner has overcalled one heart and right hand opponent has passed. What action do you take and why?

| 145. | 146. | 147. | 148. |
|---|---|---|---|
| ♠ K1042 | ♠ K1042 | ♠ K102 | ♠ K102 |
| ♥ Q85 | ♥ AQ5 | ♥ 6 | ♥ 62 |
| ♦ 82 | ♦ 82 | ♦ 852 | ♦ QJ93 |
| ♣ Q872 | ♣ Q872 | ♣ QJ10842 | ♣ J1084 |

| 149. | 150. | 151. | 152. |
|---|---|---|---|
| ♠ A2 | ♠ AKQ854 | ♠ 87 | ♠ AKQ5 |
| ♥ AJ85 | ♥ Q3 | ♥ Q854 | ♥ 97 |
| ♦ 854 | ♦ 86 | ♦ 3 | ♦ 3 |
| ♣ K1073 | ♣ K86 | ♣ J108763 | ♣ KQJ982 |

With the following hands, you have observed an opening bid of one diamond on your left. Partner has made a takeout double and right hand opponent has passed. What action do you take and why?

| 153. | 154. | 155. | 156. |
|---|---|---|---|
| ♠ Q1092 | ♠ KJ3 | ♠ 62 | ♠ KQ85 |
| ♥ 83 | ♥ AQ104 | ♥ K102 | ♥ AQ93 |
| ♦ 7 | ♦ 65 | ♦ QJ93 | ♦ 62 |
| ♣ QJ8765 | ♣ J762 | ♣ J1084 | ♣ 843 |

| 157. | 158. | 159. | 160. |
|---|---|---|---|
| ♠ KJ9874 | ♠ QJ6 | ♠ A4 | ♠ AQJ93 |
| ♥ 1075 | ♥ K9 | ♥ 632 | ♥ A64 |
| ♦ 6 | ♦ KJ108 | ♦ KQJ987 | ♦ 5 |
| ♣ 962 | ♣ J765 | ♣ 73 | ♣ QJ109 |

With the following hands, you have opened the bidding one heart and your partner has raised to two hearts. How do you continue and why?

| 161. | 162. | 163. | 164. |
|---|---|---|---|
| ♠ 8 | ♠ 8 | ♠ 8 | ♠ Q85 |
| ♥ Q8763 | ♥ AK1095 | ♥ AKJ1073 | ♥ AK1095 |
| ♦ AKQ4 | ♦ AK74 | ♦ AK7 | ♦ AK63 |
| ♣ AJ10 | ♣ K83 | ♣ K83 | ♣ 2 |

With the following hands, you have raised your partner's opening bid of one spade to two. Partner has continued by bidding three clubs. What action do you take and why?

| 165. | 166. | 167. | 168. |
|------|------|------|------|
| ♠ Q76 | ♠ Q76 | ♠ Q76 | ♠ 975 |
| ♥ Q1095 | ♥ KJ93 | ♥ 853 | ♥ KQ9 |
| ♦ 52 | ♦ J107 | ♦ KJ109 | ♦ QJ104 |
| ♣ KJ109 | ♣ 842 | ♣ J107 | ♣ J107 |

With the following hands, you are the opening bidder. What auction do you plan?

| 169. | 170. | 171. | 172. |
|------|------|------|------|
| ♠ 4 | ♠ K3 | ♠ K3 | ♠ 8 |
| ♥ AQJ6 | ♥ 5 | ♥ 94 | ♥ AJ92 |
| ♦ K53 | ♦ AQ4 | ♦ KQJ6 | ♦ KJ854 |
| ♣ AK1083 | ♣ AKQ10873 | ♣ KJ872 | ♣ AJ7 |

## Answers

1. One notrump. Even though you hold only fourteen high card points, you have tenaces in a semi-balanced hand, and the lead should come up to you rather than through you. Remember to add points for the six card suit. You then meet the requirements for the opening bid of one notrump. Anyone who opens one diamond has not learned proper evaluation. **Example 5h.**

2. One spade in any of the first three positions. If you are in fourth seat, open two spades. **Page 174.**

3. Let the rule of two, three, and four be your guide. If you are vulnerable and the opponents are not, three hearts is enough since you have only seven winners. At any other vulnerability, open four hearts. **Pages 169-173.**

4. Open two notrump. Do not let the bad doubleton dissuade you. This is the only proper description of your size and shape. **Page 17.**

5. Open two diamonds. Anyone who tries to tell you that you cannot do this with three cards in major suits does not understand weak two bids. If partner responds in a major suit your raise will promise three including a high honor card. **Page 173.**

6. One diamond. You do not have to like it—neither do I. Partner will probably respond in a major suit, which you will be happy to raise. **Page 20.**

7. Again, the vulnerability will determine your action. Unless you are vulnerable against not, you should open three diamonds. If that one vulnerability exists, you do not have enough winners to open at the three level. Open two diamonds instead. **Pages 169-173.**

8. Open one heart. Yes, you do have the strength to reverse, but that would not describe your pattern. In most auctions, your rebid will be only two diamonds despite 18 HCP. You do have extra strength that has not yet been shown, and if partner signs off, you have the right to make one more try for game. **Page 25— Example 8a.**

9. One spade. The expired standard required an opening bid of one club, but the new standard allows you to open one spade. If partner responds in a red suit at the two level, he shows game forcing values, and that allows you to rebid clubs at the three level without showing extra values. **Page 28.**

10. One notrump. This describes your balanced sixteen count. Do not let the bad doubleton cause you to misdescribe. **Page 17.**

11. One spade. If partner has passed, an opening bid of four spades would be fine. When partner has not yet passed and may have good values, you must open one spade rather than four. After partner responds and shows some values, a jump rebid of four spades will describe this hand. **Page 169.**

12. Pass in all seats except third. In third seat, open one heart. You will have given partner a good lead director and still have a shot at a fit in either major suit when one is present. **Page 29—Example 10a.**

13. One club. Yes, the diamonds are better, but if partner has a hand that needs to raise clubs, you will have shut out that possibility. Also, when you open one diamond, you tend to promise a four card holding. Do not be tempted by better diamond quality when you have three cards in each minor suit. **Page 20.**

14. Five spades. This tells partner that all you need to make more than eleven tricks is honor cards in spades. Partner will pass without spade honors, but will raise one level for every high honor in spades that he might hold. **Page 172.**

15. Do not open with a preemptive bid when you hold two defensive tricks. Pass is reasonable. If you want to open two hearts, that should not cause a problem, even though it violates partnership agreements. **Page 170.**

16. Three notrump. Gambling. You show a solid seven card minor suit and nothing else. Partner will pass with stoppers in all other suits. Your suit will be known since partner can have no honor in it. Partner may need to run without a good hand and will probably bid four clubs. Do not pass—correct to diamonds.

17. Pass in first or second seat. Open one spade in either third or fourth seat. You do have enough Pearson points to open in fourth. **Page 30.**

18. One heart. Yes, we both like the spades better, and maybe we will play there if partner responds in spades. But, you are playing a five card major system and must open by bidding the very weak heart suit because of its length. **Page 20.**

19. Pass in first or second seat. In third or fourth, you should open one club rather than in a major suit. Your four card heart suit is not good enough to bid, and a club lead is OK if you defend. **Page 29—Example 10b.**

20. One notrump. This hand passes the three tests presented in Chapter Two for opening one notrump with a five card major. There are three cards in the other major, there is no empty doubleton, and the hand is mostly texture rather than top cards. **Page 19.**

21. One notrump if you are unpassed. You will show your balanced limit raise at your next turn. If you are a passed hand, you will bid two clubs—**Drury**—to show your limit raise for hearts. **Page 79, 157.**

22. Two clubs. Natural and forcing to game. Plan to rebid clubs at your next turn to suggest a club slam if partner has a fit and good controls. **Page 54.**

23. Two notrump. This is the **Jacoby Two Notrump**. You promise four card support and at least an opening hand, and ask partner to rebid to describe. If partner shows some hand that fits, you will continue to seek a slam. **Page 156.**

24. One spade. Yes, this does seem strange. If partner has four spades and five hearts, this is the only way to reach a spade contract. If partner has a balanced hand, we will reach the best contract of one notrump. If partner does raise spades, the three-four fit will be our best place to play. This was not presented in the text, but is a common sense suggestion.

25. Three spades. This is a **splinter** raise, which is forcing to game and shows the values of a limit raise but also has four card support for partner's major suit and shortness where described. You want to play at least in a game, but when partner has the right hand, your description will allow your side to reach a fitting slam. **Page 155.**

26. One notrump. This is the **forcing notrump**. You intend to take a heart preference at your rebid to show limited values and a doubleton in support of partner's suit. **Page 73.**

27. Three hearts if not a passed hand. This is a classic limit raise for partner's heart opening bid. If passed, you will use **Drury** instead. As a passed hand, a jump raise is no longer limit—it is preemptive instead. **Page 157.**

28. One notrump. If you are not a passed hand, this is forcing for one round. You plan to bid clubs—even at the three level, if necessary—as your rebid. Your hand has no value unless your suit is the trump suit. With clubs as trumps, your hand will win five tricks. If clubs are not trumps, your hand may win no tricks at all. **Page 78—Example 43.**

29. One spade. Do not be deterred by the bad quality of your spades. Partner could easily have four good spades in addition to hearts, and spades might be the best place to play. If you do not bid spades at this turn, it will be almost impossible for your side to find spades as your trump suit. **Page 20.**

30. Two hearts. Show a minimum opening bid with four card support for hearts. **Page 22—Example 6c.**

31. Three diamonds. A **jump reverse (splinter)**. You promise four card heart support, shortness in diamonds, and values enough to play at the three level. **Page 25.**

32. Two notrump. Your first priority is to show your balanced hand with 18 or 19 HCP. Do not worry about missing a spade fit. If partner holds four spades, he will check back for that fit by using **new minor forcing**. If your values were minimum, you would need to bid spades with four of them, but not when your values are in this range. **Page 115.**

33. Two spades. This is a natural game forcing jump shift rebid. You want to be sure that once partner has responded, a game will be reached. You promise enough in values that game should be reached once there has been a response. **Page 36—Example 12d.**

34. Two diamonds. A **reverse**, forcing for one round and showing at least 16 HCP with more clubs than diamonds. **Page 24.**

35. Two clubs. You hate to rebid a suit that is only five cards long, but there is no alternative. You began with one club rather than one diamond, planning to rebid your clubs if necessary since your diamond suit is so weak. If partner had responded one spade, you might have raised despite holding only three card support. Always look to make "the least worst bad bid". **Page 25.**

36. Three hearts. You would like to **splinter** to show your heart fit with short spades, but you cannot force the auction to the four level. Partner will know that you do not have shortness in diamonds since you did not make a **jump reverse** to that suit. He may be able to infer that you have shortness in spades. **Page 26.**

37. One notrump. You hate to bid notrump with such a distributional hand, but no other bid will suffice. You cannot bid two clubs since that would be **fourth suit forcing**, and would not even show clubs as it overstated the values you hold. You cannot repeat hearts on five. One notrump is the only call that limits your values, even though it does not give a picture of your shape. **Page 89.**

38. Three diamonds. This jump preference shows game invitational values, implies only four cards in hearts, and shows a diamond fit which rates to be five long. **Page 91.**

39. Two clubs. This is **fourth suit forcing**, which is your only way to find a three card fit for your heart suit, even though your values are only game invitational. Those who insist on playing **fourth suit forcing** to game will not be able to bid this hand. **Page 41.**

40. Two notrump. This shows game invitational values, promises a stopper in the unbid suit (clubs), and implies that you have only four hearts since you did not search for a three card fit for hearts. **Page 91.**

41. Four spades. You know which game to bid and have no aspirations for slam, so go directly to game. **Page 21.**

42. Three hearts. Not forcing, but invitational to game showing six reasonable hearts. **Page 91.**

43. Two clubs. This is **fourth suit forcing**. You know that you want to play in spades, but your values are too great to just jump to game in spades. After using **fourth suit forcing**, when you show support for spades, partner will know that he has been invited to a slam since you did not jump to game when you might have done so. **Page 41.**

44. Pass. One spade should be as good a contract as any. If you bid again, your side might get higher than it wants to be. You show a good 5 to a bad 7 in HCP with this pass, and three or four spades. **Page 90.**

45. Two clubs. Again, you must use **fourth suit forcing** holding only game invitational values. A jump to two notrump at this turn would promise a club stopper, which you do not have. If partner shows support for hearts and you then bid two notrump, he will understand the nature of your hand, and will not expect a stopper in clubs. **Page 41.**

46. Four clubs. This is clearly a **splinter** in support of spades. Partner will know that you hold club shortness, four card support for spades, and the values to play at least in game in spades. **Page 13.**

47. Two diamonds. A simple preference to partner's first suit. This shows minimum response values and a good fit for diamonds. **Page 89.**

48. Four hearts. Your suit is good enough to play in game without any support from partner. It is always easy to bid a game when you know what game to bid.

49. Two hearts. Your preference shows minimum response values and a doubleton heart. Do not pass two clubs. Your partner could have as few as two. **Page 77.**

50. Three clubs. You deny a heart fit, and show game invitational values with five clubs. Since partner could have rebid clubs with as few as two, you cannot have fewer than five. **Page 81—Example 46.**

51. Two notrump. You deny a heart fit and promise game invitational values with stoppers in both unbid suits. **Page 82.**

52. Three hearts. You have a balanced limit raise for partner's heart suit. **Page 79.**

53. Pass. You have no heart fit and minimum response values. You hope that partner has at least three clubs. **Page 77.**

54. Three diamonds. You show game invitational values and a good diamond suit as you deny a fit for hearts. **Page 81—Example 47.**

55. Two spades. No, this does not show that you have spades. You denied holding spades when you responded one notrump and bypassed spades. You show game invitational values without a stopper in spades, and suggest that, if partner also has no spade stopper, there is a home in clubs, which was partner's rebid. **Page 82.**

56. Two diamonds. You could have never reached diamonds if one notrump had not been forcing. Partner would have passed and you would have played one notrump, but since your call was forcing you were able to reach your suit and show minimum values. Two diamonds should be easy, but one notrump would have been shaky at best. **Page 78—Example 42.**

57. Two notrump. Game invitational values with stoppers in the unbid suits. **Page 80.**

58. Three clubs. If clubs are not trumps, your hand will have no value. With clubs as trumps, your hand will be worth five tricks. Your call shows minimum response values and a club suit that must be trumps. **Page 78—Example 43.**

59. Two hearts. This shows minimum response values and five or more hearts. This choice is better than two spades. You may find a three card fit. Even if partner has a

doubleton, it will be better to play in hearts than in spades. If partner has a void or singleton in hearts, he will correct to two spades. **Page 78.**

60. Four spades. You had intended to jump in spades to show your limit raise. After partner either rebids spades at the two level or makes a jump shift rebid, you cannot just bid three spades since that will not show a real spade fit and game invitational values. A jump in spades is necessary in either auction. **Page 80.**

61. Two spades. You show minimum response values and at least five spades. **Page 94—Example 52.**

62. Two notrump. You ask partner to bid three clubs with the intention of passing if he does as requested. You know that there is at least a five-three club fit, and no other contract appeals. **Page 94.**

63. Two notrump. Do not bid two spades, even though you hold five of them. You know that your side should play in hearts, and you must show that fit while you limit your values. You are not strong enough to raise hearts at this turn. After partner bids three clubs as expected, your call of three hearts shows four and minimum response values. If you mistakenly bid two spades instead of two notrump, you might not get the chance to show your fit for hearts. **Page 95—Example 54.**

64. Three spades. You show values enough to play game facing a **reverse,** and that you have six spades. **Page 97—Example 56.**

65. Three notrump. You show 12 to 15 HCP, and that diamonds are stopped. **Page 96.**

66. Three hearts. This raise shows four card support and values enough to play game. **Page 95—Example 54.**

67. Two notrump. You plan to bid three notrump next if partner bids three clubs as requested. You show 9+ to 12- HCP. **Page 96—Example 55b.**

68. Three clubs. This shows your fit for partner's known five card or longer suit and is forcing. **Page 94—Example 53a.**

69. Bid two clubs, the **Stayman convention**. You plan to pass whatever partner bids. Your hand would not have been worth much at a notrump contract, but with one of your suits as the trump suit your hand will have good value. **Page 121—Example 65.**

70. Four notrump. A quantitative invitation to a slam. **Page 120—Example 64d.**

71. Two clubs—**Stayman**. Although partner will believe that you are looking for a major suit fit, when you continue by bidding three clubs, your auction will show interest in a club slam. If partner then bids three notrump, he will deny interest in the slam you have suggested. You hope that he will cue bid three diamonds, which will show that he shares your slam interest and has the diamond ace. **Page 124—Example 67c.**

72. Four clubs—**Gerber**. If partner shows three aces, you will be cold for a small slam and favored to make a grand. If he has only two aces, a small slam should be safe. **Page 137.**

73. Two clubs—**Stayman**. If partner bids two diamonds, you will bid two notrump as a game invitation. If partner bids either major suit, you will raise to the three level to invite. **Page 122.**

74. Three notrump. With 4-3-3-3 distribution, you should not use **Stayman** even though you do have a four card major suit. **Page 123.**

75. Two hearts—a **Jacoby Transfer**. After partner bids two spades, you will bid two notrump to confirm exactly five spades and invite a game. If partner makes a super acceptance, you will carry on to game happily. **Page 128.**

76. Two clubs—**Stayman**. If partner bids either major suit, you will raise to game. If partner bids two diamonds to deny a four card major, you will jump to three spades to show five and force to game. **Page 124.**

77. Two diamonds—a **Jacoby Transfer**. After partner bids two hearts, you will describe your hand and force to game by bidding three diamonds. **Page 129.**

78. Five notrump. You invite a grand slam and force at least six notrump. **Page 120.**

79. Four hearts—a **Texas Transfer**. You will then use **Blackwood** to find out about controls for a possible spade slam. **Page 130.**

80. Three diamonds. This invitational response shows a good suit and nothing else. If partner has the diamond king and stoppers in all of the other suits, he will bid three notrump. Without a diamond fit or with an unstopped suit, he will pass and you will declare three diamonds. **Page 134.**

81. Two clubs—**Stayman**. You will bid game in hearts if partner shows four, or jump to three notrump if partner denies four hearts by bidding either two diamonds or two spades. **Page 124.**

82. Two hearts—a **Jacoby Transfer**. After partner bids two spades, you will raise to three spades to invite game. **Page 128.**

83. Four diamonds—a **Texas Transfer**. You will pass and let partner play four hearts. **Page 130.**

84. Two diamonds—a **Jacoby Transfer**. You will pass and let partner play two hearts. **Page 128.**

85. Three notrump. The indicated contract. **Page 118.**

86. Four spades. You show the desire to play game in spades and nothing more. **Page 115.**

87. Three diamonds—**new minor forcing**. You hope to find a three card fit for your spade suit. **Page 115.**

88. Three hearts. You promise five-five in the majors. If you held only four hearts, you would use **new minor forcing** instead. **Page 116—Example 62a.**

89. Pass. Your response was as light as it could possibly be. You are high enough. **Page 114.**

90. Four notrump. A quantitative raise inviting a notrump slam. **Page 118.**

91. Four clubs—**Gerber**. If partner has three or more aces, a slam looks inviting. **Page 137.**

92. Three spades. An invitation to slam since you did not use **fast arrival**. You hope that partner will cue bid in clubs to show interest in the slam you have suggested. **Page 115—Example 61b.**

93. Two clubs—**new minor forcing**. You hope to find a three card fit for your heart suit. **Page 110.**

94. Three notrump. You have no eight card major suit fit and do have the values to be in a game. **Page 104.**

95. Two hearts. Placing the contract. Partner holds either two or three hearts, and your suit will be better than notrump. **Page 104.**

96. Two clubs—**new minor forcing**. When you next bid three diamonds, your auction will be forcing suggesting a slam in diamonds. **Page 111.**

97. Three clubs. This shows a weak hand with only four hearts and six clubs. This is exactly where you would like to play this hand. **Page 113.**

98. Three hearts. A game invitation promising six hearts. **Page 110—Example 60c.**

99. Two notrump. A natural game invitation. **Page 104—Example 57a.**

100. Four hearts. Only ten HCP, but plenty of tricks facing partner's balanced minimum opening bid. **Page 45.**

101. Overcall one notrump. A perfect description. **Page 191.**

102. Overcall one heart. Not a great hand but you certainly want partner to lead hearts. **Page 194—Example 105c.**

103. Double for takeout. A fairly classic minimum with support for all unbid suits. **Page 206.**

104. Two clubs—**Michaels**. You promise five-five in the major suits and 6 to 11 HCP. **Page 212.**

105. Double. Partner will believe that you have support for all unbid suits until you next bid hearts. Then, you will have shown a hand too good for an overcall. **Page 211.**

106. Double. Yes, you would have opened one notrump, but when the opening bid has been in clubs you should not overcall in notrump. You have only one stopper in clubs and it is not flexible. You must spend it early. A better description is to show support for the unbid suits. If the opening bid had been in any other suit, an overcall of one notrump would have been fine. **Page 191.**

107. Overcall one heart. You are at the one level with a chunky suit and length in the suit that has been bid in front of you. Those are the requirements for an overcall on a four card suit. **Page 195.**

108. Jump to two notrump. This is the **unusual notrump**—showing at least five-five in diamonds and hearts. A preempt in two suits. **Page 192.**

109. One notrump. A minimum response with stoppers in spades. **Page 219.**

110. Two diamonds. This is a free bid showing at least a five card suit, and game invitational values of at least a good nine HCP. **Page 221.**

111. Make a **negative double**. You show at least four hearts and the values to invite partner to bid at the two level. **Page 223.**

112. Two spades. You promise a limit raise (or better) for partner's suit. **Page 220.**

113. Three hearts. A preemptive jump raise. After the overcall you would show a limit raise (or better) for hearts by making a cue bid. Therefore, a jump raise becomes preemptive rather than limit. **Page 220.**

114. Two notrump. A natural invitation to game showing club stoppers and no good fit for hearts. Alternately, you might pass and wait for partner to reopen with double, which you would convert to penalty. **Page 219.**

115. Three clubs. Again, the cue bid shows a good raise for partner's suit. **Page 220.**

116. Two spades. This free bid shows at least game invitational values and a five card or longer suit. **Page 221.**

117. Two hearts. Without the overcall you might have passed. But, after the overcall, you should stretch to raise your partner's suit. **Page 220.**

118. Make a **negative double**. This promises four spades and the values to ask partner to bid at the two level. **Page 223.**

119. Four diamonds. Clearly a **splinter** in support of hearts. This is the same action you would have taken without the overcall. **Page 155.**

120. Four hearts. Again, the same call you would have made without the overcall. **Page 153.**

121. One spade. Do not redouble just because you have ten points. One spade is natural and forcing. If you redouble and the opponents preempt, you may not have a chance to show both of your suits. **Page 230.**

122. One notrump. The same call you would have made without the double. You show a balanced minimum response without a four card major. **Page 229.**

123. Two notrump. After double, this shows a limit raise (or better) for partner's suit. **Page 230.**

124. Two spades. A natural preemptive response after the double. **Page 230.**

125. Redouble. You plan to double the opponents no matter where they land. **Page 231.**

126. One spade. Make your natural response. Ignore the double. **Page 230.**

127. Three diamonds. After the double, this is a preemptive call. **Page 230.**

128. Two diamonds. An easy natural single raise. **Page 230.**

129. Two notrump. After the double, this shows a limit raise (or better) for partner's suit. **Page 230.**

130. Two hearts. Stretch to raise in competition. **Page 230—Example 127e.**

131. One notrump. Natural and non-forcing because of the double. **Page 229.**

132. Two clubs. Because of the double, this is not forcing. It shows shortness in hearts and a suit of at least five card length. **Page 230.**

133. Three hearts. After the double, raises are preemptive. **Page 230.**

134. Four clubs. Your **splinter** is not affected by the double. **Page 155.**

135. Redouble. Show that you have values and bid diamonds at your next turn. A bid in diamonds after the double would not be forcing. **Page 231.**

136. One spade. Natural and forcing. Ignore the double. **Page 230.**

137. Two hearts. Your cue bid of one of RHO's suits promises a stopper for play in notrump and at least game invitational values. **Page 233.**

138. Three notrump. You have the values to play game facing partner's opening bid and stoppers in both suits shown by the cue bid. **Page 233.**

139. Two diamonds. Natural and non forcing after the cue bid. **Page 233.**

140. Three clubs. This will show a limit raise for partner's suit. **Page 233.**

141. Three spades. This shows a single raise under pressure. You would cue bid if your values were those of a limit raise or more. **Page 228.**

142. Double. You promise that you can punish at least one of the suits shown by the opponents. **Page 228.**

143. Three diamonds. This is a cue bid showing a limit raise (or more) for partner's suit. **Page 228.**

144. Three hearts. You show a good suit with less than game invitational values. **Page 228—Example 126d.**

145. Two hearts. Raise partner's overcall whenever possible. **Page 197.**

146. Two diamonds. Cue bid to show some good hand. This time it is a good three card raise, which is the expected hand. If partner rebids two hearts, you will pass. **Page 198.**

147. Two clubs. This is a non-forcing corrective call. You do not relish playing in hearts and have a good suit of your own. **Page 197.**

148. One notrump. Natural and not forcing. **Page 197.**

149. Three diamonds. The jump cue bid shows a power raise for partner's suit with four card support. **Page 198.**

150. Two spades. Your jump promises opening bid values and a good six card suit. **Page 198.**

151. Three hearts. Jump raises of overcalls are always preemptive. **Page 198.**

152. Two diamonds. You must establish a force in order to first show clubs, then spades. **Page 198.**

153. One spade. Always bid a major suit when possible in response to a takeout double. Do not make the error of bidding clubs just because you hold more clubs than spades. If game is possible, it surely will be in the major suit rather than the minor. **Page 208—Example 115e.**

154. Two hearts. Jump to show game invitational values. **Page 208.**

155. One notrump. Your balanced minimum includes a double stopper in diamonds. **Page 208.**

156. Two diamonds. Do not guess which major to bid. Your cue bid asks partner to name the suit, and promises at least game invitational values. **Page 208.**

157. Three spades. Your double jump response is preemptive. **Page 208.**

158. Two notrump. Invite game and show that diamonds are well stopped. **Page 208.**

159. Pass. Your trump stack will serve you well. **Page 207—Example 114a.**

160. Four spades. You belong in game facing a takeout double, and you know what game to bid. **Page 208—Example 115a.**

161. Three hearts. Your game try asks partner for good trumps. **Page 162.**

162. Three clubs. A natural game try asking for help in clubs. **Page 162.**

163. Three clubs again. You know that you will play at least in game. If partner has good clubs and shows that in response to your try for game, you will know that the secondary fit makes slam a better shot. If you jump to game, you will not get this information. **Page 240.**

164. Two spades. Always make your game try without bypassing any suit in which you need help. A game try in diamonds would not find out about help in spades. **Page 162.**

165. Four spades. Partner has asked for help in clubs and you have a great holding in that suit. Do not do less than bid game. **Page 163.**

166. Three spades. Partner needs help in clubs and you have none. Hope that three spades is not too high. **Page 163.**

167. Three diamonds. Your help for clubs is suspect, but you do have a holding that might be useful. Make a counter offer. Bid three diamonds. **Page 163.**

168. Three notrump. With poor spades and maximum values, you suggest what might be the only makeable game. **Page 161.**

169. Open one club. If the response is one diamond, rebid one heart. If the response is one heart, make a jump raise to three hearts. If the response is either one spade or one notrump, your rebid should be a reverse to two hearts. **Page 24.**

170. Open one club. If the response is one spade or one notrump, reverse to two diamonds. Your hand is too good for a jump rebid in clubs. If the response is one heart, jump rebid three notrump. This jump rebid promises a source of tricks in clubs, stoppers in the unbid suits, and suggests shortness in the suit of partner's response (This complex is detailed in *Advanced Bridge Bidding for the Twenty First Century*). **Page 24.**

171. Open one diamond. If the response is one spade or one notrump, rebid two clubs. If the response is one heart, you might rebid one notrump since you do hold a stopper in spades. If you open one club, you may have to rebid clubs, which would not describe, as well as allowing for the opportunity to bid both minor suits. You are not strong enough to open one club and then reverse to diamonds. **Page 25.**

172. Open one diamond. If the response is one heart, you will have to choose between the underbid of two hearts and the overbid of three hearts. If the response is either one spade or one notrump, your best rebid is two clubs. Partner will take a "false preference" to diamonds when his minor suit holdings are two-three. A rebid of the bad five card diamond suit would not be as good. **Page 25.**

We hope that you have done well with these problems, and that the entire book has brought you a complete—if simplified—picture of the standard bidding methods of today. Look forward to *Advanced Bridge Bidding for the Twenty First Century*. With it, you will upgrade to the best of bidding tools that are available today.